Unique Focus

Linguistik Aktuell/Linguistics Today (LA)

Linguistik Aktuell/Linguistics Today (LA) provides a platform for original monograph studies into synchronic and diachronic linguistics. Studies in LA confront empirical and theoretical problems as these are currently discussed in syntax, semantics, morphology, phonology, and systematic pragmatics with the aim to establish robust empirical generalizations within a universalistic perspective.

General Editors

Werner Abraham
University of Vienna / Rijksuniversiteit
Groningen

Elly van Gelderen
Arizona State University

Advisory Editorial Board

Cedric Boeckx
Harvard University

Christer Platzack
University of Lund

Guglielmo Cinque
University of Venice

Ian Roberts
Cambridge University

Günther Grewendorf
J.W. Goethe-University, Frankfurt

Lisa deMena Travis
McGill University

Liliane Haegeman
University of Lille, France

Sten Vikner
University of Aarhus

Hubert Haider
University of Salzburg

C. Jan-Wouter Zwart
University of Groningen

Volume 123

Unique Focus. Languages without multiple wh-questions
by Marina Stoyanova

Unique Focus

Languages without multiple wh-questions

Marina Stoyanova
University of Frankfurt

John Benjamins Publishing Company
Amsterdam / Philadelphia

The paper used in this publication meets the minimum requirements of American National Standard for Information Sciences – Permanence of Paper for Printed Library Materials, ANSI z39.48-1984.

Library of Congress Cataloging-in-Publication Data

Stoyanova, Marina.
  Unique focus : languages without multiple wh-questions / by Marina Stoyanova.
    p. cm. (Linguistik Aktuell/Linguistics Today, ISSN 0166-0829 ; v. 123)
Includes bibliographical references and index.
  1. Grammar, Comparative and general--Interrogative. 2. Focus (Linguistics) 3.
    Grammar, Comparative and general--Syntax. I. Title.
P299.I57S76   2008
415--dc22   200800342
ISBN 978 90 272 5506 8 (Hb; alk. paper)

John Benjamins Publishing Co. · P.O. Box 36224 · 1020 ME Amsterdam · The Netherlands
John Benjamins North America · P.O. Box 27519 · Philadelphia PA 19118-0519 · USA

TABLE OF CONTENTS

vi

ACKNOWLEDGEMENTS

This monograph constitutes a revision of my doctoral dissertation submitted at the department "Neuere Philologien" at the University of Frankfurt. I would like to thank the La/LT-Series Editors, Werner Abraham and Elly van Gelderen, and the Editorial Director, Kees Vaes, for their interest in this book and helpful comments. Writing this book would not have been possible without the precious help of many people who I kindly want to thank. First of all, I am indebted to Joachim Sabel and Helen Leuninger for their valuable scientific support, wise advice and for the many linguistic discussions. I had the pleasure to profit from the comments and advice of many other linguists. I am grateful to Giorgio Banti, Željko Bošković, Lisa Lai-Shen Cheng, Mara Frascarelli, Jost Gippert, Günther Grewendorf, Kleanthes Grohmann, Liliane Haegeman, Joost Kremers, Aniko Liptak, Maarten Kossmann, Marten Mous, Rick Nouwen, Christian Plunze, Monika Rathert, Anna Roussou, Rainer Voßen, Ede Zimmermann and Malte Zimmermann. I thank my colleagues at the Graduate School 'Sentence types: Variation and interpretation' at the University of Frankfurt: Lana Ahlborn, Sonja Ermisch, Verena Mayer, Florian Remplik, Magda Roguska, Andreas Runkel, Magda Schwager, Blasius Achiri Taboh, Marc-Oliver Vorköper and Melani Wratil. I very much appreciated the help of my informants Noureddine Elouazizi, Eugenia Marchisio, Elisabetta Passinetti, Robert Plaice, Patricia Ronan and Cabdelqadir Ruumi. Special thanks go to my friends Bossila Dontcheva, Julia Graf, Winnie Kraushaar, Thorsten Lülfing, Sevetlana Pankau, Mila Tconeva, Milena Wende and Dina Zacharieva. And last but not least, I thank all the members of my family, especially my parents Margarita & Stefčo Stoyanovi, Karo, Emilia Aleksieva, Marinka Stoyanova and Ekaterina Vǎlcheva for their immense emotional support.

ABBREVIATIONS

1 = first person
2 = second person
3 = third person
ABS = absolutive case
ACC = accusative case
ADP = verbal adposition
ADV = adverbial
ASP = aspect
AT = agent topic
CM = cleft marker
COMP = complementizer
COND = conditional
COP = copula
CS = construct case
CT = circumstantial topic
DAT = dative case
EXPL = expletive element
F = feminine
FM = focus marker
FS = free state
FUT = future tense
GEN = genitive case
IMP = imperative
M = masculine
NEG = negation

NOM = nominative case
OCL = object clitic
PART = participle
PAST = past tense
PERF = perfective aspect
PL = plural
PRED = predicative
PRES = present tense
PROG = progressive
PRT = particle
PP = past participle
Q = question particle, yes/no-
    particle or interrogative
    morpheme
QD = interrogative determiner
REFL = reflexive
REL = relative
REST = restricted paradigm
SCL = subject clitic
SG = singular
SUB = subordinate verbal forms
SUBJ = subjunctive
TT = theme topic
VGP = verbal group
Bold = information focus and wh-
    phrases
CAPITALS = contrastive focus

CHAPTER 1
INTRODUCTION

This book represents both an empirically and theoretically oriented study of language grammar. It shows how typological research may be done by means of generative syntactic theory, i.e. the following investigation illustrates how typological variation within languages may be accounted for by theoretical means.

A common and not very well investigated property of some languages that do not belong to the same language family is the non-existing option to build multiple wh-questions. This specific language property constitutes the core of the following investigation. The languages, which have been reported to exhibit this phenomenon, are Italian (Calabrese 1984, 1987, Rizzi 1982, 1997), Somali (Lecarme 1999, Svolacchia et al. 1995, Svolacchia & Puglielli 1999), Berber (Calabrese 1987) and Irish (Adams 1984, McCloskey 1979).

1.1   The Central Problem: The Languages without Multiple Wh-Questions
Before starting to examine the specific properties of wh-interrogatives in the languages without multiple wh-questions (Somali, Berber, Italian and Irish) I will consider the current typology of multiple wh-questions. According to the three major strategies of multiple wh-question formation languages have been divided into three types.[1]

Some languages make use of the so-called ex-situ strategy according to which all wh-phrases in a multiple wh-question form a sequence of adjacent elements that occupy a sentence initial position (cf. Rudin 1988 and Boeckx & Grohmann 2003, among others). These are the *multiple wh-fronting languages*:

(1)   **Koj kakvo** kupi?   (Bulgarian)
       who what   bought
       'Who bought what?'

---

[1] Subtype internal differences are not relevant for the current proposal.

The in-situ strategy defines a language type that does not show any kind of movement of wh-elements. All wh-items in a multiple wh-question remain in their base positions (cf. Cheng 1997, among others). These languages are referred to as the *wh-in-situ languages*:

(2)   Taroo-ga **dare-ni**   **nani-o**   ageta no?   (Japanese)
      Taroo-NOM who-DAT   what-ACC   gave Q
      'Who did Taroo give what?'
      (Richards 1997:13)

The third language type adopts a mixed version of the pure ex-situ and in-situ strategy, henceforth the *mixed language type*. Multiple wh-questions show a surface structure like (3). One wh-phrase is realised at the beginning of the sentence while other wh-elements appear in-situ (cf. Cheng 1997, among others):

(3)   **Wer** hat   **was** gekauft?   (German)
      who has   what bought
      'Who bought what?'

There is, however, a fourth language type which does not use any of the three outlined strategies of multiple wh-question formation. Consider the following examples:

(4)a. **Maxáy**   sameeyeen?   (Somali)
      what-FM-SCL   did
      'What did they do?'
   b. *****yaa**   **goormuu**   yimid?
      who-FM   time-which-FM-SCL   came
      'Who came when?'
   c. *****yaa**   yimid **goorma**?
      who-FM   came   time-which
      'Who came when?'
      (Svolacchia & Puglielli 1999)

(5)a. **May**   t-sghu   terbatt?   (Berber)
      what-CM3FSG-bought   girl
      'What did the girl buy?'
      (Calabrese 1987)

b. ***W manwn** i(g)   yzwn?
   who whom   CM   kissed-PART
   'Who kissed whom?'
   (Noureddine Elouazizi, p.c.)

c. ***Wiy**   yzrin   **may**?
   who-CM   seen-PART   what-CM
   'Who saw what?'
   (Cole & Tenny 1987)

(6)a. **Che cosa**   ha   fatto, Carlo?   (Italian)
      what   have-3SG   done Carlo
      'What did Carlo do?'

b. ***Chi che cosa**   ha   fatto?
   who what   have-3SG   done
   'Who did what?'
   (Rizzi 1997)

c. ***Che cosa** hai   dato **a chi**?
   what   have-2SG   given to whom
   'What did you give to whom?'
   (Calabrese 1987)

(7)a. **Caidé**   aL   thug tú   dó?   (Irish)
      what   COMP   give you   to-him
      'What did you give him?'

b. ***Cé caidé**   aL   rinne?
   who what   COMP   did
   'Who did what?'

c. ***Cé** aL   rinne **caidé**?
   who COMP   did   what
   'Who did what?'
   (McCloskey 1979:61, 71)

The grammatical examples (4a), (5a), (6a) and (7a) show the only position in which wh-phrases in Somali, Berber, Italian and Irish are licensed properly. This is a position left-adjacent to a focus marker in Somali (cf. 4a). In Berber, the wh-item appears left-adjacent to a cleft marker (cf. 5a). In Italian, the wh-item is immediately followed by the finite verb (cf. 6a). The Irish example (cf. 7a) shows that a complementizer appears to the left of the wh-word. The ungrammatical examples (4b), (5b), (6b) and (7b) provide evidence that multiple wh-fronting is not possible. The observation that a wh-phrase cannot be left in-situ is represented by the examples (4c), (5c), (6c) and (7c). Hence, the mixed strategy cannot be applied in Somali, Berber, Italian and Irish either.

The central task of this investigation is to determine the place of languages like Somali, Berber, Italian and Irish within the language typology based on the criterion of multiple wh-question formation. As the examples in (4), (5), (6) and (7) illustrate, all considerable strategies of deriving multiple wh-questions found across different language types give rise to ungrammaticality in Somali, Berber, Italian and Irish. The pure multiple wh-in-situ strategy (the Japanese type) is automatically excluded from consideration because the examined languages obligatorily front wh-elements in single wh-questions (cf. 4a, 5a, 6a and 7a). Moreover, the canonical position of a wh-item is structurally marked: A position followed by a focus marker in Somali, by a cleft marker in Berber, by the finite verb in Italian and by a complementizer in Irish. Two central questions arise. First, why is it impossible to front one wh-phrase and leave another one in-situ (the German type) in Somali, Berber, Italian and Irish? Second, why is multiple wh-fronting (the Bulgarian type) not an available option either?

In what follows I argue that due to specific internal properties of these languages there is no syntactic mechanism for the derivation of multiple wh-questions. Therefore, languages like Somali, Berber, Italian and Irish constitute a separate type. The current typology of multiple wh-questions has to be revised in order to capture the observed language variation. I will show that there are primarily two typologically distinct language types. These are the languages that allow multiple wh-questions and the languages in which multiple wh-questions do not appear (as in Somali, Berber, Italian and Irish). I account for the observed typological variation within languages in the framework of the minimalist syntactic theory as developed by Chomsky (1995, 2000, and 2001). As we will see, in languages like Somali, Berber, Italian and Irish wh-interrogative systems exactly parallel the available focusing mechanisms typical of these languages. This observation is expressed by the formulation of the Head-Adjacency Generalisation in section (3.5.1.):

(8)   The Head-Adjacency Generalisation
        Languages that do not allow multiple wh-questions are languages that
        license wh-phrases only through an overtly established spec-head rela-
        tionship with a head element endowed with a focus feature:
        [$_{\text{SpecFocP}}$ wh-phrase [$_{\text{Foc}°}$ X°] [...]]

I account for the absence of multiple wh-questions by the fact that multiple focusing is abandoned from the grammars of the languages under discussion. In order to do so I propose the Uniqueness Hypothesis in section (3.5.2.):

(9) The Uniqueness Hypothesis
Languages that license wh-phrases only in a unique structural focus
position are languages without multiple wh-questions. The notion of
uniqueness has to be understood as the interaction of the following
three parameters:
a. no focus in-situ[2]
b. no multiple specifiers of a FocP or alternatively no clustering of focused constituents
c. no FocP-recursion

The analysis is sketched here briefly. I assume that wh-phrases in languages
that do not admit multiple wh-questions have an uninterpretable strong focus
feature (for theoretical discussion of the assumption that morphological features which trigger syntactic movement may reside on the dislocated elements
themselves see Lasnik 1999:128, for its application Bošković 1998, 1999).
This implies that the focus feature of wh-phrases in these languages must be
checked before spell-out. Therefore, wh-elements in the languages without
multiple wh-questions move to the specifier of a functional head Foc° in order
to establish an agreement relation with its interpretable focus feature. As a result of this operation, the wh-elements check and eliminate their uninterpretable focus feature against the interpretable focus feature of Foc°. Suppose
the syntactic derivation begins with a numeration containing more than one
wh-element. Given the fact that wh-phrases have to check an uninterpretable
strong focus feature and under the observation that in Somali, Berber, Irish and
Italian focus is realised in a unique structural position marked through head-
adjacency, multiple wh-questions cannot be licensed in these languages (see
for details of the analysis chapter 4.).

---

[2] Many different assumptions concerning the notion of focus and its syntactic representation
have been made in studies on the word order and clausal structure of Italian. For the sake of
better understanding and avoiding misunderstandings, I will refer to some prominent investigations on the left periphery of Italian. Rizzi (1997) proposes a structural position only for contrastive focus, which is located in the clausal left periphery. Along the lines of his system, pure
information focus always appears in-situ while contrastive focus may optionally remain in-situ.
According to Benincà & Poletto (2002), both pure information and contrastive focus may occupy different dedicated positions in the left periphery. Belletti (2002) assumes that contrastive
focus is a part of the clausal left periphery while pure information focus belongs to a lower
clausal area, namely a FocP located between VP and IP. I will discuss these possibilities in
subchapter (3.1.) and show that there is good reason to believe that focus cannot be realised in-
situ in Italian. It is in a structurally marked position and represents a unique syntactic category
in the grammar of Italian as stated in (9).

1.2   Chapter Outline

The book is organised as follows. In subchapter (1.3.) I first outline the theoretical framework (cf. section 1.3.1.) I adopt for the discussion and the analysis of the phenomenon under investigation. Then I address the current theory of wh-questions (cf. section 1.3.2.) and in addition the theory of focus which is closely related to the analyses of wh-questions (cf. section 1.3.3.). In chapter (2.) I review three already proposed analyses of the ungrammaticality of multiple wh-questions. The major chapter (3.) represents the relevant phenomena related to the grammar of wh-questions in Italian (cf. subchapter 3.1.), Somali (cf. subchapter 3.2.), Berber (cf. subchapter 3.3.) and Irish (cf. subchapter 3.4.). In subchapter (3.5.) I outline the crucial generalisations on the syntax of wh-questions in the languages without multiple wh-questions and propose a working hypothesis to account for the ungrammaticality of multiple wh-questions. In chapter (4.) I verify the working hypothesis and propose a feature checking analysis of the languages without multiple wh-questions. In the last chapter (5.) I provide an overview of the argumentation and propose a revision of the typology of multiple wh-questions.

1.3   Theoretical Preliminaries

1.3.1 The Framework

The discussion and the analysis I propose in this study of wh-questions in Somali, Italian, Berber and Irish are anchored in a feature checking mechanism as developed in the *Minimalist Program* (Chomsky 1995, 2000, 2001). According to this theory, syntactic derivations are driven by the need to check morphological features. Morphological features may be interpretable or uninterpretable. Uninterpretable features must be checked and deleted before they enter the interface levels of grammar: PF and LF. Interpretable features do not need to be checked. The syntactic derivation begins with a *numeration* consisting of a set of lexical items chosen from the *lexicon*. There are three options involved in the syntactic derivations. *Merge* is an operation that takes two items from the numeration and creates a complex item. This complex item can be merged again with other elements in order to create more complex items. The process continues until all elements of the numeration are used up. *Move* is a last resort operation triggered by the need to check *strong* features of syntactic elements. Move applies when there is no available element in the numeration which can be merged and thereby check a strong feature. When the uninterpretable feature of a syntactic item is *weak*, feature checking is achieved through the operation *agree*. Agree establishes a relation at distance between a morphological feature on a syntactic head and a phrasal element with a matching feature (note that the concept of agree I adopt belongs to elaborations of the minimalist program from after Chomsky 1995). Another similar concept of move expressed along the lines of the *probe-goal* system (Chomsky 2000, 2001) is the following one. Move is assumed to be a twofold operation which consists of agreement between a *probe* (a syntactic head with an uninterpretable feature) and a *goal* (a syntactic object with a matching interpretable feature), and subsequent merge which is triggered by an additional *EPP*-feature of the probe. This amounts to saying that merge is the less costly operation and it is preferable to move. Sticking to the Chomsky's (1995) theoretical model, I further assume that movement proceeds overtly, successive-cyclically and is induced by the need to check uninterpretable strong features of functional heads (C°, T°, D° etc.). Adopting an idea of Lasnik (1999:128), I assume that features which trigger movement may reside on dislocated elements themselves (e.g., on D° of a DP).

1.3.2 The Theory of Multiple Wh-Questions
I will consider three accounts for the typology of wh-questions and discuss the problems these standard assumptions face when confronted with languages like Somali, Berber, Italian and Irish. This overview substantiates the necessity of theoretical and typological revision. The first one is Cheng's (1997:22) *Clausal Typing Hypothesis*. This is an account for the typological variation of wh-in-situ languages and languages with wh-movement:

(10) The Clausal Typing Hypothesis
Every clause needs to be typed. In the case of typing a wh-question, either a wh-particle in C° is used or else fronting of a wh-word to SpecCP is used, thereby typing a clause through C° by Spec-head agreement.[3]

In other words, languages like Japanese, which exhibit yes/no-particles, are wh-in-situ languages. Languages like German or English do not have yes/no-particles. Therefore, clausal typing is achieved through wh-movement to SpecCP. This also implies that wh-movement cannot be optional (for analysis of languages like French or Egyptian Arabic with optional wh-fronting see Bošković 1998, Cheng 1997, Cheng & Rooryck 2000, Poletto & Pollock 2000, Rizzi 1991 and Sabel 2004).

What does an analysis like this reveal about the syntax of multiple wh-questions? In the case of Japanese-like languages, the licensing of wh-in-situ is not restricted to one wh-item. In the case of English-like languages, movement of one wh-word to SpecCP is for the purposes of clausal typing. Other wh-

---

[3] The term wh-particle refers to particles which mark yes/no-questions. In the following, I adopt the term *yes/no-particle*.

items may remain in-situ. In the case of Bulgarian-like languages, fronting of all wh-phrases is for independent reasons. Cheng (1997:71) assumes that interrogative wh-words in Bulgarian have a null determiner that has an interrogative force: $[_D \, \emptyset \, _{[+WH]}]$. She proposes that this determiner has to be licensed by $C°$, which is marked for [+WH]. Thus, the licensing of $[_D \, \emptyset \, _{[+WH]}]$ requires fronting of all wh-words (for a similar proposal in minimalist terms see Grewendorf 2001 and Sabel 2001). Analyses in terms of a *wh-Criterion* (May 1985, Rizzi 1991) make similar predictions about the syntax of multiple wh-questions.[4]

Sabel (2004) discusses several problems connected with this approach. One of these problems also arises in Somali, Irish and Berber due to the specific properties of wh-questions in these languages. These three languages exhibit overt yes/no-particles; nevertheless, wh-phrases obligatorily appear in a left-peripheral position (for extensive discussion and examples see subchapter 4.3.).

The second approach is based on the assumption that wh-questions are related to focus constructions. The idea to analyse wh-movement as an instance of focus movement is not new (Horvath 1986, among others). Many languages of the world confirm the fact that wh-question formation is triggered by the need to check focus features. Such analyses are often traced back to the (semantic) fact that a wh-element is inherently focused. The wh-word is the focus of the interrogative clause, i.e. the wh-phrase designates what is not presupposed as known. Horvath (1986:118) assumes a universal principle according to which focus is a syntactic feature that is assigned to a non-echo wh-phrase. In addition, several syntactic arguments have been given for the assumption that wh-fronting takes place for focusing reasons. For example, Brody (1990) assumes a functional category Focus which projects into a Focus Phrase (FP) that is generated between IP/VP and CP. He argues for a *Focus-Criterion* in analogy to the *wh-Criterion* (May 1985, Rizzi 1991) in order to account for the crosslinguistic variation with respect to the position of focused constituents in the overt and covert syntax (for covert focus movement see e.g., Puskás 2000):

(11) The Focus-Criterion
      a. At S-Structure and LF the Spec of FP must contain a +f-phrase.
      b. At LF all +f-phrases must be in a FP.
      (Brody 1990)

In Hungarian, where the Focus-Criterion has to be fulfilled in the overt syntax (and of course at LF), the focused category must move in the overt syntax. It

---

[4] The wh-Criterion (Rizzi 1991):
   A. A wh-operator must be in a Spec-head configuration with $X°_{[+WH]}$.
   B. An $X°_{[+WH]}$ must be in a Spec-head configuration with a wh-operator.

cannot stay in-situ as in English, where the Focus-Criterion may apply at LF. Thus, we have two types of languages with respect to the mechanisms involved in focus licensing. There are languages in which focus is licensed in-situ and languages in which focus is licensed in a designated position.[5] A final important distinction with respect to realising focus concerns the fact that some languages have more than one possibility to mark focus. German has a focus position in SpecCP but focus may also be realised in-situ. Korean is assumed to exhibit more than one focus position (cf. Choe 1995). Hungarian is argued to have a recursive FocP (cf. Horvath 1995 and É. Kiss 1998a).

The predictions of focus-based analyses about the derivation of wh-questions are similar to those of the Clausal Typing Hypothesis. In languages without a designated focus position wh-phrases are supposed to appear in-situ (e.g., Japanese, cf. 2). Languages that exhibit a structurally marked focus position usually license wh-phrases into that position (e.g., Hungarian, cf. 13). In languages that have both possibilities to realise focus, wh-items may be found both in-situ and in a structurally marked position (e.g., Malagasy, see subchapter 4.3.). Nevertheless, there are some unclarities connected with focus-based approaches. The optionality of wh-movement in a language like Malagasy remains obscure. The distribution of wh-items in a multiple wh-question is also not precisely defined in such analyses. It is not clear what happens in multiple wh-questions in e.g., a language like German which has both possibilities to realise focus, i.e. within the C-projection and in-situ. In other words, we cannot tell within a focus-based approach if wh-fronting in German is for focusing or for clausal typing purposes. The next analysis sketched below casts light on these unclear issues.

A third approach combines the two basic ideas about the syntax of wh-questions discussed above. Sabel (2000, 2003 and 2004) argues that wh-question formation is triggered by the need to check two kinds of features: wh-features and focus features. According to him strong wh- or focus features trigger wh-movement. Weak wh- or focus features do not trigger wh-movement. Optional wh-movement is analysed as optional realisation of strong or weak wh- or focus features in the C-system. Even when both strong wh- and focus features give rise to the same effect, i.e. wh-fronting takes place in both cases, there are still differences between a derivation driven by need of satisfying

---

[5] Several assumptions with respect to the notion of a focus position have been made in linguistic literature. Languages that exhibit a structurally marked focus position are, according to É. Kiss (1995), the *discourse configurational languages*. Languages may vary with respect to the realisation of the focus feature in I° or C° as proposed by Bhatt & Yoon (1991) but it is also possible that in some languages this feature heads its own projection FocP (see Rizzi 1997, Benincà & Poletto 2002, Belletti 2002, among others). Which of these possibilities is realised is a question of language parameterisation.

either a focus or a wh-feature. Thus, the fact that languages like Malagasy and Iraqi Arabic exhibit partial wh-movement and wh-in-situ in embedded interrogative clauses is accounted for by the assumption that the wh-feature in these languages is always weak but the focus feature may optionally be strong. The opposite feature constellation appears in languages like French and Duala, i.e. the focus feature is always weak and the wh-feature may optionally be strong. In these languages partial wh-movement and wh-in-situ in indirect questions are impossible (for detailed discussion see Sabel 2004).

What happens in multiple wh-questions according to this analysis? Japanese-like languages have weak wh- and focus features in C°. C° does not attract any wh-phrase. The wh- or alternatively the focus feature in C° is checked through c-command (binding) of the wh-elements in-situ.[6] Consequently, these languages have multiple wh-in-situ questions. Languages like German and English, which have a strong focus and a strong wh-feature in C° respectively, require wh-movement to C°. The strong feature in C° is eliminated through movement of one wh-element to SpecCP. Therefore, C° does not attract other wh-items. Since the wh-phrases in these languages have interpretable features, they do not need to move to C°. In a multiple wh-question the second and subsequent wh-phrases remain in-situ. In languages like Bulgarian and Malagasy the strong wh- and the strong focus feature in C° respectively trigger wh-fronting to C°. In a clause containing more than one wh-phrase all wh-items undergo raising to C°. This fact is accounted for by the assumption that wh-phrases in these languages bear a strong wh- or focus feature. The strong wh- and focus features on the wh-phrases themselves force the formation of a wh-cluster prior to wh-movement to SpecCP (for details see Grewendorf 2001, Sabel 2001 and 2004). Thus, we get multiple wh-fronting constructions (for other possibilities of multiple wh-question formation in Malagasy see Sabel 2004).

Although Sabel (2004) admits that the languages without multiple wh-questions deserve a separate status in the typology of multiple wh-constructions, there are still many questions concerning the grammar of these languages which need to be discussed precisely, such as, for example, why multiple wh-questions are blocked in the grammar of these languages.

The main question of the current investigation will be what happens in languages like Somali, Italian, Irish and Berber, which do not allow multiple wh-questions. What kinds of features are responsible for the derivation of wh-questions in these languages? As we will see wh-question formation is an in-

---

[6] Note that this approach assumes that covert wh-movement does not exist.

stance of focusing into a designated structural position. Why is wh-in-situ not possible? Why do we not find multiple wh-questions like those found in Bulgarian (a language with multiple wh-fronting to SpecCP, cf. 12) or Hungarian (a language with a recursive FocP, cf. 13)?

(12) [$_{CP}$**Koj**$_i$ **kakvo**$_j$ [$_{IP}$ t$_i$ kupi t$_j$]?   (Bulgarian)
      who what   bought
      'Who bought what?'

(13) [$_{FocP}$**Ki** [$_{Foc°}$ vert$_i$]...meg...[$_{FocP}$ **kit** [$_{Foc°}$ t$_i$][$_{VP}$ ...t$_i$...]]]?   (Hungarian)
      who   beat   PRT   whom
      'Who beat whom?'
      (É. Kiss 1998b)

The following chapters will cast light on the above questions and will additionally introduce many interesting linguistic phenomena from the typological point of view, which are connected with the grammar of wh-questions in the languages without multiple wh-questions. To end the introductory chapter, let me say some words about the theory of focus, especially about different focus phenomena and their relation to wh-questions.

1.3.3 The Theory of Focus

It is clear that the concept of a wh-feature is strictly connected with wh-questions. But what does the notion of focus mean exactly? Some clarifications are necessary in order to avoid misunderstandings emerging from the theory-specific use of the term focus. In this study I apply the term *focus* as developed in É. Kiss (1998a). She argues that two basic types of focus have to be distinguished from each other: *information focus* and *identificational focus*. Information focus is the unmarked kind of focus. It is related to the expression of contextually new, not presupposed information and it is typically not associated with syntactic movement. Identificational focus has quantificational properties and involves an operator which expresses exhaustive identification. A strong piece of evidence for this interpretation is provided by the fact that identificational focus may be accompanied by focusing particles as *only*, but not by universal quantifiers, *even*- and *also*-phrases. In syntactic terms '...the constituent called identificational focus acts as an operator which moves into a scope position in the specifier of a functional projection and binds a variable' (cf. É. Kiss 1998a). Its function is defined as follows: 'An identificational focus represents a subset of the set of contextually or situationally given elements for which the predicate phrase can potentially hold; it is identified as the exhaustive subset of this set for which the predicate holds.' (cf. É. Kiss 1998a). Identificational focus is [±contrastive]. A [+contrastive]-interpretation is given when the identificational focus operates on a closed set of entities whose members are known to the participants of the discourse. A [-contrastive]-interpretation is given when the identificational focus operates on an open set of entities (for discussion of other proposals see É. Kiss 1998a and references cited there).

What kind of relation exists between the two kinds of focus (information and identificational focus) and the grammar of wh-questions? As we will see in the discussion of wh-questions and focus constructions in Italian (cf. subchapter 3.1.), wh-questions in this language seem to pattern syntactically with contrastive focus realised in a designated left-peripheral position. However, this apparent similarity is puzzling since the interpretation of wh-phrases and wh-questions has nothing to do with the semantics of contrast. I will show that information focus (crucially non-contrastive focus) also appears in a dedicated syntactic position in the languages under investigation. In order to examine the nature and the distributional patterns of the two basic types of focus, i.e. information vs. identificational focus, in Somali, Italian, Berber and Irish I will examine typical environments of their use. Wh-questions and answers to wh-questions will be referred to as clauses involving the appearance of information focus. As for the syntactic properties of identificational focus I will consider contexts which clearly signal its [+contrastive]-interpretation. In other words, in the following investigation I will work with the terms *information focus* and *contrastive focus*. Since all the languages I am dealing with, i.e. Somali, Berber, Irish and Italian, have a designated structural focus position, to ease representation I will adopt a split version of the CP along the lines of Rizzi (1997). Within this representational model, there are separate projections for information types coded in the C-system. ForceP expresses the relation of a clause to superordinate structures: to a higher clause or to the discourse. Fin(iteness)P is related to the propositional content (expressed by the IP) and reflects an observation that there are certain 'agreement' rules between the C and I (for more on the content of ForceP and FinP see Rizzi 1997). The projections Top(ic)P and Foc(us)P are refer to the information structure of a clause and express the linguistic fact that old and new (or contrastive) information can appear into structurally marked positions. Consider example (14) from Italian which illustrates the split version of the CP:

(14)

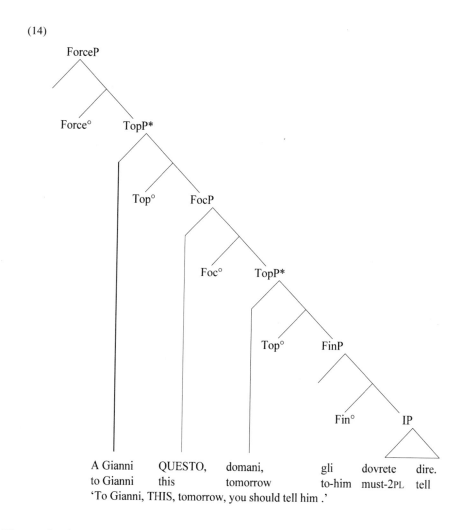

```
A Gianni      QUESTO,      domani,          gli      dovrete     dire.
to Gianni     this         tomorrow         to-him   must-2PL    tell
'To Gianni, THIS, tomorrow, you should tell him .'
```

The projections I will be mainly concerned with are FocP (for focused elements) and TopP (for topic phrases). Using the term topic, I refer to the syntactic representation of old, contextually given or presupposed information (for
detailed classification of different kinds of topics see Büring 1997 and Frascarelli & Hinterhölzl 2004, among others).

Let us now turn to the already proposed analyses of the ungrammaticality of
multiple wh-questions and get better acquainted with this phenomenon observed in Somali, Berber, Italian and Irish.

CHAPTER 2
PREVIOUS ANALYSES OF THE UNGRAMMATICALITY OF
MULTIPLE WH-QUESTIONS

Several rather heterogeneous analyses have been proposed in the literature in order to explain the ungrammaticality of multiple wh-questions. It is important to point out that there is no uniform treatment of the problem. The proposals discussed below are connected with different ideas based on theoretical assumptions as stated in the earlier versions of the *Principles & Parameters Model* (since Chomsky 1981) as well as in its recent versions beginning with the *Minimalist Program* (Chomsky 1995 and subsequent developments of the theory). Each of the earlier treatments of the ungrammaticality of multiple wh-questions either concentrates on a single language or represents a comparative analysis of two languages. The following sections sketch the lines of argumentation of the three analyses. Adams' (1984) analysis is an attempt to explain the ungrammaticality of multiple wh-questions in Italian and Irish (see subchapter 2.1.). Calabrese's (1987) approach, based on his analysis of Italian (Calabrese 1984), compares Italian with Berber (see subchapter 2.2.). The ideas represented in Lecarme (1999), Svolacchia et al. (1995) and Svolacchia & Puglielli (1999) focus on Somali (see subchapter 2.3.).

2.1   The Condition on COMP Adjunction

Adams (1984) takes the following observation made by Rizzi (1982) as a starting point of her analysis of the ungrammaticality of multiple wh-questions in Italian and Irish:

(15) a. *Mi domando **chi** ha   incontrato **chi**.
          I   wonder   who have-3SG met   whom
          'I wonder who met who.'
      b. ??Non so   ancora **chi** ha   fatto **che cosa**?
          not know yet   who have-3SG done what
          'I don't know yet who did what.'
          (Rizzi 1982:51)

Regarding the marginal acceptability of some examples (indicated by '??' in 15b), Rizzi claims that certain interpretative rules for wh-words in interrogatives render sentences containing more than one wh-element ungrammatical.[7] This rather poorly defined restriction is responsible for the ungrammaticality of multiple wh-questions (see 15a, b).

Rizzi's ideas are further developed in Adams' (1984) comparative analysis of the ungrammaticality of multiple wh-questions in Italian and Irish. As a formal alternative of the *Doubly-Filled Comp Filter*, she formulates the so-called *Condition on COMP Adjunction* (henceforth the CCA). This filter operates at different points of the derivation across different languages and determines at which representational level of the grammar adjunction to COMP is prohibited:[8]

(16)   The Condition on COMP Adjunction:
       $*[_{COMP}\ \alpha\ COMP]$

Making further the assumptions that S (IP) is a universal bounding category and that at LF the CCA identifies interrogative operators and their traces but not relative operators and their traces she elaborates a classification of language types according to the CCA:[9]

Table 1. Language Types according to the CCA

Level of representation	English, French	Italian	Irish	Bulgarian
S-Structure	+	-	+	-
LF	-	+	+	-

As illustrated in Table (1.) adjunction to COMP in Italian is allowed at S-Structure but not at LF. These specifications of the CCA are firstly designed to explain the ungrammaticality of multiple wh-questions. Multiple wh-questions involving fronting of all wh-items (cf. 6b) or fronting of one wh-item and leaving further wh-elements in-situ (cf. 6c) are ungrammatical in Italian. Secondly,

---

[7] Note that an account for the ungrammaticality of multiple wh-questions based on differences of interpretation suggests that there are specific semantic requirements for wh-questions that are only valid for Italian. This outcome is undesirable because it goes against the principles of universal grammar. Given the assumption that LF as a grammatical level of representation is universal, there cannot be LF conditions that are valid for Italian but not for any other language.

[8] Adams (1984) states the Doubly-Filled COMP Filter as follows (cf. Chomsky & Lasnik 1977, Chomsky 1981):
       (i) $*[_{COMP}\quad \alpha\quad \beta]$

[9] The original table as proposed by Adams (1984) has been slightly modified for the current purposes of the discussion. The symbol '+' indicates at which stage of the derivation the CCA is active (i.e. adjunction to COMP is impossible); whereas the symbol '-' signals at which representational level the CCA is inactive (i.e. adjunction to COMP is possible).

they explain why relativising out of a wh-question is permitted. As (17) shows
Italian allows relativisation out of wh-islands:[10]

(17) Il   solo incarico **che** non sapevi   **a chi**   avrebbero
      the   only charge   that   not knew-2SG   to whom would-3PL
      affidato è   poi   finito   proprio a te.
      entrust is-3SG   then ended   exactly to you
      'The only charge that you didn't know to whom they would entrust
      has been entrusted exactly to you.'
      (Adams 1984)

Given Adams' additional assumption that the CCA does not identify relative
operators at LF, the derivation is not ruled out at that level as the grammatical
example (17) indicates. However, the explanation for the ungrammaticality of
multiple wh-questions in Italian developed by Adams is problematic when we
consider extraction of D-Linked wh-phrases out of wh-islands.[11] Adams' proposal wrongly predicts that (18a) is ungrammatical.

(18) a. **A quale   dei   tuoi figli**$_i$ non ti   ricordi
         to which of   your sons not you   remember
         quanti   soldi   hai   dato t$_i$?
         how-much   money   have-2SG   given
         'To which one of your sons don't you remember how much money
         you gave?'
      b. *****Chi**$_i$ ti   domandi   **chi**   t$_i$ ha   incontrato t$_i$?
         whom   you   wonder   who   have-3SG   met
         'Who do you wonder who met?'
      c. ??**Chi**$_i$ non   sai   t$_i$ **che cosa**   t$_i$ ha   fatto?
         who   not   know-2SG   what   have-3SG   done
         'Who don't you know what did?'
         (Rizzi 1982:70; 51)

---

[10] The account which Rizzi (1982) offers for the case of relativisation out of a wh-question in
(17), is that S' (CP) and not S (IP) is the bounding node in Italian. Since COMP cannot be
doubly filled in Italian the only possible derivation is the one in which the relative pronoun
crosses two S (IP) nodes. The intention of Adams' statement that the CCA does not identify
relative operators and their traces is to account for the grammaticality of clauses like (17) and
at the same time to exclude clauses like (18b and c).

[11] The possibility of island violations of this kind is due to a certain property of D-Linked wh-
phrases. The complex wh-phrase *'a quale dei tuoi figli'* originating in the indirect question can
undergo long extraction without giving rise to an intervention effect induced by the presence of
another wh-phrase *'quanti soldi'* in the specifier position of the embedded clause. The nature
of D-Linking should not be of interest at this point of the investigation (cf. Rizzi 1982, 1990,
2000, see also Grewendorf 2002 for discussion and references).

According to Adams' analysis, sentences like (18b and c) are ungrammatical in Italian. The account for the ungrammaticality of (18b and c) is analogous to the analysis of multiple wh-questions like (15a and b) developed on the basis of the CCA. The LF representations [$_{SpecCP}$ chi chi] for (15a) and [$_{SpecCP}$ chi che cosa] for (15b) are illicit because they violate the CCA. Similarly (18b and c) have illicit LF representations [$_{SpecCP}$ chi t$_i$] and [$_{SpecCP}$ t$_i$ che cosa] respectively. But consider a clause like (18a). It shows the same constellation as in (18b and c), but example (18a) is still grammatical. This undesirable effect indicates that the CCA is not correct.

Another unfortunate outcome of Adams' proposal is the fact that a multiple wh-question like the following one should be possible in Italian:

(19) *__Quele professore__ vuole   assumere qualcuno
      which professor   want-3SG to-hire   someone
      che parla   __quale__ __lingua__?
      that speak-3SG which   language
      'Which professor wants to hire someone who speaks which
      language?'
      (Brunetti 2003:109)

Since Adams assumes that the CCA does not identify relative operators and their traces at LF, the wh-phrase *quale lingua* 'which language' inside the relative clause is supposed to be able to adjoin to the relative operator in the embedded COMP at LF. This is, however, impossible as (19) shows. The CCA does not provide clear judgements about the status of clauses like (19). Why cannot wh-phrases stay in-situ in Italian take an interrogative scope?[12]

Irish presents a slightly different situation. According to Adams' classification, Irish does not allow adjunction to COMP at both S-Structure and LF given the

---

[12] Complex NP-islands are not a problem for wh-arguments in-situ crosslinguistically (see Cheng 1997). Consider an example that suggests that wh-elements in-situ are generally prohibited in Italian (see for contrast 18a):

    (i) *__Chi__ crede   che   Giovanni abbia   baciato __quale ragazza__?
        who think-2SG that Giovanni have-3SG-SUBJ kissed   which girl
        'Who thinks that Giovanni kissed which girl?'
        (Eugenia Marchisio, p.c.)

Consequently, the right analysis of the ungrammaticality of multiple wh-questions in Italian has to take this crucial fact into account. Adams fails to observe this important restriction in the syntax of wh-questions of Italian. The account I propose easily excludes clauses like (19). According to my analysis *quale lingua* has to check its strong focus feature against a head with an appropriate interpretable feature, i.e. it has to adjoin to the matrix C° position. This is, however, impossible in Italian (for the technical details of the analysis see chapter 4.).

fact that relativisation and questioning out of wh-islands are illicit (cf. 20a and b):

(20) a. ***fear$_i$**   nachN   bhfuil   fhios   agam
          a man   NEG-COMP is   knowledge at-me
          cén   **cineal**   **mná**   aL   phósfadh **t$_i$**
          which sort of a   woman COMP   marry
          'a man which I don't know what kind of a woman would marry'
     b. ***Cén**   **sagart$_i$** nachN   bhfuil   fhios   agat   **caidé**
          which priest NEG-COMP is   knowledge at-you   what
          aL   dúirt **t$_i$**?
          COMP   said
          'Which priest don't you know what said?'

However, McCloskey (1979:32) notes that examples like (20a, b) become grammatical when an appropriate pronoun appears in the embedded position instead of the trace (see for discussion and examples subchapter 3.4.). The CCA cannot explain this observation about Irish.

Adams' approach is an attempt to explain the typological differences between multiple wh-questions involving fronting of all wh-elements (the Romanian/Bulgarian type) and multiple wh-questions with wh-in-situ (the English type). One striking problem of this analysis is the fact that the CCA does not have an available option to explain the existence of typical wh-in-situ languages like Japanese. There is no possible value of the CCA in Table (1.), which renders any movement to COMP at S-Structure illicit but allows all wh-elements to move to COMP at LF as usually assumed for wh-in-situ languages. Note further that French, which Adams classifies together with English, is in fact a wh-in-situ language with optional wh-fronting (for discussion see Bošković 1998, Sabel 2000 and Cheng & Rooryck 2000, among others). Since all these crucial distinctions cannot be made within the CCA, Adams approach is obviously not the right solution for a typological account of multiple wh-questions.

Another problem of the CCA is its false prediction that Bulgarian freely allows for wh-extraction out of a wh-island. Given the fact that Bulgarian is a multiple wh-fronting language and the CCA does not hold at any level of its grammar (see Table 1.), adjunction to an already filled COMP should be possible. But consider the following example (for more examples from Bulgarian see Rudin 1988,):

Why bother with Adams (1984)? Old terminology + structure

(21) ***Na kogo**$_i$ ne   znaeš   **koj** šte   podari t$_i$ kniga   za
      to whom   NEG know-2SG who will give   a-book for
      roždennia den?
      birthday
      'Who don't you know to whom will give a book for the birthday?'

Example (21) exactly represents the constellation observed in Italian (cf. 18b and c). However, Bulgarian is not like Italian in any other ways. As we know, Bulgarian is a multiple wh-fronting language (for discussion of multiple wh-fronting languages see Boeckx & Grohmann 2003).

Let us look at a non-multiple fronting language like Swedish that allows extraction out of wh-islands. In this respect it behaves like Bulgarian, a multiple fronting language. Argument extraction out of wh-islands in Swedish and Bulgarian is possible for relative and D-Linked wh-phrases. Compare Swedish (cf. 22b) with Bulgarian (cf. 22a):

(22) a. ?**Koja ot tezi knigi**   se   čudiš   **koj** znae
         which of these books   REFL wonder-2SG who know-3SG
         koj prodava?
         who sell-3SG
         'Which of these books do you wonder who knows who sells?'
         (Rudin 1988)
      b. **Vilken film** var   det   du   gärna   ville   veta
         which   film was   it   you   gladly wanted know
         vem som hade regisserat?
         who that had   directed
         'Which film did you want to know who had directed?'
         (Engdahl 1986)

The CCA is an analysis that relates the possibility of extraction out of wh-islands to the possibility of multiple adjunction to COMP. It therefore wrongly predicts that Swedish is a multiple wh-fronting language like Bulgarian (for a discussion of Swedish and Bulgarian see Bošković 2003).

Next, the classification of the other languages that do not allow multiple wh-questions is also problematic. Somali behaves like Irish with respect to long distance wh-dependencies across syntactic islands. Such structures are acceptable in both languages. It is therefore reasonable to put it into the language group to which Irish belongs according to the CCA. But there is still a problem for the CCA. While embedded wh-questions in Somali do not occur at all, long distance wh-dependencies are still possible (cf. subchapter 3.2. for data and discussion). This rather puzzling fact cannot be explained by the CCA.

Irish poses a further problem for the analysis proposed by Adams. She claims that the CCA is fulfilled in Irish at both levels, S-Structure and LF. This is, however, not correct. Like Berber, Irish has a special strategy of wh-question formation. Wh-questions in Irish are instances of clefts. These constructions show a linear word order consisting of the wh-phrase followed directly by a complementizer in Irish and a cleft marker in Berber (cf. subchapter 3.3. for Berber and subchapter 3.4. for Irish). This fact clearly contradicts Adams (1984). Therefore, the CCA as a modification of the Doubly-Filled COMP-Filter has to be valued negatively at least at S-Structure.[13]

Finally, any semantically motivated account for the language variation with respect to the possibility of multiple wh-questions is on the wrong track. It is a common hypothesis in generative grammar that all languages share the same interpretational principles, i.e. the LF rules are universal. Hence, typological differences between multiple wh-questions, i.e. the possibility to move wh-phrases or leave them in-situ, cannot be due to language-specific interpretative conditions. This means that a language in which wh-adjunction to $C°$ at LF is prohibited cannot exist, as Adams wrongly proposes for Italian and Irish. I will argue that the restrictions that explain the exceptional behaviour of the languages without multiple wh-questions have to be located in the lexicon. The wh-elements as lexical items are endowed with specific morphological features which force their distribution in designated syntactic positions. As we will see, wh-questions correspond to specific focus constructions in Somali, Berber, Italian and Irish. I will interpret this fact in the following way: In order to get a legitimate LF representation every wh-phrase in these languages has to check its strong focus feature in the overt syntax, i.e. before the derivation enters the semantic component of grammar. The account I will propose in chapter (4.) is

---

[13] Note that Adams (1984) discusses cases like Middle English in which an interrogative wh-word is followed by the neutral complementizer *that* (for further examples from other languages cf. Adams 1984):

    (i) Men shal wel knowe who that I am.

She assumes that the complementizer is semantically featureless. It may therefore be freely inserted at any level. It may cooccur with a wh-element in PF (provided the CCA does not apply at that level in the given language) while at the same time being absent at LF. This explanation is not acceptable for languages like Irish and Berber because, as we will see in the next chapter, the wh-question formation in languages without multiple wh-questions involves a derivational mechanism that crucially depends on the specific licensing conditions of focus constructions. Thus, the head elements found left-adjacent to the wh-phrases in Somali, Berber and Irish are not featureless and therefore not optional. Rather, as licensors of focus features they are obligatory (see chapter 4.).

related to an important idea expressed by the next analysis (cf. subchapter 2.2.). This is the idea that wh-question formation has to do with the language-specific syntactic mechanisms for the representation of new information, referred to as *information focus*.

2.2 Wh-Questions as Instances of Unique Information Focus

Calabrese (1984) relates the fact that it is not possible to host more than one wh-element in a single clause in Italian to the fact that it is not possible to have more than one focus of new information in the same sentence. This correlation is derived from the information structure typical of Italian sentences. He assumes a rule of new information feature assignment, called the *N-feature* and a principle of grammar, which requires that an interrogative wh-expression must receive an N-feature by the following rule:

(23) If there is a wh-expression, then it must receive an N-feature, otherwise it is a relative wh-expression.

The rules of N-feature assignment are stated as follows:

(24) Assign the N-feature either to a sentence S or to the last constituent α in the linear order of S (where α is either a predicate or an argument of S).

The two principles indicate that only one wh-expression per clause can receive the N-feature and thus sentences containing more than one wh-phrase are ungrammatical:

(25) ***Chi** ha   scritto   **che cosa?**
      who have-3SG   written   what
      'Who wrote what?'

The same derivational mechanism renders sentences containing more than one focus of new information ungrammatical (cf. 26).[14]

---

[14] Belletti (2002) discusses similar examples with contrastive focus stress on the initial focused phrase and information focus interpretation of the element in bold:
   (i) *A GIANNI ho   regalato   **un libro.**
       to Gianni   have-1SG given   a   book
       'I gave a book to Gianni.'
   (ii) *UN LIBRO ha   letto   **Gianni**.
        a   book   have-3SG read   Gianni
        'Gianni read a book.'
Belletti (2002) assumes the existence of two distinct focus positions in Italian, i.e. a left-peripheral FocP for contrastive focus and a clause internal FocP between IP and VP for infor-

(26) ***Mario** ha   scritto   una   **lettera**.
       Mario have-3SG   written   a   letter
       'Mario has written a letter.'

However, there are additional restrictions that are necessary to account for data like the following:

(27) a. Carlo_i   è   stato ucciso t_i
           Carlo   be-3SG   been killed
           'Carlo has been killed.'
      b. Lo_i   hai   visto t_i.
           it   have-2SG   seen
           'You have seen it.'

The interpretation of the examples indicates that either the whole sentence or the VP can be interpreted as new. The fronted elements that bind the postverbal traces cannot be instances of new information. Calabrese proposes that the rule of N-feature assignment applies at S-Structure to case marked constituents only. Therefore, the traces of the fronted elements in the examples above cannot be checked by the rule of N-feature assignment. Calabrese claims that the NP and the object clitic move for case reasons, i.e. a movement which is different from wh-movement. But note that under the standard account objects receive their case inside the VP through government. Under the so-called VP-internal hypothesis, subjects may also receive their case inside the VP, a fact supported by the existence of postverbal subjects in Italian (see e.g., Rizzi 1982). These assumptions pose a problem for Calabrese's account (for more

---

mation focus. Nevertheless, given the ungrammaticality of (i) and (ii) she suggests that there is a constraint which excludes two focused items in Italian regardless of their semantics. The constituents *un libro* 'a book' and *Gianni* can only have a topic interpretation. An additional argument in favour of this hypothesis is presented by the absence of a weak crossover effect with postverbal subjects in wh-questions (for discussion of weak crossover effects see Rizzi 1997, Benincà & Poletto 2002 and subchapter 3.1.):

  (iii)   Attualmente, **in quale suo_i**   **appartamento**   vive   Gianni_i?
           at present   in which his   apartment   live-3SG   Gianni
           'In which of his apartments does Gianni live at present?'
  (iv)   *?Attualmente,   **in un suo_i**   **appartamento**   vive   Gianni_i.
           at present   in one his   apartment   live-3SG   Gianni
           'Gianni lives in one of his apartments at present.'

Note that the wco-effect is present in (iv). This indicates that the DP *Gianni* has operator properties, i.e. it has moved to an operator position, as standardly assumed. This in turn means that postverbal subjects in Italian are in fact not in-situ, but have moved to a focus position. The fact that two foci are generally impossible (cf. 26, i and ii) in Italian suggests that the language has only one focus position per clause. This is actually the possibility I will argue for (see subchapter 3.1.).

information about the status of preverbal subjects see e.g., Belletti 1999, among others, see also Chomsky 2000, 2001 for case assignment at long distance).

The necessity of wh-movement in wh-questions remains unexplained in this account. Suppose that the wh-phrase receives the N-feature in its case position. Then, wh-movement seems to be triggered by some other need that indicates that the processes of N-feature assignment and wh-movement do not belong to the same type of syntactic derivation. Calabrese does not discuss these differences (see Rizzi 1997 for an account of differently motivated movements to the left periphery).

The comparative analysis of wh-questions in Italian and Berber proposed by Calabrese (1987) implements the crucial idea from Calabrese (1984) that wh-interrogatives and focused elements constitute related syntactic and semantic phenomena. Since multiple information foci are impossible in Italian, multiple wh-questions are not expected to appear either. In Berber the focus of new information is realised by the means of clefting. Multiple foci would be possible in Berber only if more cleft sites were available in a single clause. But this is not the case. Wh-questions in Berber are parasitic on clefting and multiple wh-questions are ungrammatical for the same reason that multiple foci are.

Calabrese (1987) proposes two rather complex licensing mechanisms for both focus and wh-constituents. The first one requires adjacency between the focused or the wh-element and the verb and a specific rule of endo-government that reflects his claim that new information is represented inside the VP:

(28)   Focus is assigned to a constituent endo-governed by the verb.

The definition of endo-government is stated as follows:

(29) α endo-governs β in $[_\gamma \ldots \alpha \ldots \beta \ldots]$ if
    (i) $\alpha = X^\circ$
    (ii) γ is a maximal projection of α and
    (iii) α c-commands β.

If VP is the maximal projection of V, then V endo-governs only the constituents inside the VP. This amounts to saying that focus is assigned to a constituent endo-governed by the verb.

Additionally, adjacency between the verb and the element bearing new information is crucial in order to account for the distributional pattern of wh-arguments and arguments bearing new information in Italian:

(30) a. *Ha   scritto quella lettera **Maria**.[15]
           have-3SG written that   letter   Maria
           'Maria has written that letter.'
      b. Ha   scritto **Maria,** quella lettera.
           have-3SG written Maria   that   letter
           'Maria has written that letter.'

In (30a) the rule of endo-government as stated in (29) seems to be observed for the subject, but it cannot be new information because it is not adjacent to the verb as in (30b). The same is true for wh-arguments as the contrast between (31a) and (31b) indicates:

(31) a. **Che cosa** Carlo ha   scritto a Maria?
           what   Carlo have-3SG written to Maria
           'What did Carlo write to Maria?'
      b. **Che cosa** ha   scritto Carlo a Maria?
           what   have-3SG written Carlo to Maria
           'What did Carlo write to Maria?'

In the case of wh-questions (cf. 31b) the wh-item is to the left of the verb, i.e. it is not endo-governed by the verb. Nevertheless, it is the focus of new information. Regarding these facts, it is not clear whether the rule of endo-government is crucial for the distribution of wh-phrases. It seems that the only case in which the notion of endo-government becomes important is the assignment of information focus in declaratives. Consider again an example which shows that preverbal subjects cannot be the focus of new information in Italian:

---

[15] Belletti (2002) proposes a different account for the marginal acceptance ('??' according to Belletti's judgements) of VOS sequences in Italian. She analyses such clauses as instances of clause internal remnant topic movement. The VO sequence is interpreted as topic, which occupies the clause internal topic position located to the left of the clause internal focus position. The subject fills the low new information focus position. Belletti stipulates that VOS sentences (cf. i) in Italian are degraded because objects have to move out of their case position. She provides examples (cf. ii) which show that removing the object from that position rescues the sentence (see also Brunetti 2003:125ff for further discussion on VSO / VOS sequences):

   (i) ??[TopP [t_i ha   letto il romanzo]_VP [FocP **Gianni_i**]   t_VP]
                        has-3SG read the novel   Gianni
            'Gianni has read the novel.'
   (ii) L'ha   letto **Gianni**.
        it-have-3SG read   Gianni
        'Gianni has read it.'

(32) a. **Quanto   tempo** è   passato…?
         how much time   be-3SG passed
         'How much time has passed…?'
      b. Sono   passate **molte   settimane**.
         be-3PL passed   a lot of weeks
         'A lot of weeks have passed.'
      c. #**Molte settimane** sono   passate.
         a lot of weeks   be-3PL passed
         'A lot of weeks have passed.'

Both endo-government and adjacency have to be observed in the case of focused subjects (cf. 32b). This is shown by the contrast between (32b) and (32c). However, the wh-subject does not need to satisfy the endo-government requirement as (32a) shows. Moreover, satisfying the endo-government requirement is not enough for the licensing of wh-phrases in Italian (cf. example 87). To sum up, there is an obvious difference between the distributional pattern of wh-phrases in wh-questions and information focus in answers to wh-questions. The analysis Calabrese proposes fails to capture this difference neatly. I will account for these differences in subsection 3.1.1.4.

Next, I will review the application of the relevant focus assignment rules in Berber. Wh-questions and new information focus are both expressed by a cleft construction:

(33) a. **May**   t-sghu   terbatt?
         what-CM3FSG-bought   girl
         'What did the girl buy?'
      b. (d) **adil**   ay   t-sghu   terbatt.
         COP   grapes   CM   3FSG-buy   girl
         'It is grapes that the girl bought.'

The endo-governing element in Berber is the copula *d*, which is optional in declaratives and does not appear in wh-questions at all. Calabrese proposes a rule of copula deletion in wh-questions which applies to the phonological part of the grammar. But if endo-government is crucial for the licensing of focus then we expect to find strong evidence for its existence, i.e. deletion is not supposed to be possible. Calabrese's account of the facts is rather ad hoc and poses a problem for the additional adjacency requirement between the endo-governing element and the focused item.

The second licensing mechanism was created to account for the appearance of focused elements in a final position (for examples see Calabrese 1987) and wh-adjuncts, especially for wh-phrases like *perché* 'why' and *come* 'how' in Italian as well as for *maymi* 'why' and *mani* 'where' in Berber. He assumes that such adjunct wh-questions in Berber are not instances of clefts:

(34)   Assign focus to a sentence peripheral ungoverned constituent.

Consider the examples Calabrese provides as an illustration of (34) in Italian (cf. 35a) and Berber (cf. 35b):[16]

(35)   a. **Perché** Carlo ha   detto queste cose?   (Italian)
          why   Carlo have-3SG said these things
          'Why did Carlo say these things?'
       b. **Maymi** x-s   tetsit?   (Berber)
          why   on-him   laughed-2SG
          'Why did you laugh at him?'

The third crucial rule Calabrese proposes excludes the application of both mechanisms of focus assignment. This mechanism is responsible for the ungrammaticality of multiple wh-questions. The following ungrammatical multiple wh-questions in Italian (cf. 36a) and Berber (36b) illustrate that an interaction of both rules of focus assignment is blocked:

(36)   a. ***Maymi**   **may**   t-sghu   terbatt?   (Berber)
          why   what-CM   3FSG-bought girl
          'Why did the girl buy what?'
       b. ***Perché** hai   comprato **che cosa**?   (Italian)
          why   have-2SG   bought   what
          'Why did you buy what?'

The basic idea of Calabrese's account for the ungrammaticality of multiple wh-questions is correct. Wh-questions are undoubtedly closely related to the linguistic mechanisms for the representation of information / identificational focus (cf. e.g., Horvath 1986 and É. Kiss 1998a, among others). However, recent investigations of the information structure and particularly of the expression of focus in Italian reveal further puzzling facts. In Rizzi's (1997) split-C theory wh-elements are in a complementary distribution with contrastively focused

---

[16] However, Calabrese does not show convincingly that the wh-adjunct *maymi* 'why' in Berber is not an instance of a cleft. As pointed out by Guerssel (1984) and Choe (1987), the morphophonological rules in Berber are very complex and it is not always possible to reconstruct the original morphological structures before phonological contraction has taken place. Since there is no strong evidence against a cleft analysis of wh-adjuncts in Berber I will assume that they are like wh-arguments instances of clefts (see also section 3.3.4.)

elements located in a designated left-peripheral focus projection (see also Benincà & Poletto 2002 for a modified version of the left periphery). Based on the following cooccurrence restrictions Rizzi (1997) argues for the complementary distribution of wh-items and contrastively focused elements:

(37) a. *__Che cosa__,   A GIANNI   hai   detto?
          what   to Gianni   have-2SG   told
          'What TO GIANNI did you tell?'
     b. *A GIANNI,   __che cosa__   hai   detto?
          to Gianni   what   have-2SG   told
          'TO GIANNI what did you tell?'

The position of contrastive focus is syntactically different from the position of information focus. According to Rizzi's assumption, there are two structurally distinct types of focus in Italian. There is a unique left-peripheral position for contrastive focus which is not the same as information focus. The latter is assumed to belong to the VP (cf. Belletti 2002 and Calabrese 1992).[17] By establishing a syntactic correlation between wh-phrases and contrastively focused elements Rizzi (1997) contradicts Calabrese's (1984, 1987) generalisation that wh-interrogatives pattern with information focus. But note that a correlation between contrastive focus and wh-questions is not expected in the semantics. The fact that this correlation does not hold semantically (at least in the unmarked cases) is supported by examples showing question and answer pairs. A neutral wh-question cannot be answered by a contrastive focus construction as the pattern in (38) shows.

(38) a. __Che cosa__   hai   letto?
          what   have-2SG   read
          'What have you read?'
     b. Ho   letto __il__   __libro__.
          have-1SG   read the   book
          'I have read a book.'
     c. #IL   LIBRO   ho   letto (non il   giornale)
          the book   have-1SG   read not the   magazine
          'THE BOOK I have read, not the magazine.'
          (Belletti 2003)

---

[17] Recall that Belletti (2002) proposes a decomposed VP-periphery with the same structure as the clausal left periphery developed by Rizzi (1997). She assumes that contrastive focus is only a left-peripheral phenomenon. Information focus is located in a clause internal low FocP located between the IP and VP layer and does not appear elsewhere (for extensive discussion of different approaches to focus in Italian see subchapter 3.1.).

In other words, wh-questions and their appropriate answers do not seem to display identical syntactic structures. All these facts indicate that a better data survey is needed in order to explain the exact relation between focus constructions and wh-questions in Italian (see subchapter 3.1. for a detailed discussion of the problem). The question, which automatically arises, is whether wh-questions in Italian correspond to the syntactic expression of contrastive focus or of information focus.

For the analysis in chapter (4.), I adopt Calabrese's (1984, 1987) idea for a strict correlation between wh-question formation and the syntactic representation of information focus. By developing the notion of uniqueness, I provide evidence that languages without multiple wh-questions are languages that display a unique focus position. Multiple wh-questions are not allowed to appear in the grammars of languages with a unique focus position because the expression of (both information and contrastive) focus is restricted to a single structurally marked position.

2.3   Wh-Questions in a Clitic Polysynthetic Language

The last approach to the ungrammaticality of multiple wh-questions I will discuss is based on Somali. Somali is assumed a discourse configurational polysynthetic SOV language of a particular subtype. Since it does not fit Baker's (1996) Polysynthesis Parameter neatly, Svolacchia & Puglielli (1999) refer to it as a 'clitic polysynthetic language'. This term reflects an observation that Somali shares some similarities with the pronominal argument languages (also called non-configurational languages) defined in Jelinek (1984). A basic feature of that language type is a pronominal argument structure. Pronominal clitics occur in the A-positions and are assigned θ-roles there. Full NPs appear in adjoined A'-positions associated with the IP-internal pronominal position that determines their interpretation. Basically, the difference between a pronominal argument language (Jelinek 1984) and a polysynthetic language (Baker 1996) is the appearance of overt pronominal elements in the argument positions in the former language type, but not necessarily in the latter. Argument positions in a polysynthetic language are filled with empty elements, which may have the status of either empty pronouns or traces. To sum up, Somali is assumed to be a kind of mixed language type (see also section 3.2.1.).

Lecarme (1999) proposes an account for the ungrammaticality of multiple wh-questions in Somali based on its specific property that argument positions are occupied by pronominal elements. Let us review the lines of her argumentation.

First, if Somali is a pronominal argument language, then wh-expressions cannot occur in argument positions (see also Svolacchia et al. 1995 and Svolacchia & Puglielli 1999). Since wh-phrases cannot appear in-situ at all, the Japanese type of multiple wh-questions is excluded.

Second, according to her, it also follows that there are no multiple wh-questions like those in English. Recall that English represents the mixed strategy, i.e. only one interrogative phrase moves to SpecCP while others remain in-situ.

Third, considering the fact that there is only one focus marker per clause and the observation that a wh-phrase has to be in a focus position in Somali, Lecarme argues that only one wh-phrase can be licensed in SpecCP (cf. for discussion subchapter 3.2.). In other words, multiple fronting of wh-phrases (the Bulgarian type) is not allowed either. This claim is, however, problematic. Richards (1997) proposes a theory for multiple wh-fronting languages in terms of multiple specifiers of a single head. Sabel (2003) argues for a cluster formation of wh-elements in a language like Malagasy as an alternative possibility. A correct analysis must show that both possibilities are not possible in Somali. Next, as another way to derive multiple wh-questions focus recursion has been proposed for a discourse configurational language like Hungarian (É. Kiss 1998b). This option needs to be dismissed from the syntax of Somali as well. Therefore, the exact properties of the focus position in Somali need to be determined more precisely.

Finally, Lecarme claims that given the indefinite, non-referential nature of wh-expressions in Somali they cannot be licensed in adjunct positions. Her claim entails the assumption that any wh-phrase in Somali is base generated in an adjunct position and moves afterwards to SpecCP.[18] A second one cannot stay in an adjunct position where it is base generated (see also Baker 1996:71 for Mohawk, Reinhart 1995, 1998 and Tsai 1994 for a crosslinguistic survey on wh-adverbs). If we assume that every wh-phrase behaves syntactically like a wh-adjunct, then the licensing of a second wh-phrase in-situ is blocked for the same reasons as the licensing of a wh-adjunct in-situ in a language like English.[19] Furthermore, according to an observation made by Bošković (1998) multiple wh-questions containing two wh-adjuncts are not possible in a multi-

---

[18] I provide counter evidence in subchapter (3.2.) and show that wh-questions in Somali do not show movement properties.
[19] The relevant observation is represented by the following English example:
   (i) *Who fixed the car how?

ple wh-fronting language like Serbo-Croatian.[20] If Somali is a language in which all wh-phrases behave syntactically like wh-adjuncts and it is also true that for some reasons two wh-adjuncts per clause are illicit as in the case of Serbo-Croatian, it follows independently from Lecarme's proposal that it is not possible to derive a multiple wh-question in Somali. However, languages like German allow wh-adjuncts to stay in-situ and admit more than one wh-adjunct per clause (see Bošković 2000, 2002 and Müller & Sternefeld 1996 for discussion). Therefore, it is not clear how to treat Somali in crosslinguistic typological aspects.

Moreover, accounts of that kind entail a stronger claim, i.e. any pronominal argument language disallows multiple wh-questions. The question whether this prediction is born out or not needs to be examined carefully (for a discussion and an alternative analysis of a potential pronominal argument language such as Navajo that admits multiple wh-questions cf. Barss et al. 1991). I will show that a focus-based account for the ungrammaticality of multiple wh-questions is a more plausible solution.

Note also that an analysis of Somali as a polysynthetic language faces several problems with the standard definition of polysynthetic languages. Baker (1996) argues for a slightly different language type from that defined in Jelinek (1984). Wh-phrases in a polysynthetic language can be base generated in argument positions. But following the descriptive generalisation that no NP/DP may be in an A-position at the level of S-Structure, he argues that all wh-phrases are forced to move to SpecCP. Thus, polysynthetic languages allow multiple wh-questions of the Bulgarian type:[21]

(39) a. Tak-hróri   **úhka nahótʌ** wa'-e-hnínu-'   (Mohawk)
         2SSIMPER/SO-tell who what   FACT-FsS-buy-PUNC
         'Tell me who bought what.'

---

[20] The following example illustrates that multiple wh-questions containing two wh-adjuncts are judged ungrammatical in Serbo-Croatian:
    (i) *__Zašto__   je __kako__ istukao   Petra?
        why   is how   beaten   Peter
        'Why did he beat Peter how?'
        (Bošković 1998)

[21] Detailed arguments that Mohawk is an overt wh-movement language are represented in (Baker 1996:66-83). Wh-phrases are restricted to a left-peripheral clausal position. Wh-questions obey syntactic islands such as the complex NP- and adjunct islands. Additionally wh-questions give rise to weak crossover effects. In fact, Mohawk is more like Serbo-Croatian with respect to wh-question formation since it does not show superiority effects (see for examples Baker 1996:93 and for discussion of the differences between Bulgarian and Serbo-Croatian Rudin 1988, among others).

b. #**Úhka**   wa'-e-tsh´Ʌri-'   **nahótʌ?**
   who   FACT-FsS-find-PUNC   what
   'Who found what?'
   (Baker 1996:71f)[22]

The second wh-phrase in (39b) can only have an echo interpretation. To conclude, it is not very clear what kind of language Somali really is, a pronominal argument language in Jelinek's (1984) terms or a polysynthetic language in Baker's (1996) terms. As shown, both kinds of analyses make different predictions about possible derivations of wh-questions. In order to avoid confusion resulting from the unclear typological status of Somali, I will propose an analysis based on a focus theory.

In this chapter I have discussed three analyses of the ungrammaticality of multiple wh-questions and the problems connected with them. Adams' (1984) proposal for Italian and Irish is based on a modified version of the doubly filled COMP filter, the CCA. Her analysis has generated diverse problems with the typological classification of other languages that do not show multiple wh-questions as well as with certain wh-constructions from Italian and Irish. Although Calabrese's (1984, 1987) approach is basically on the right track, I have shown that a better data examination is necessary in order to justify the hypothesis that wh-questions in Italian and Berber are closely related to focus constructions. Finally, I have argued that Lecarme's (1999) ideas concerning the ungrammaticality of multiple wh-questions in Somali give rise to problems connected to the unclear typological status of this language.

---

[22] The abbreviations in the glosses correspond to the original ones as stated in Baker (1996:517ff): 2 = second person, S = singular, S = subject, IMPER = imperative, O = object, FACT = factual (aorist), F = feminine (indefinite), PUNC = punctual.

CHAPTER 3 THE OVERVIEW
WHAT IS POSSIBLE IN WHICH LANGUAGE?

This chapter discusses in detail the group of languages that do not allow multiple wh-interrogatives. I will focus especially on the relevant syntactic phenomena from Italian (cf. subchapter 3.1.), Somali (cf. subchapter 3.2.), Berber (cf. subchapter 3.3.) and Irish (cf. subchapter 3.4) that accompany the major issue under investigation, i.e. the unavailable option of deriving multiple wh-questions. The whole section consists of four parts each devoted to one of the languages without multiple wh-questions and a summary part (cf. subchapter 3.5.) with the important conclusions and the working hypotheses.

The following important questions should be answered in the course of research (see also the summary in subchapter 3.5.):

Q1   Are there specific syntactic phenomena that correlate with the unavailable option to build multiple wh-questions and what are they?
Q2   How do the relevant syntactic phenomena interact with each other?
Q3   Which language properties block the formation of multiple wh-questions?
Q4   Are there other similarities between Italian, Somali, Berber and Irish and what are they?
Q5   Is a uniform analysis of the phenomenon possible?

3.1   Italian
Standard Italian is assumed to be a *pro*-drop language with a SVO base structure and free subject inversion (cf. Rizzi 1982, among others).

3.1.1 Wh-questions and Focus Constructions
As pointed out by Calabrese (1984, 1987) and Rizzi (1997), focus constructions and wh-questions in Italian show many similarities in their syntactical behaviour. Calabrese connects the distribution of wh-phrases to that of information focus. Rizzi, however, shows that wh-elements behave syntactically as contrastively focused constituents. This discrepancy has posed a problem for Calabrese's (1984, 1987) analysis of wh-interrogatives in Italian (see subchap-

ter 2.2.). Therefore, the syntactic properties of wh-questions in Italian have to be examined carefully.

3.1.1.1   Wh-Questions and Contrastive Focus. Rizzi (1997) develops a theory of the fine structure of the clausal left periphery which splits the clausal C-projection into several different layers, each reserved for a specific function expressed by the C-system. Consider the structural hierarchy of the topic and focus field:

(40) [... [$_{Top*}$ [$_{Foc}$ [$_{Top*}$ ... [$_{IP}$ ...]]]]]

First, a clause in Italian may contain several topics (cf. 41a) but only one structural contrastive focus position is available (compare 41b and 41c).

(41) a. Il   libro, a Gianni, domani,   glielo   darò
         the book to Gianni tomorrow to-him-it give-1SG-FUT
         senz'altro.
         for sure
         'The book, to John, tomorrow, I'll give it to him for sure.'
      b. IL TUO LIBRO ha   letto (, non il   suo).
         the your book   have-1SG read   not the   his
         'YOUR BOOK I read (, not his).'
      c. *A GIANNI IL   LIBRO darò   (, non a Piero,
         to Gianni   the   book give-1SG-FUT   not to Piero
         l'articolo).
         the article
         'TO JOHN THE BOOK I'll give, not to Piero, the article.'

More than one wh-phrase in the left periphery of a clause is also impossible (cf. 42b). With this respect wh-elements pattern with contrastively focused elements (compare 41c and 42b):

(42) a. **Che cosa** ha   fatto, Gianni?
         what   have-3SG done Gianni
         'What did Gianni do?'
      b. ***Chi che cosa** ha   fatto?
         who what   have-3SG done
         'Who did what?'

Second, contrastively focused elements and wh-phrases are mutually excluded. The following examples show that wh-phrases and focused constituents cannot occur in one and the same clause:

(43) a. *Che cosa,   A GIANNI   hai   detto?
         what   to Gianni   have-2SG   told
         'What TO GIANNI did you tell?'
     b. *A GIANNI,   che cosa   hai   detto?
         to Gianni   what   have-2SG   told
         'TO GIANNI what did you tell?'

To sum up, wh-phrases and contrastively focused elements display the same syntactic properties. Following this observation, Rizzi (1997) concludes that wh-phrases and contrastively focused constituents are licensed in the same structural position of the left periphery and therefore have a complementary distribution.[23] This position cannot host more than one element. Given this observation, Rizzi argues for a unique focus position in the left periphery of Italian. According to him, this specific property of the information structure in Italian ensures that neither multiple wh-questions nor multiple contrastive foci, nor both wh- and contrastively focused elements can occur in one and the same clause.

Wh-questions and focus constructions show two other similarities that are worth mentioning. Following Lasnik & Stowell (1991), Rizzi uses the *weak crossover* effect (henceforth the wco-effect) as a diagnostic tool for quantificational operators. As the examples indicate, both contrastively focused elements (cf. 44a) and wh-constituents (cf. 44b) give rise to a wco-effect; hence, they are instances of an identical syntactic pattern.

---

[23] Hungarian is also a language that licenses wh-elements in a structurally marked focus position adjacent to the verb. É. Kiss (1998b) has argued that Hungarian has a recursive focus projection. This structure corresponds to the derivation of multiple wh-questions in Hungarian. Another possibility of deriving multiple wh-questions in Hungarian is multiple fronting of wh-elements with a surface structure similar to that of Bulgarian multiple wh-questions. In this construction, however, only the wh-phrase immediately adjacent to the verb is interpreted as focused. The initial wh-phrase is assumed to be in a different position, crucially not in the focus position (see also Surányi 2004 for interpretative differences between the two kinds of multiple wh-questions in Hungarian and the discussion in chapter 4.). A possibility of intermediate base generation of wh-elements in the topmost left-peripheral embedded position (probably a topic position) and additional focus fronting to the matrix focus position as a mechanism of long wh-extraction will be discussed for Berber in subchapter (3.3.). This possibility is not available in Italian because long wh-extraction is the result of movement to intermediate specifiers. These movement operations are traditionally assumed to be feature triggered. There is strong evidence that wh-questions in Italian are instances of a movement operation triggered by a focus feature. Typically of focusing this kind of constituent displacement shows indices of operator movement (see examples 44a, b vs. 45). Therefore, a strong topic feature will not attract a bare wh-phrase that is not marked for topicality. The parametric possibility that wh-elements may appear in positions different from the canonical focus position is available in some languages but not in Italian as the ungrammatical examples (cf. 43a, b) indicate.

(44) a. ??GIANNI$_i$,   sua$_i$ madre   ha   sempre   apprezzato t$_i$
        Gianni$_{Obj}$ his   mother$_{Subj}$ have-3SG   always   appreciated
        (, non Piero).
        not Piero
        'GIANNI his mother always appreciated (, not Piero).'
        (Rizzi 1997)
    b. *Chi$_i$ hanno   visto i   suoi$_i$ genitori?
        who$_{Obj}$ have-3PL   seen the   his   parents$_{Subj}$
        'Who did his parents see?'
        (Frascarelli 2000:90)

According to Rizzi's (1997) model of the left periphery, both contrastively focused constituents and topics are located there. What is relevant for the discussion now is to distinguish wh-elements from topics and thus support the claim that wh-phrases and contrastively focused elements share the same structural position. The wco-effect can serve as a distinctive test for this purpose as well. The following example shows that contrary to wh-phrases and contrastively focused elements, topic elements do not give rise to a wco-effect.

(45) Gianni$_i$,   sua$_i$ madre   lo$_i$ ha   sempre   apprezzato.
        Gianni   his   mother him   have-3SG   always   appreciated
        'Gianni, his mother always appreciated him.'

A further difference concerns the deeper syntactic position that elements located in the left periphery are related to. Wh-phrases and contrastively focused constituents have to bind a variable trace whereas topics are related to resumptive clitics (see Rizzi 1997 for comments on the nature of empty categories). This distinction also follows from the different nature of the elements in the left periphery. Following the wco-test as a diagnostic tool, contrastively focused elements and wh-phrases are quantificational operators while topics are not.

To summarise Rizzi's (1997) observations: As instances of the same derivational mechanism wh-questions and contrastive focus constructions pattern with each other. Next, I will discuss Calabrese's observation about the parallel behaviour of wh-questions and information focus.

3.1.1.2 Wh-Questions and Information Focus. Recall Calabrese's (1984, 1987) generalisation, which connects the syntactic structure in wh-questions to that of declarative constructions with information focus. Let us now examine briefly the syntactic properties of information focus in Italian. Frascarelli (2000:90) shows that wco-effects also appear in syntactic structures involving pure information focus. Consider the syntactic behaviour of information focus as in (46) which gives an answer to the wh-question in (44b):

(46) ?*I   suoi₁ genitori hanno   visto **Luigi**₁.
     the his parents have-3PL   seen Luigi
     'His parents saw Luigi.'

The licensing of parasitic gaps provides a further piece of evidence for the similarity between wh-constituents and information focus. Since the element expressing information focus (cf. 47b) is the exact mirror image of the wh-constituent (cf. 47a), Frascarelli concludes that information focus has to be analysed as an LF operator whose variable trace licences the parasitic gap (cf. also Brunetti 2003):

(47) a. **Che cosa**₁ hai   buttato via senza   leggere [e₁]?
        what   have-2SG thrown away without reading
        'What did you throw away without reading?'
     b. Ho   buttato via senza   leggere [e₁]
        have-1SG thrown away without reading
        un   libro di   statistica₁.
        a   book about statistics
        'I threw away without reading a book about statistics.'

Interestingly, contrastive focus is able to license parasitic gaps as well (cf. Frascarelli 2000 and Brunetti 2003).

(48) UN LIBRO DI   STATISTICA₁ ho   buttato via
     a   book about statistics   have-1SG thrown away
     senza   leggere[e₁].
     without reading
     'It is A BOOK ABOUT STATISTICS I have thrown away without reading.'
     (Brunetti 2003)

Consider next a wh-question and its most appropriate answer in Italian. The examples (49a and b) show that in the unmarked case the most appropriate answer to a true wh-question is expressed by means of information focus. This fact is also pragmatically supported. A request for information is a clause containing information focus rather than contrastive focus (cf. 49b and c; see also the discussion in subchapter 2.2.).

(49) a. **Chi** e   partito / ha   parlato?
         who be-3SG   left   / have-3SG   spoken
         'Who has left / spoken?'
     b. E'   partito **Gianni** / ha   parlato **Gianni**.
        be-3SG left   Gianni   have-3SG   spoken   Gianni
        'Gianni has left / spoken.'
     c. #GIANNI e   partito / GIANNI   ha   parlato
        Gianni   be-3SG   left   GIANNI   have-3SG   spoken
        (, non   Maria).
        not   Maria
        'GIANNI has left / spoken, (not Maria).'
        (Belletti 2003)

Furthermore, Calabrese (1984, 1987) shows that information focus is unique. In this respect, it shares another property with contrastive focus:

(50) a. ***Mario** ha   scritto una **lettera**.
         Mario   have-3SG   written a   letter
         'Mario has written a letter.'
     b. ***Franco**   è   partito **alle cinque**.
         Franco   is-3SG   left   at   five
         'Franco has left at five o'clock.'

The problem that was mentioned in the discussion of Calabrese's (1984, 1987) analyses for Italian and Berber (cf. subchapter 2.2.) appears again. As far as both syntactic and semantic constraints on the licensing of wh-phrases are concerned, it is not clear enough how to treat wh-questions in Italian. It seems to be the case that wh-questions are similar to both contrastive focus (mainly from a syntactic point of view) and information focus (from both the syntactic and the semantic point of view). The question that has to be answered is if there is good reason to make a syntactic distinction between contrastive and information focus in Italian. Table (2.) sketches the syntactic properties of information focus, contrastive focus and wh-elements in Italian discussed so far:

Table 2. Syntactic Correlations in Focus Constructions and Wh-Questions in Italian

Types of information structure	Wco-effect	Licensing of Parasitic gaps	Uniqueness	Left-peripheral[24]
Information focus	+	+	+	-
Contrastive focus	+	+	+	+
Wh-elements	+	+	+	+

To recapitulate the discussion of this section, wh-questions pattern with the syntactic representation of both information and contrastive focus. What remains to be explained are the observations listed in last column of Table (2.):

A) Is there a positional distinction between information and contrastive focus in Italian?
B) Why do wh-phrases seem to occupy the position of contrastively focused elements in Italian?

3.1.1.3 How many Focus and Wh-Positions? Consider now some further theoretical proposals for the expression of focus in Italian. Recent developments of the split-C theory show that Italian apparently has a left-peripheral position for information focus which differs from that of contrastive focus. The absence of clitic resumption and the wco-effect have been proposed as diagnostics for contrastive focus in Italian (Rizzi 1997). Consider the examples below reported by Benincà & Poletto (2002):

(51) a. *A   GIANNI,   **un libro di poesie**$_i$,   lo$_i$ regalerete.
         to   Gianni   a   book of poems   it   give-FUT-2SG
         'TO GIANNI, a book of poems, you will give it.'
      b. Un   libro di poesie$_i$,   A GIANNI,   lo$_i$ regalerete.
         a   book of poems,   to Gianni   it   give-FUT-2SG
         'You will give a book of poems to Gianni'

(52) a. *A MARIA,   **Giorgio**$_i$,   sua$_i$ madre   presenterà.
         to Maria   Giorgio   his   mother   introduce-FUT-3SG
         'His mother will introduce Giorgio TO MARIA.'

---

[24] The inconsistencies which we observe in the last column will be the topic of the next subsections. I will show that there is only an apparent positional difference between contrastive, information focus and wh-phrases in Italian (see subsection 3.1.1.4.).

b. Gianni$_i$, suo$_i$ padre l$_i$'ha   licenzato.
   Gianni his   father   him-have-3SG fired
   'Gianni has been fired by his own father.'

The examples indicate that elements appearing after contrastive focus behave
differently from topic phrases. A phrase below contrastive focus cannot be
resumed by a clitic pronoun (cf. 51a) and gives rise to a wco-effect (cf. 52a).
Since elements located below contrastive focus do not share the typical properties of topic phrases in Italian (compare the prefocal topics in 51b and 52b),
they cannot be topics at all. They display, rather, the syntactic properties of
contrastive focus but differ from it with respect to intonation. Therefore, such
elements are assumed to be instances of information focus. Relying on these
observations Benincà & Poletto (2002) conclude that there is no topic layer
below focus. The focus field consists of a projection for contrastive focus and a
following one for information focus (for details see Benincà & Poletto 2002).

(53) [TOPIC FIELD   [CONTRASTIVE FOCUS   [INFORMATION FOCUS   [IP …]]]]

Benincà & Poletto (2002) stipulate that the position of information focus in
Standard Italian is not accessible unless the focus field has already been activated by the presence of a contrastively focused element as shown by the contrast between (54a) and (54b). Therefore, sentences with information focus in
an initial position are not acceptable in Standard Italian (cf. 54b and c):

(54) a. A   GIORGIO, **questo libro**, devi   dare.
         to   Giorgio this   book must-2SG give
         'You must give this book TO GIORGIO.'
      b. *__Antonio__ sono.
          Antonio be-1SG
          'I am Antonio.'
      c. Sono **Antonio**.
         be-1SG Antonio
         'I am Antonio.'

Since Italian has two available designated focus positions in the left periphery
we expect that wh-items, given their semantic nature of requiring new information, should target the position of information focus rather than that of contrastive focus. If the hypothesis that elements located below contrastive focus represent information focus remains true, we expect to find structures with a wh-
phrase following a contrastively focused phrase. This is, however, not the case
as the data reported by Rizzi (1997) indicate (cf. 55b):

(55) a. ***Che cosa**,   A GIANNI   hai   detto?
          what   to Gianni   have-2SG   told
          'What TO GIANNI did you tell?'
    b. *A GIANNI,   **che cosa**   hai   detto?
          to Gianni   what   have-2SG   told
          'TO GIANNI what did you tell?'

It is not the case either that an appropriate answer to a wh-question shows a clausal structure like (54a) which substantiates the assumption that left-peripheral information focus in Standard Italian is only possible in the presence of contrastive focus. Benincà & Poletto (2002:fn. 7) do not address these questions at all. Therefore, I conclude that this approach does not cast any light on the distribution of wh-phrases in Italian (see for further discussion of this proposal Brunetti 2003:123ff).

The puzzle gets more complicated when we look at the following examples:

(56) a. **Perché** QUESTO   avremmo   dovuto   dirgli,
          why   this   have-1PL-COND   must-PART   say-him
          non   qualcos'altro?
          not   something-else
          'Why THIS we should have said to him, not something else?'
    b. **Come   mai** IL   MIO LIBRO gli   ha   dato,
          how   come the   my   book   him   have-2SG   given
          non   il   tuo?
          not   the   yours
          'How come MY BOOK you gave to him, not yours?'

(57) a. ***QUESTO perché** avremmo   dovuto   dirgli,
          this   why   have-1PL-COND   must-PART   say-him
          non qualcos'altro?
          not something-else
          'THIS why should we have said to him, not something else?'
    b. *IL   MIO LIBRO **come mai** gli   ha   dato,
          the my   book   how come him   have-2SG   given
          non il   tuo?
          not the   yours
          'MY BOOK how come did you give to him, not yours?'
    c. **Perché** ha   detto che   si   dimetterà?
          why   have-3SG   said that be-3SG-FUT   resign
          'Why did he say that he would resign?'
          (Rizzi 1999)

Using the distributional patterns in the examples (56a and b) Rizzi (1999) argues that wh-elements like *perché* 'why' and *come mai* 'how come' occupy a position different from that of wh-phrases like *chi* 'who' or *che cosa* 'what' (cf. 55a and b). He labels this position as Int(errogative) and locates it hierarchically higher than FocP (see also Calabrese's 1987 discussion of wh-adjuncts in Berber and Italian and subchapter 2.2.):

(58)   FORCE (TOP)* **INT** (TOP)* **FOC** (TOP)* FIN   IP

Given the observation that wh-arguments occupy the position for contrastive focus, FocP in Rizzi's (1997) system, i.e. a position different from that of *perché* 'why', we expect that a combination of a wh-phrase like *perché* 'why' with a wh-argument will give rise to a grammatical sentence. The expectation is, however, not borne out:

(59)   a. *__Perché__ hai   comprato   **che cosa**?
           why   have-2SG bought   what
           'Why did you buy what?'
           (Calabrese 1987)
       b. *__Perché che cosa__   hai   comprato?
           why   what   have-2SG bought
           'Why did you buy what?'

[handwritten margin note: Not only positions but feature compatibility]

Since the theory Rizzi develops does not give a full explanation for the strange behaviour of such elements I will treat them as an exception. Cheng (1997:61) has proposed to analyse wh-adjuncts in Egyptian Arabic as topic phrases directly merged into an available position in the left periphery of the interrogative clause. The same claim does not seem to hold for wh-adjuncts in Italian. The fact that they cannot be combined with a further wh-phrase (cf. 59a and b) suggests that they must check a focus feature; hence, they have to be in a focal position. I therefore propose that [*perché QUESTO*] and [*come mai IL MIO LIBRO*] represent a kind of complex contrastive wh-phrase with a structure analogous to D-Linked wh-phrases like [*quale libro*] 'which book' (see subsection 3.1.2.4. for discussion of D-Linked wh-phrases). I assume that a non-referential wh-adjunct like *perché* or *come mai* may serve as a modifier of a contrastive phrase. An advantage of this assumption is that it preserves the original statements, i.e. a wh-phrase has to be in a focal position in the clausal left periphery (FocP), FocP cannot host more than one element in Italian, and is the locus of both focused elements and wh-phrases.

3.1.1.4 Towards a Unification of Focus. An interesting idea that may cast light on the puzzle of contrastive vs. information focus and especially on the distribution of wh-elements is the analysis of focus constructions in Standard Italian proposed by Brunetti (2003). She argues against Benincà & Poletto (2002) and Belletti (2002), who suggest a structural distinction between contrastive and information focus (for detailed discussion of Belletti's proposal see Brunetti 2003). Brunetti (2003) claims instead that the distinction between contrastive and information focus is not true for any level of grammar. I do not fully agree with this strong claim. Many linguists share the intuitive idea that pure new information and contrastively (or exhaustively) represented pieces of information can be clearly distinguished from each other at the level of semantic interpretation. Therefore for the purpose of my analysis I will confine myself to the discussion of the syntactic correlation between contrastive and information focus only. We have seen that both contrastive and information focus show the same syntactic behaviour with respect to licensing of parasitic gaps and wco-effects (cf. Table 2.). Therefore, I conclude that focus may be treated as a unique category in the syntax of Italian. First, recall question (A) from subsection (3.1.1.2.): Do we find a positional distinction between information focus and contrastive focus in Italian? Contrastive focus is allowed in the left periphery and inside the clause (in-situ) (cf. 60a and b). Information focus is not allowed in the left periphery (cf. 61c, d). Wh-phrases obligatorily undergo fronting and are cannot appear in-situ (cf. 61a and b). Why is this the case?

Second, I come back to question (B) from subsection (3.1.1.2.): Why do wh-phrases seem to occupy the position of contrastively focused elements in Italian? Earlier approaches to the grammar of wh-questions also make a connection between movement of wh-phrases and movement of phrases expressing (identificational) focus (see Horvath 1986, among others). A number of languages, which move focused phrases overtly, are analysed as languages with focus fronting of wh-phrases. This analysis has been convincingly applied to, among other languages, Aghem, Basque, Hungarian and Quechua (see Horvath 1986, É. Kiss 1995). Stjepanović (1999) shows that Serbo-Croatian fits into this line of analysis. Bošković (2002) draws a parallel between multiple wh-fronting in Bulgarian and fronting of focused phrases (cf. also Sabel 2003 for an analysis of multiple wh-fronting in Malagasy as focus movement). In order to account for the optional fronting of focused phrases in the Slavic languages Bošković assumes a minor difference in the lexical specification of wh-phrases and focused phrases. Thus, wh-phrases have a strong focus feature while focused phrases can either have a strong or weak focus feature (for details and examples cf. Bošković 2002). I will apply the idea that typological differences within the grammar of wh-questions may be expressed in terms of different feature specifications of the relevant elements selected from the lexicon. This assumption enables me to explain why wh-phrases seem to occupy a position for contrastively focused elements even if it is more natural to connect wh-items semantically and pragmatically with the notion of information focus. Furthermore, the most used unmarked answers to wh-questions in Italian indicate a clear connection with the semantics of information focus. Consider the relevant examples from Italian:

(60) a. GIANNI   ha   parlato (non Maria).
        Gianni   have-3SG spoken   not Maria
        'GIANNI has spoken, not Maria.'
     b. Ha   parlato GIANNI (non Mario).
        have-3SG spoken   Gianni   not Mario
        'GIANNI has spoken, not Mario.'
        (Belletti 2003)

Contrastive focus usually moves to the left periphery (cf.60a) but apparently, it can stay in-situ (cf. 60b). Information focus cannot be expressed in a left-peripheral position in Italian as the contrast between (61c) and (61d) shows:

(61) a. [FocP **Che cosa**   hai   letto]?
              what   have-2SG read
        'What have you read?'
     b. *[GroundP   Hai   letto [FocP **che cosa**]]?
                     have-2SG read   what
        'What have you read?'
     c. [GroundP   Ho   letto [FocP **il   libro**]].
                   have-1SG read   the book
        'I have read a book.'

d. *[$_{FocP}$ **Il**   **libro** ho   letto].[25]
    the   book have-1SG   read
    'I have read the book.'

e. #[$_{FocP}$ IL LIBRO ho   letto] (non il   giornale)
    the   book have-1SG   read not the   magazine
    'THE BOOK I have read, not the magazine.'
    (Belletti 2003)

Example (61c) poses the main problem. Why does the correct answer to a wh-question (cf. 61c) not show the same structure as the wh-interrogative (61a)? Alternatively, why is (61d) not the correct answer to (61a)? I propose that both kinds of focused elements, i.e. contrastive and information focus move to the same structural position of the clausal left periphery on par with wh-elements. According to this proposal, the difference between (61c) and (61e) is not the position of information focus in (61c) or that of contrastive focus in (61e). 'il libro' in (61c) and 'IL LIBRO' in (61e) are both located in the same position of the left periphery. What is different is the position of the remnant IP in (61c) and (61e). After the information focus in (61c) moves to the left periphery, the IP left behind undergoes remnant IP-movement in order to check the topic or background features (cf. Poletto & Pollock 2000 and Belletti 2002 for a different account). The same process seems to apply optionally in contrastive focus constructions (cf. 60a vs. b).

What still remains to be explained is why remnant IP-movement is optional in contrastive focus constructions and why it is obligatory in pure information focus constructions. As stated above, sentences with information focus are usually uttered as answers to wh-questions. Following Brunetti's (2003:113) argumentation for ellipsis in answers to wh-questions, I assume that a wh-question creates an information structure containing not presupposed informa-

---

[25] This sentence is grammatical with a clitic pronoun attached to the auxiliary:
    (i) Il libro, l'ho   letto.
    the book   it-have-1SG   read
    'I have read the book.'
The sentence in (i) has a typical topic interpretation of the constituent *il libro*, which is additionally supported by the presence of an object clitic. The ungrammaticality of (61d) indicates that when a strong topic or background feature enters the derivation, it has to be checked, otherwise ungrammaticality will follow. Cecchetto (2000) claims that only in the case of direct objects like in (i) the presence of a clitic is obligatory (see for analysis of clitic left dislocation constructions in Italian as a movement operation Cecchetto 2000). Therefore, the absence of a clitic leads to ungrammaticality in (61d). Following his observation on the distribution of clitics in Italian, I claim that (61c) shows the same information structure as (i). The status of *ho letto* 'I have read', in (61c), actually a moved remnant IP, is the same as *il libro* 'the book' in (i): background information or a topic. The difference is that a topicalised remnant IP does not need to be resumed by a clitic.

tion represented by the wh-element and background information.[26] Further-more, let me suggest that in an answer to a wh-question a functional category Ground° with a strong feature (or alternatively with an +EPP-feature) is se-lected from the lexicon. This strong feature will force the remnant IP to move to the ground layer in answers to wh-questions (cf. 61c). Consider another op-tion: since the background information has already been activated through the wh-question, a Ground° with a weak feature (or alternatively with an -EPP-feature) may be selected from the lexicon in the numeration of the answer as well. In this case, remnant IP-movement will not apply at all. We expect to find an answer with a syntactic structure like (62a):

(62) a. *Il   **libro** ho   letto.[27]
          the book   have-1SG read
          'I have read the book.'

     b. **Il**   **libro** [ho   letto.]
          the   book   [have-1SG   read]
          '[I have read]the book.'

This is, however, not attested for Standard Italian. What happens in a structure with a weak ground feature (or alternatively with an -EPP-feature) is deletion of the background information as represented in (62b). Therefore, answers to wh-questions usually consist of a single phrase and not of a complete clause. An answer consisting of a single phrase is derived through an ellipsis of the background material. This assumption is independently motivated by the prin-ciples of economy that are active in natural languages. Arguments in favour of movement prior to background information ellipsis in fragment answers, such as preposition stranding and wh-island sensitivity, are discussed by Brunetti (2003:107ff) in detail. Now we are able to answer questions (A) and (B) from subsection (3.1.1.2.). We do not find a positional distinction between informa-tion and contrastive focus in Italian. Both kinds of elements are located in the same position within the clausal left periphery, FocP. Wh-phrases in Italian are

---

[26] Brunetti (2003:113) proposes the following ellipsis rule:
    (i) Ellipsis of background material in a sentence applies if the elided material has an an-tecedent which is also background material.

[27] Brunetti (2003:121) provides contexts where information focus fronting may occur. The following example is uttered 'out of the blue' and the sentence does not have broad focus but narrow focus on *uno studente* 'a student':
    (i) Sai'   l'ho   scoperto: **Uno** **studente** aveva   rubato
         know-2SG it-have-3SG found-out   a   student   have-PAST-3SG- stolen
         quel   libro.
         that   book
         'You know, I found it out: A student stole that book.'

also located in this position. The functional projection FocP in Italian is unique in the sense that it cannot host more than one element.

Another logical question arises with respect to the optionality of remnant IP-movement: why do we not find wh-questions in Italian like the following?

(63) a. *Ha   comprato **che cosa**, Gianni?
    have-3SG bought   what   Gianni
    'What did Gianni buy?'

   b. ***Chi** crede   che Giovanni abbia   baciato
    who thinks that Giovanni have-COND-3SG kissed
    quale ragazza?[28]
    Which girl
    'Who thinks that Giovanni has kissed which girl?'
    (Eugenia Marchisio, p.c.)

A well-known property of root wh-questions in Standard Italian is the so-called *residual V2-phenomenon* (cf. Rizzi 1991). Following this observation, (63a) is not possible because the verb has not moved to Foc°, which is crucial at least for root wh-questions in Italian. Standard Italian exhibits V2 remnants in wh-questions and imperatives (see Wratil 2004 for discussion of imperatives). (63b) indicates that wh-in-situ is not possible at all (for more on the position of the finite verb and root vs. embedded wh-questions see the section 3.1.2.).

Although the concept of remnant IP-movement is theoretically problematic, as pointed out by Belletti (2002) and Brunetti (2003:chapter 6), it can still plausibly account for the fact that the licensing position for focus is unique in Italian, which in turn explains the ungrammaticality of multiple wh-questions. Moreover, postverbal focus in Italian has certain properties which call for an operator movement analysis (weak crossover effects and licensing of parasitic gaps discussed in subsection 3.1.1.2.). Therefore, it is natural to propose that information focus moves out of its base position. Within Belletti's (2002) system there are two independent focus projections. One of them belongs to the C-domain. The other one is located between IP and VP. Given the observation that wh-questions in Italian are closely related to the syntactic mechanism of focusing we cannot explain with this syntactic model why it is not possible to licence wh-elements in either position and thus derive multiple wh-questions in the same way it is possible e.g., in Hungarian (for discussion of Hungarian multiple wh-questions with recursive FocP see chapter 4.). Belletti (2003:45f)

---

[28] *Quale ragazza* 'which girl' cannot be interpreted as a real interrogative phrase. It may have an echo reading, but I am dealing with real wh-questions only.

notes that left-peripheral focalisation is not compatible with clause internal focalisation. This fact is attributed to an independent rule that a sentence can only contain one focused element. This constraint does not seem to make a distinction as to the kind of focus in question (see also the discussion of sub-chapter 2.2.) She does not discuss multiple wh-questions in Italian at all (cf. Belletti 2002:fn. 61). Therefore, I have argued that there is only one focus position in Italian, namely FocP located in the left periphery.

According to Brunetti's (2003:150ff) approach a focused phrase is always the complement of a C-head hosting an intonational focus morpheme. She adopts a CP-structure for DPs along the lines of Manzini & Savoia (2002) and Starke (2001).[29] Every focused DP and wh-phrase has an intonational focus morpheme in C°. Thus in order to exclude multiple wh-questions this approach also has to postulate an independent constraint that should filter out syntactic structures with more than one DP containing an intonational focus morpheme. Brunetti (2003) does not address this problem at all.

As Brunetti (2003:159) herself notes, the optionality of remnant IP-movement dispenses if we assume semantically different topic layers in the sense of Frascarelli & Hinterhölzl (2004). Then, even when the focused material precedes the remnant IP in the surface structure (as in wh-questions), the remnant IP is in a certain topic position below focus. Crucially, derivations of this kind prove the observation that focus is a unique syntactic category in the grammar of Italian. The uniqueness of focus in turn offers a plausible account for the ungrammaticality of multiple wh-questions in languages without multiple wh-questions such as Italian, Somali, Berber and Irish.

The account in terms of differences within the feature specifications of lexical items I have proposed for Standard Italian can capture the differences among the Italian varieties discussed by Poletto & Pollock (2000). Poletto & Pollock observe that bare wh-phrases like *che* 'what', *andé* 'where', *chi* 'who' and *come* 'how' in Bellunese must occur in a sentence-final position:

---

[29] Brunetti assumes that the intonational morpheme is realised on a left-peripheral head of a DP as shown in (ii):

    (i) **Che cosa** è   arrivato?

          what   is-3SG arrived

          'What arrived?'

    (ii) [$_{IP}$ È [$_{VP}$ arrivato   [$_{SpecCP}$ [$_{C°}$ Focus] [$_{DP}$ **l'Intercity**]]]]

            is-3SG arrived   the Intercity

          'The Intercity arrived.'

(64) a. Ha-tu   magnà   **che?**
       have-2SG-you eaten   what
       'What did you eat?'

      b. ***Che**   ha-tu   magnà?
       what   have-2SG-you eaten
       'What did you eat?'

(65) a. Se-tu   'ndat **andè?**
       be-2SG   gone   where
       'Where did you go?'

      b. ***Andè**   se-tu 'ndat?
       where   be-2SG gone
       'Where did you go?'

By contrast, wh-phrases like *qual* 'which' and *quanti* 'how much' can appear in a sentence initial position:

(66) a. **Qual**   avé-o   ciot?
       which   have-2SG-you taken
       'Which one did you take?'

      b. Avé-o   ciot **qual?**
       have-2SG-you taken which
       'Which one did you take?'

(67) a. **Quant**   avé-o   laorà?
       how much have-2SG-you worked
       'How long did you work?'

      b. Avé-o   laorà? **quant?**
       have-2SG-you worked how   much
       'How long did you work?'

Following the authors, I also assume that wh-phrases in Standard Italian and in its varieties move to the left periphery. Primary evidence for wh-movement in the above examples is the presence of Subject Clitic Inversion (for detailed argumentation cf. Poletto & Pollock 2000 and subsection 3.1.2.3.).[30] Expressed

---

[30] It is important to note that Poletto & Pollock (2000) do not analyse Subject Clitic Inversion as head movement but as remnant IP-movement. The possibility to place adverbials between the verb and the clitic elements is taken as a crucial evidence for the analysis they propose. The authors also discuss arguments in favour of wh-movement such as island sensitivity and emergination of dative complements among other phenomena. Therefore, I agree with the authors that wh-movement has taken place in examples like (64a), (65a), (66b) and (67b). Note further that for theoretical reasons there is no need to decide whether head movement or rem-

along the lines of a feature checking analysis, wh-phrases always have a strong focus feature which needs to be checked against Foc°. I suggest that the differences between the two types of wh-elements can be explained if we assume that the left periphery of Bellunese also involves strong features that need to be checked. Poletto & Pollock (2000) propose that among force, topic and focus, so-called *ground features* are also a part of the left periphery. Thus, the discrepancy between wh-phrases like *che* 'what' (cf. 64 a, b and 65a, b) and *qual* 'which' (cf. 66a, b and 67a, b) can be captured if we assume different lexical specifications of the wh-phrases. After checking its own strong feature against Foc°, the latter phrase but not the former is able to check the strong ground feature of the left periphery in Bellunese. Therefore, in the case of (64a) and (65a) remnant IP-movement to GroundP applies, in (66a) and (67a) the strong ground feature is checked by subsequent movement of the wh-phrase *qual* 'which' to GroundP.[31] Note, that *which*-phrases have a D-Linked character, which means that they represent to some extent background information as well (see Munaro 1998, 2003).

In this section I have argued that focus is a unique category in the grammar of Italian. I have discussed two alternative approaches to focus in Italian (cf. Belletti 2002 and Brunetti 2003) and shown that an approach that favours a single designated left-peripheral position and does not syntactically differentiate between contrastive and information focus can better prove the observation that multiple wh-questions do not occur in Italian.

3.1.1.5 The Syntax of Embedded Focus and Wh-Constructions. There are some distributional differences between main and embedded wh-phrases and focused constituents (for more differences between root and embedded wh-questions in Italian see section 3.1.2.). Contrary to what happens in main questions, a wh-element is compatible with a contrastively focused element in embedded ones (compare 68a and b):

---

nant IP-movement takes place in Bellunese. The choice between head and phrasal movement is a question of language parameterisation as proposed by Pesetsky & Torrego (2000) who claim that an EPP-feature (in their terms a feature which triggers dislocation in general) may be eliminated either by head or by phrasal movement and trace back this possibility to principles of derivational economy (for details see their proposal). Whether head or remnant IP-movement takes place in Bellunese is not relevant for the purposes of my analysis. Note also that according to the translation, the information status of the wh-phrases in the examples from Bellunese is the same as of real wh-interrogatives.

[31] I propose to modify the original argumentation and integrate the analysis of the cases mentioned here into the account of Poletto & Pollock for the syntactic behaviour of D-Linked wh-phrases (for technical aspect of the analysis, e.g., deriving Subject Clitic Inversion as well as for the application of different checking operations involved cf. Polletto and Pollock 2000 and subsection 3.1.2.3.).

(68) a. *A GIANNI **che cosa** hanno detto (, non a Piero)?
to Gianni what have-3PL said not to Piero
'TO GIANNI what did they say (, not to Piero)?'
b. ?Mi domando A GIANNI **che cosa** abbiano ditto
I wonder to Gianni what have-3PL-SUBJ said
(,non a Piero).
not to Piero
'I wonder TO GIANNI what they said (, not to Piero).
(Rizzi 1997)

The contrast between main and embedded interrogatives may suggest that the wh-element can occupy an independent position distinct from FocP in embedded questions (cf. Rizzi 1997:fn. 18). Rizzi (1999) claims for the presence of a position below focus in embedded constituent questions occupied by wh-elements:

(69) …Force…Int…Foc…Wh…

One can alternatively say that the contrastively focused element *A GIANNI* 'to Gianni' in (68b) has undergone movement to the matrix clause for some discourse pragmatic reasons. Therefore, the grammaticality of the sentence is improved. Frascarelli (2000:121) also discusses similar cases. She assumes that the different behaviour of embedded wh-phrases and focused elements is due to some semantic-pragmatic factors inherent to the nature of embedding (see also Poletto 2000 and Barbosa 2001). Note further that in all embedded constructions, in which phrases with contrastive interpretation and wh-elements cooccur, subjunctive is the preferred mood. All these differences between matrix and embedded clauses are poorly investigated. Consider also the contrast between (70a) and (70b). As the judgements about the grammaticality indicate (compare the notations '??' and '*'), embedded multiple wh-questions are slightly improved in comparison with root multiple wh-questions:

(70) a. ??Non so ancora **chi** ha fatto **che cosa**.
NEG know-1SG yet who have-3SG done what
'I do not know yet who did what.'
(Rizzi 1982:51)
b. *Chi ha scritto **che cosa**?
who have-3SG written what
'Who wrote what?'
(Calabrese 1984)

Possibly 2 people → 2 ≠ judgements

I conclude that for some still unclear reasons the left periphery in Italian does not display a unified structure, which appears in both root and embedded contexts. Further problems arise from the fact that some varieties of Italian allow constructions that seem to be ungrammatical in others. Even Standard Italian varies from speaker to speaker. All these issues will not be discussed here. The problematic cases need extensive research which is not necessary for the purposes of this investigation.

What is important for the current discussion is the fact that wh-questions always seem to parallel focus constructions. The observation that a contrastively represented element may appear together with a wh-item in an embedded clause is paralleled by the behaviour of answers to paraphrased multiple wh-questions. In Italian the most appropriate way to express what is meant by a multiple wh-question (e.g., Who gave a book to whom?) is a clause like (71):

(71) **A chi**   ha   dato un libro ognuno   di loro?
      to whom   have-3SG   given a book everyone of them
      'To whom did every one of them give a book?'
      (Giorgio Banti, p.c.)

The single wh-clause (71) paraphrases a multiple wh-question that typically requires a pair list answer:

(72) [ContrTopGIANNI] ha   dato un libro [InfFoca   Maria],
              Gianni   have-3SG   given a book   to Mary
      ALBERTO a Susanna
      Alberto   to Susanna
      'Gianni gave a book to Maria, Alberto to Susanna...'
      (Giorgio Banti, p.c.)

The constituent *ognuno di loro* 'every one of them' can only refer to a contextually given set of elements. Therefore, it cannot express new information. In the pair list answer the elements that belong to the presupposed set are contrasted to each other. *GIANNI* is contrasted to *ALBERTO*. The phrases *a Maria* 'to Maria' and *a Susanna* 'to Susanna', which correspond to the wh-phase in the wh-question, represent new information. The intonation curves of these constituents confirm the assumed information structure of the clause (Mara Frascarelli and Giorgio Banti, p.c.). The observation that only one focal element may appear in a single clause in Italian is supported by the fact that the elements in capitals in (72) represent a kind of contrastive topic in answers to wh-questions like (71) (for discussion of contrastive topic cf. Büring 1997, Frascarelli & Hinterhölzl 2004, see also Molnar 2001 for a proposal of an independent phrase).[32] I conclude from these observations that when a contrastively represented element appears with a wh-phrase in the same clause, the contrastive element is non-focal. It belongs rather to some subclass of topic constituents, most probably contrastive topics. Thus, only one element expressing focused information may appear within the clausal structure of Italian.

3.1.1.6 Ideolectal Variation and Multiple Wh-Questions. It is worth mentioning that the judgements concerning multiple focus and wh-constructions in Italian vary from speaker to speaker. An interesting observation pointed out by Frascarelli (2000:92) is that multiple contrastive foci in Italian are acceptable for some speakers:

(73) GIOVANNI   ha   dato un bacio A MARIA
      Giovanni   have-3SG given a kiss   to Maria
      (non Antonio a Luisa).
       not Antonio to Luisa
      'GIOVANNI gave a kiss to MARIA (not Antonio to Luisa).'

However, this possibility is subject to severe constraints. The following restrictions prove the marked character of the constructions. First, it is not possible to realise the subject in a postverbal position as (74) shows.

(74) *Ha   dato GIOVANNI   un bacio A MARIA
       have-3SG given Giovanni   a kiss   to Maria
       (nonAntonio a Luisa).
        not Antonio to Luisa
      'GIOVANNI gave a kiss to MARIA (not Antonio to Luisa).'

Second, multiple foci have to observe the superiority constraint, especially when one of the focused elements is the subject it has to be realised in the left periphery.

---

[32] Note that in a multiple wh-question like 'Who bought what?' both wh-elements may refer to contextually not given or presupposed sets of elements. The pair list answers to that kind of wh-questions can contain two focal elements which are instances of new information (see also Rooth 1992 on the semantics of multiple wh-questions and their answers). Furthermore, Frascarelli & Hinterhölzl (2004) note that contrast is not an inherent property of either focus or topic, but a functional feature that is licensed in an A'-position in the CP-system, where either topic is merged or focus can move.

(75) *A MARIA   ha   dato GIOVANNI   un bacio
      to Maria   have-3SG given Giovanni   a   kiss
      (non   a Luisa Antonio).
      not   to Luisa Antonio
      'TO MARIA gave GIOVANNI a kiss (not to Luisa Antonio).'

Furthermore, when the subject is not one of the two focused constituents the clause is not acceptable at all:

(76) a. *A MARIA   ha   dato (Giovanni) UN   BACIO.
         to Maria   have-3SG given Giovanni a   kiss
         'Giovanni gave TO MARIA A KISS.'
     b. *UN BACIO ha   dato (Giovanni) A MARIA.
         a   kiss   have-3SG given Giovanni to Maria
         'Giovanni gave A KISS TO MARIA.'

Finally, when more than two constituents are focused the structure is unacceptable:

(77) *GIOVANNI ha   dato un bacio A MARIA IERI.
      Giovanni   have-3SG given a kiss to Maria   yesterday
      'GIOVANNI gave a kiss to MARIA YESTERDAY.'

Frascarelli (2000) reports that the same restrictions are true for multiple wh-questions:

(78) a. **Chi** ha   dato   **che cosa**   a Maria?
         who have-3SG given what   to Maria
         'Who gave what to Maria?'
     b. *?**Che cosa** ha   dato **chi** a Maria?
         what   have-3SG given who to Maria
         'What did who give to Maria?'
     c. *?**Chi**   ha   dato **che cosa**   a Maria   **dove**?
         who   have-3SG given what   to Maria   when
         'What did who give to Maria?'

A multiple wh-question like (78a) parallels a multiple focus construction like (73). The ungrammatical multiple wh-question in (78b) violates the superiority condition in the same way as the multiple focus construction in (75) does. Example (78c) structurally corresponds to (77).[33]

Whatever explanation one adopts for the marginally acceptable constructions with multiple foci in Italian, it is important that the correlation with wh-questions is preserved. The conclusion that wh-questions and clauses containing focused constituents are related syntactic phenomena still holds. The paradox of a syntactic parallelism between wh-questions and both contrastive and information focus goes away with the assumption that both kinds of focus are licensed in the same position. I have shown that information and contrastive focus do not display any differences with respect to their syntactic behaviour. Therefore, I have argued for a unique focus position in Italian. → so (78a)

3.1.2 Defining the Structural Properties of the Wh-Position
We have seen that there is good reason to believe that focused and wh-elements share the same syntactic properties: wco-effects, uniqueness and licensing of parasitic gaps (see Table 2.). In this section I will propose that the proper licensing of wh-elements relies crucially on head-adjacency, i.e. a wh-element in Italian is licensed in the specifier position of a functional head endowed with a focus feature. Let us now move to some differences between wh-questions and focus constructions concerning their relative order with respect to the finite verb.

3.1.2.1 The Finite Verb in Wh-questions and Focus Constructions of Main Clauses.
The position of the finite verb is closely related to the syntax of wh-interrogatives. In Italian V-to-C movement obligatorily takes place in matrix wh-questions. This phenomenon has often been considered a consequence of the wh-Criterion (Rizzi 1991).[34] But note that wh-questions and contrastive focus constructions discussed by Rizzi (1997) do not behave in the same way with respect to verb movement:

(79) a. Il premio Nobel, **a chi**   lo daranno?
     the prize Nobel, to whom it give-3PL-FUT
     'The Nobel Prize, to whom will they give it?'

---

[33] Note that multiple wh-questions like (70a and b) are identical with examples like (78a). Rizzi and Calabrese judge the former ungrammatical. The contrast underpins Frascarelli's (2000) thesis that Standard Italian shows a great number of ideolectal differences.

[34] The wh-Criterion (Rizzi 1991):
   A. A wh-operator must be in a Spec-head configuration with $X°_{[+WH]}$.
   B. An $X°_{[+WH]}$ must be in a Spec-head configuration with a wh-operator.

    b. ***A chi,**   il premio Nobel, lo daranno?
       to whom   the   prize Nobel, it give-3PL-FUT
       'To whom, the Nobel Prize, will they give it?'

(80) a. QUESTO Gianni ti   dirà
        this   Gianni to-you say-3SG-FUT
        (, non quello che pensavi).
        not   that   what you-thought
        'THIS Gianni will say to you (, not what you thought).'
      b. ***Che cosa** Gianni ti   dirà?
        what   Gianni to-you say-3SG-FUT
        'What Gianni will say to you?'
        (Rizzi 1997)

The contrast between (79a) and (79b) shows that topics are not licensed in a position following the wh-phrase in Italian interrogatives. As (80b) illustrates subjects are not found in that position either. If the wh-Criterion has to be fulfilled in the overt syntax in Italian, the ungrammaticality of the wh-questions (cf. 79b and 80b) is expected. A wh-operator and a functional head bearing a wh-feature have to be in a spec-head relation. In root questions wh-elements move to the specifier position of a functional projection of the left periphery. The verb moves to the head position of the same projection.[35] Both movement operations follow directly from the wh-Criterion. In contrast, focusing does not necessarily involve V-to-C movement (compare 79a with 80a). Note that Rizzi (1997) assumes a Focus-Criterion parallel to the wh-Criterion (see also Brody 1990 for another formulation of the Focus-Criterion).[36] He claims that 'the focus feature is inherently possessed by the Foc° head and no movement of an inflectional head is required' (Rizzi 1997). According to Chomsky's (1995) terminology, his proposal can be translated in the following way: In focus constructions Foc° has a weak feature focus feature. Therefore, movement of an inflectional head into this position is not necessary (cf. Rizzi 1997:fn. 17, 18; see also the discussion of Calabrese's 1984, 1987 analysis in subchapter 2.2.).

I will interpret these observations slightly differently. As an instance of a residual V2 phenomenon wh-questions constitute an exception in a non-V2-language like Italian. The lexicalisation of the functional head in whose specifier wh-elements are properly licensed, namely Foc°, is simply a remnant V2-

---

[35] Rizzi (1997) assumes that the resumptive clitics in clauses involving topic constituents are head elements (see 79a).

[36] The Focus-Criterion (Brody 1990):
    A. At S-Structure and LF the Spec of a FocP must contain a [+Focus]-phrase.
    B. At LF all [+Focus]-phrases must be in a FocP.

property which also shows up in imperatives (see Rizzi 1991 for a crosslinguistic survey of V2-phenomena in wh-questions and Wratil 2004 for the same effects in imperatives in the West-Germanic and Romance languages). In theoretical terms, along the same lines as Chomsky (1995), one can assume that Foc° in root interrogatives has a strong wh-feature which requires V-to-C movement. The stipulation of the latter property of Foc° in root interrogatives in Italian captures the observations leaving the reasons for the verb placement asymmetry between focus and wh-phenomena still unclear. Such reasons lie in the historical development of the language. I will continue to assume that both wh-phrases and their non-interrogative focused counterparts appear in the specifier position of a head bearing a focus feature, i.e. a Foc°. The head of the former construction is lexicalised through V-to-C movement while in the latter construction this is not obligatory (see also the discussion on embedded wh-questions in subsection 3.1.2.2.).[37] For the time being I will leave the theoretical discussion of head movement aside because the core of the investigation, namely why is it impossible to derive multiple wh-questions in certain languages, remains within the domain of phrasal categories.

3.1.2.2 The Finite Verb in Wh-Questions and Focus Constructions of Embedded Clauses. In embedded contexts the contrast between focus constructions and wh-interrogatives is weaker. Rizzi (1991, 1999) observes that the V-to-C movement as a consequence of the wh-Criterion is not obligatory in embedded questions. In indirect questions other elements may come between the wh-phrase and the finite verb. In (81b) a topic phrase appears between the wh-element and the finite verb:

(81) a. Mi   domando, il   premio Nobel, **a chi**
          I   wonder   the   prize   Nobel   to whom
          lo potrebbero   dare.
          it can-3PL-COND give
          'I wonder, the Nobel Prize, to whom they could give it.'
      b. ?Mi domando **a chi,**   il   premio Nobel,
          I   wonder to whom   the   prize   Nobel
          lo   potrebbero   dare.
          it   can-3PL-COND give
          'I wonder to whom, the Nobel Prize, they could give it.'

---

[37] Alternatively, Conni 2001 proposes that C° in root interrogatives can be represented as a syncretic head bearing both strong wh- and agreement features which require V-to-C movement. Conni 2001 follows a proposal of Giorgi & Pianesi 1997 who assume that syncretic heads have only one specifier available in order to exclude constructions like (80b). This assumption, however, does not comply with the observation in (80a).

There is a clear contrast between (81b) and (80b). Why is it that the head-adjacency between the wh-element in an embedded wh-question does not have to be met? Rizzi (1991) argues that a wh-feature on an embedded C° is present in embedded wh-questions due to the selectional properties of the matrix verb. Hence, the wh-Criterion is fulfilled and embedded V-to-C movement is not necessary.

3.1.2.3 An Account for the Differences between Main and Embedded Clauses.
Poletto & Pollock (2000) propose an account for the differences between main and embedded interrogatives using a split clausal left periphery. They suggest that there are two kinds of interrogative constructions in Italian: the so-called *Subject Clitic Inversion* (SCLI) which is found in both main and yes/no-questions and *Stylistic Inversion* (SI), a well-known phenomenon from French interrogatives that is manifested mostly in indirect questions of Standard Italian.

Consider now wh-interrogatives with SCLI. Since Italian is a *pro*-drop language subject clitics are not legitimate PF objects.[38] Thus, SCLI involves a *pro* subject in a postverbal position, while the subject NP, *Gianni*, in (82a) occupies a sentence peripheral position separated from the entire clause by a pause. This phenomenon is known as 'emergination' (see also Calabrese 1992).

(82) a. **Cosa** ha   *pro*   fatto, Gianni?
         what have-3SG   he   done Gianni
         'What did Gianni do?'

---

[38] Poletto & Pollock (2000) assume that the left periphery in Romance is invariant. Empty subject pronouns in Standard Italian are in the same position as overt clitic subject pronouns in French (cf. i) or in some Italian dialects (cf. ii). In clauses involving analytical verb forms inverted subject pronouns occupy a position between the auxiliary verb and the past participial. The same form of SCLI should also be available in Standard Italian with *pro* subjects.
    (i) **Qu**'a-t-il   fait?   (French)
        what-has-he done
        'What did he do?'
    (ii) Ha-tu   magnà **che**?   (Bellunese)
        have-2SG-you eaten   what
        'What did you eat?'

     b. ***Cosa** Gianni ha   fatto?[39]
        what Gianni have-3SG done
        'What Gianni has done?'

In indirect questions SCLI is not possible. Subordinated structures usually display SI (cf. 83a), which is optional for some speakers (cf. 83b).[40] Preverbal subjects in embedded questions with subjunctive, future and conditional predicates are grammatical for all speakers (cf. 83c). Differences between the judgments are found with indicative predicates (cf. 83b) (cf. Rizzi 1991 and Poletto 2000).

(83) a. Mi   hanno   chiesto **cosa** ha   fatto Gianni.
           me   have-3PL asked   what have-3SG done Gianni
           'They asked me what Gianni has done.'
      b. (??)Mi hanno   chiesto **dove**   Gianni è andato ieri.
             me have-3PL asked   where   Gianni is gone yesterday
           'They asked me where Gianni went yesterday.'
      c. Mi   chiedo **cosa** Gianni avrebbe   fatto
           me   ask   what Gianni have-3SG-COND done
           in quell frangente.
           in that   occasion
           'I wonder what Gianni would have done on that occasion.'
           (Poletto 2000:157)

Working on the theoretical assumption that the left periphery in Romance has a complex structure with different contextually dependent strong features that need to be checked (cf. 84), Poletto & Pollock (2000) account for the differences between matrix and indirect questions.

---

[39] Note that wh-questions like (i) do not occur in Italian either:
    (i) ***Che cosa**   ha   il direttore detto?
         what   have-3SG the director said
        'What did the director say?'
Rizzi (1991) accounts for the ungrammaticality of (i) in terms of case theory. He assumes that I (AgrS) can only assign nominative to the subject under a spec-head configuration. V-to-C movement destroys the spec-head relation. Therefore, the subject is not properly licensed in the specifier of I (see Barbosa 2001 for a different account). A difference between Rizzi's (1991) analysis of wh-questions and the proposal under discussion is the assumption that postverbal subjects in examples like (82a) are not outside of the clause but VP-internal.
[40] SI is a syntactic phenomenon in which the subject occurs in a non-canonical displaced position. Unlike subject NPs in SCLI-constructions, which appear in an extraposed position, the subject NP in SI-constructions occurs inside the clause in a postparticipial or a postinfinitival position (for examples, discussion and further references cf. Poletto & Pollock 2000).

(84) $[_{Op2P}Op2°[_{ForceP}Force°[_{GroundP}Ground°[_{TopP}Top°[_{Op1P}Op1°[_{IP}...]]]]]]$[41]

Their analysis implements the basic idea from Kayne (1998) that movement proceeds overtly and phrasal movement in many cases replaces head movement. Compare the derivation of a root wh-interrogative (cf. 85a, b) with that of an embedded one (cf. 86a, b):

(85) a. **Dove**   è   *pro* andato?
         where   is-3SG   gone
         'Where did he go?'

      b. $[_{Op2P}$ **dove**$_i[_{ForceP} [_{IP}t_k$ è $t_j]_i][_{GroundP}$ *pro*$_k$ $[_{TopP}$ [andato $t_i]_j[_{Op1P} t_i$ ... $t_l]]]]]$

(86) a. Mi   hanno   chiesto **dove**   è andato Gianni.
         me   have-3PL   asked   where   is gone   Gianni
         'They asked me where Gianni went.'

      b. $[_{Op2P}$**dove**$_i[_{ForceP} t_i[_{GroundP} [_{IP}t_j$ è andato $t_i]_k [_{TopP}$Gianni$_j[_{Op1P} t_i...t_k]]]]]$

In Standard Italian wh-phrases always occupy the upper Op2-position. The interrogative feature of ForceP in matrix questions is checked via remnant IP-movement to SpecForceP, which has SCLI as a consequence (cf. 85a, b). In embedded interrogatives the interrogative feature in ForceP is lexically checked by the selecting matrix verb. Therefore, remnant IP-movement to SpecForceP is not necessary (cf. 86a, b). SI emerges as a consequence of the latter derivation. In the cases of SI, the IP undergoes remnant movement to GroundP (cf. 86a and b). It follows from the different target positions for remnant IP-movement in both constructions, SCLI vs. SI, that the subject also occupies different positions. In main questions with SCLI the *pro*-subject is located in GroundP and in the embedded structures involving SI the subject NP is supposed to move to TopP (compare 85b and 86b). In embedded wh-questions with preverbal subjects as in (83c), the subject moves to GroundP instead of the remnant IP (for discussion and definition of the semantic content of the left-peripheral positions cf. Poletto & Pollock 2000). Eliminating V-movement from the derivation of wh-questions in Italian, this rather complex proposal captures the anti-adjacency effects between the wh-phrase and the finite verb in embedded contexts.

---

[41] The assumption of two operator positions in the left periphery of Italian follows from the detection of doubling constructions in some Italian dialects (Poletto & Pollock 2000):

      (i) **Cossa** ha-lo   fat   **che**?   (Bellunese)
          what   have-3SG-he   done   what
          'What did he do?'

To conclude, in both matrix and embedded interrogatives the wh-phrases appear in the specifier of the same functional head. Sticking to the less complicated representational model from Rizzi (1997) I will continue to refer to this position as FocP. According to Poletto & Pollock (2000) the differences between clauses in which the verb appears adjacent to the wh-element (or the focused phrase) and the ones in which the verb is not adjacent to the wh-element or the focused phrase is not a result of the different position of the wh-element (or the focused phrase) and that of the verb. The wh-element (or the focused phrase) is always in the specifier of a functional head Foc°. The verb does not move from the IP at all. The things that move around are different phrasal elements (maximal projections) like IP, DP etc. Thus, the wh-phrase fills the specifier of Foc°. This head element remains non-lexicalised.

One problem for this analysis of matrix wh-questions in Standard Italian arises from the observation that constructions in which the wh-phrase occupies the lower Op1 position do not occur (compare 85a, b and ii in fn. 38 with 87):

(87) *Ha   comprato **chi**, il   libro?
       have-3sg bought   who the book
       'Who bought the book?'
       (Elisabetta Passinetti, Eugenia Marchisio, p.c.)

This fact suggests that the head-adjacency is crucial for the proper licensing of a wh-item in Italian. Secondly, the availability of two operator positions which may host wh-elements leaves the ungrammaticality of multiple wh-questions unexplained. Thirdly, the analysis of Poletto & Pollock (2000) also faces typical problems related to the theory of *Relativized Minimality* (see Rizzi 1990). In order to avoid these problems I will stick to a V-to-C movement analysis of root wh-interrogatives in Italian assuming this effect to be a remnant V2-phenomenon (see also subsection 3.1.2.1.).

3.1.2.4 The Nature of D-Linked Wh-Phrases. D-Linked and non D-Linked wh-phrases represent a further contrast with respect to inversion effects. SCLI is not crucial in questions with D-Linked wh-items (for more on the nature of D-Linking see Rizzi 2000).

(88) a. **Quale libro** ha   *pro* letto, Gianni?   (SCLI)
         which book have-3SG   read Gianni
         'Which book did Gianni read?'
      b. **Quale libro** ha   letto Gianni?   (SI)
         which book have-3SG   read Gianni
         'Which book did Gianni read?'

c. **A quale   politico**   nessuno ha   dato il proprio voto?
   to which   politician   nobody have-3SG   given the his   vote
   'Which politician did nobody vote for?'
d. ?(?)**Quale ragazzo** Gianni ha   visto ieri?
   which boy   Gianni have-3SG   seen yesterday
   'Which boy did Gianni see yesterday?'

Non D-Linked wh-phrases in Italian are defect according to the generalisation of Poletto & Pollock (2000) and therefore not capable of checking the interrogative feature in ForceP of main interrogatives. The latter is checked either lexically or via remnant IP-movement to ForceP as shown in the previous subsection (3.1.2.3.). D-Linked wh-phrases on the contrary are able to check all strong features activated in the left periphery of an interrogative clause, thus opening up the possibility of SCLI (cf. 88a), SI (cf. 88b) and also of non-inverted subjects (cf. 88c and d).

Let me conclude the observations from this section. I will continue to assume that wh-phrases and focused constituents are licensed in one and same position of the clausal left periphery, i.e. FocP. Thus, both wh- and focused phrases require a head-adjacency configuration as a licensing mechanism reminiscent to the wh-Criterion (Rizzi 1991) or to the Focus-Criterion (Brody 1990). In the case of focused elements, wh-phrases in embedded clauses and D-Linked wh-items, the functional head does not need to be identified by a lexical material. In other words, in the latter cases the finite verb does not move to that functional head. Thus, two representations of the distributional pattern of wh-phrases are possible for Italian:

(89) a. $[_{FocP}$ wh- /focused phrase $[_{Foc°}$ $V_i°]$ $...[_{IP}$ $...t_i]]$
      b. $[_{FocP}$ wh- /focused phrase $[_{Foc°}$ $\emptyset$] $...[_{IP}$ $...V°]]$

What we have seen in this section allows us to make the following descriptive generalisation. As a language that does not admit multiple wh-questions, Italian licences wh-items into a structurally marked position as indicated in (89a, b). In other words, Italian is not a wh-in-situ language. We will also see in the next chapters that the other languages without multiple wh-questions (Somali, Berber and Irish) are not wh-in-situ languages.[42] This fact constitutes a crucial parametric property of the language type under investigation. Next, I provide a

---

[42] Note that for Somali the use of the term 'not a wh-in-situ language' is problematic. I will argue in subchapter (3.2.) that Somali uses a base generation strategy for focusing and wh-question formation. Focused and wh-elements are base generated into a left-peripheral focus position. The term 'not in-situ' should be understood as referring to 'not being in an IP-internal position', 'not being in an argument position' or 'belonging to the left periphery'.

brief overview of some Italian dialects that offer additional support for the syntactic representation of wh-questions in Italian as shown in (89 a, b).

3.1.3 The Dialectal Variation of Interrogative Constructions.

Poletto (2000) examines the dialectal variation of North-Italian wh-questions. Some different strategies of deriving wh-questions across the dialects have been pointed out: questions without SCLI, questions with the so-called '*fa*-support' and SCLI, questions involving a complementizer structure and SCLI, and a formation of wh-questions in interaction with the focal particle *pa*.[43]

Questions without SCLI are rare among the North-Italian dialects. Like in Standard Italian, it is not possible to insert a full DP between the wh-phrase and the verb. I take this crucial fact as an indication that the verb moves into some position of the left periphery adjacent to the wh-item and thus forms a syntactical relation with it (cf. 90a vs. 90b):

(90) a. **Unde**   i   van?   (Caserta Ligure - Ligurian)
         where   they go
         'Where are they going?'
    b. ***Unde** Mario   (l) va?
         where Mario   he goes
         'Where is Mario going?'
         (Poletto 2000: 56f)

The most conservative type of interrogative structures in the North-Italian dialects is the one involving *fa*-support and SCLI.

(91) a. **Come** *fa*-l comportas?   (Mono - Eastern Lombard)
         how   do-he behave
         'How is he behaving?'
    b. **Quanta** *fe*-t   majan?
         how much do-you eat
         'How much are you going to eat?'
         (Poletto 2000: 49)

Another very common structure resembles a reduced cleft construction in which a complementizer follows the wh-item (for more on reduced clefts see subchapters 3.3. and 3.4.). This possibility of building wh-questions is found

---

[43] The syntactic phenomenon called '*fa*-support' is very similar to the English '*do*-support' which is analysed as movement of the dummy verb into the C° position (for discussion and references cf. Poletto 2000:49f).

only in the varieties that have the same phenomenon in embedded interrogatives.

(92) a. **Chi** *che* maja?   (Monno - Eastern Lombard)
      who   that   eats
      'Who is eating?'
   b. I ho   domanda   **col** *che* l'ha   fat.
      I have   asked   what that he-has   done
      'I asked him what he did.'
      (Poletto 2000:86)

A full wh-cleft construction showing similar behaviour to the wh-questions involving a complementizer is also a widespread phenomenon in Italian dialects.

(93) a. **Ch** el   *c*   a   fiv   adess?(Albosaggia - Alpine Lombard)
      what is-it that SCL do   now
      'What are you doing now?'
   b. Al so   ca   **chi** *c*   a   l'è   c   a   l'è   ruat.
      I know not who that SCL SCL-is that SCL SCL-is come
      'I don't know who has come.'
      (Poletto 2000:62)

In the next construction, a focal particle *pa* occurs in different positions of the wh-clause: to the left (cf. 94a) or to the right (cf. 94b) of the inflected verb in matrix clauses. It is excluded in embedded interrogatives (compare 94e with f) and in matrix questions containing a complementizer (cf. 94c, d). Different dialects show interpretative variations in questions containing the particle *pa*. In Fassano for instance *pa* marks a rhetorical question whereas in Badiotto its presence signals a real question (for more on this topic and for interpretative differences of questions formed by means of a complementizer across the Italian dialects cf. Poletto 2000:65ff).

(94) a. **O'la** *pa*   tu   vas?   (Perra di Fassa - Rhaetoromance)
      where   PRT you   go
   b. **O'la**   vas-to *pa*?
      where   go-you PRT
      'Where on earth are you going?'
      (Poletto 2000:46)
   c. *****Olà**   che *pa*   tu   vas?
      where that PRT you   go
      'Where are you going?'

> d. *Olà   *pa*   che   tu   vas?
>   where   PRT   that   you   go
>   'Where are you going?'
>   (Poletto 2000:47)
> e. Dime   **co**   che   tu   l   fas?
>   tell-me   what   that   you   it   do
> f. *Dime   **co**   l   fas   to   *pa?*
>   tell me   how   it   do   you   PRT
>   'Tell me how you do it.'
>   (Poletto 2000:46)

Taking the fact that the wh-phrase is adjacent to the verb (cf. 90a and 91a, b), to a complementizer (cf.92a, b) or to a focal particle (cf.94a) as supporting evidence, I interpret this distribution as a spec-head configuration. Consequently, the wh-phrase is in the specifier position and the head is lexicalised either by the verb, the complementizer or the focal particle (for a different account of the distribution of the focal particle see Poletto 2000:47ff). Thus, the position of the wh-phrases in North-Italian varieties briefly described in this subsection strongly suggests that in Italian wh-elements are obligatorily licensed in spec-head relationship even in those cases when the head position is not lexicalised, as shown for Standard Italian (see section 3.1.2.).

3.1.4 The Anti-Agreement Effect

An interesting additional phenomenon accompanies the syntax of both wh-questions and focus constructions in two Italian dialects (Trentino and Fiorentino): the so-called *anti-agreement effect*. Anti-agreement also occurs in relative clauses (see Brandi & Cordin 1989, Ouhalla 1993 and Mereu 1999, among others). Basically, an invariable 3SG-form of the verb is required for the focussing, questioning or relativising of subjects regardless of the φ-features of the subject. Subject clitics, otherwise obligatory, are dropped in these contexts. Brandi & Cordin hypothesise that the subject clitics are the spelling out of the AgrS-element of a Split-INFL and suggest that these dialects belong to the group of *pro*-drop languages. The following examples from Trentino show the anti-agreement effect in wh-questions and focus constructions:[44]

---

[44] To ease representation I will ignore the Fiorentino dialect. I refer the interested reader to Brandi & Cordin (1989). Consider the inflectional paradigm for Trentino of the verb *parlo* 'to speak':

	Singular:	Plural:
1.	parlo	parlem
2.	te parli	parlé
3.	(M)el parla	i parla
	(F) la parla	le parla

Trentino lacks 1SG/PL, and 2PL subject clitics.

(95) a. LA   MARIA è   vegnù,   no   la   Carla.
        the   Maria COP   come-PP-SG   not   the   Carla
        'Maria came, not Carla.'
     b. *LA MARIA la   è   vegnuda,   no la Carla.
        the Maria SCL COP   come-PP-FSG   not the Carla
        'Maria she came, not Carla.'

(96) a. **Quante   putele** è   vegnù   con   ti?
        how many girls   COP   come-PP-SG   with   you
     b. ***Quante   putele** le   è   vegnude   con ti?
        how many   girls   SCL   COP   come-PP-PL with   you
        'How many girls came with you?'

Such phenomena are not attested for wh-questions and focus constructions in
Standard Italian. I will come back to the discussion of similar phenomena in
Somali (subchapter 3.2), Berber (subchapter 3.3.) and Irish (subchapter 3.4.)
later. Since anti-agreement effects do not count as relevant syntactic properties
for wh-questions in Standard Italian, they are not of interest here (see for further discussion on Trentino subsection 3.2.6.2.).

3.1.5 Concluding Remarks on the Syntax of Wh-Questions in Italian
To conclude the observations of subchapter (3.1.), two important generalisations have been made about Italian. First, as discussed in section (3.1.1.) there
are many pieces of evidence that the information structure in wh-questions
parallels that of focus constructions. It has been argued that both wh-questions
and declaratives containing focused elements are instances of the same syntactic pattern. I have shown that Italian is a language which obligatorily licenses
focal elements in a designated structural position in the left periphery of the
clause. A crucial property of this focus position is that it cannot host more than
one element. Unlike Rizzi (1997) who claims that only contrastive focus is
unique, I have argued for a syntactic unification of focus in the grammar of
Italian (see also Brunetti 2003). Thus, Italian allows for only one focused constituent or wh-element per clause. Second, I have characterised the position of
focused or wh-elements as left-adjacent to a head element endowed with a focus feature. We have seen that this functional head is sometimes filled by lexical material, and sometimes not (see sections 3.1.2 and 3.1.3. for discussion).
The SpecFocP in Italian can either host one contrastively focused phrase, one
element expressing information focus or one wh-item. Since no other clausal
position is capable of licensing focus in Italian, multiple wh-phrases cannot
occur in the grammar of the language.

3.2 Somali

3.2.1 Preliminaries to the Syntax of Somali

Several introductory notes are necessary for the better understanding of the syntax of Somali (for detailed information see Lecarme 1999, Svolacchia et al. 1995, Svolacchia & Puglielli 1999 and Saeed 1999). Somali is assumed to be a discourse prominent SOV polysynthetic language (see È. Kiss 1995 for the definition of discourse prominent languages and Baker 1996 for the definition of polysynthetic languages). It is, however, not an example of the classical polysynthetic type but rather a pronominal argument language (also called non-configurational language) as defined in Jelinek (1984). A basic feature of that language type is a pronominal argument structure (for discussion see also sub-chapter 2.3.). Pronominal clitics occur in the A-positions and are assigned θ-roles there. All clitic elements in Somali must precede the verb in a fixed linear order. The pronominal clitics are either enclitics or proclitics, depending on their lexical properties. Subject clitics are enclitics attached to the right of the so-called *focus markers*. Object clitics are proclitics that are either adjacent to the verb or combined with right adjacent prepositions. Together they form the so-called *verbal group*. Saeed (1999:164) describes its structure in the following way:

(97) [$_{\text{VGP}}$ SCL OCL1 ADP ADV1 ADV2 OCL2 V]

Full NPs appear in adjoined A'-positions associated with an IP-internal pronoun position that determines their interpretation (see for discussion Lecarme 1999, Saeed 1999: chapter 7 and subsection 3.2.1.2.).

Most of the clauses in Somali exhibit overt focus markers, also called focus particles or indicator particles (for discussion of the terminological differences cf. Svolacchia et al. 1995 and Saeed 2000). In the following I adopt the expression focus marker. Three basic syntactic structures have been reported in the grammars of Somali. I will briefly review their use in the following subsections and concentrate on the focus construction which parallels wh-questions in Somali.

3.2.1.1 The waa-Focus Construction.
Positive declarative sentences with verbal focalisation in which all nominal phrases are unfocused are represented with the focus marker *waa* (see Andrzejewski 1975). Saeed (1984:179), however, claims that *waa*-structures are neutral with respect to the discourse function of focus. According to him, the particle *waa* serves as sentence type identification and is classified in his terminology as a *positive declarative marker*. The distribution of *waa* is shown by the following example:

(98) a. Cali warqáddíi **wuu** **íi** **dhiibay**.
         Ali letter-the FM-SCL me-to passed
      b. Warqáddíi Cali **wuu** **íi** **dhiibay**.
         letter-the Ali FM-SCL me-to passed
      c. **Wuu** **íi** **dhiibay** Cali warqáddíi.
         FM-SCL me-to passed Ali letter-the
      d. **Wuu** **íi** **dhiibay** warqáddíi Cali.
         FM-SCL me-to passed letter-the Ali
         'Ali passed the letter to me.'
         (Saeed 1999:229)

The verb and the preverbal elements attached to it form the verbal group. The focus marker *waa* immediately precedes the verbal group. This order remains unchanged in (98a-d). What can change is the position of other NPs, DPs or APs.

3.2.1.2 The bàa/ayàa-Focus Construction. Nominal focalisation involves the focus marker *bàa/ayàa*:[45] The focused element must be to the left of the verb followed by the adjacent focus marker. The order of other nominal constituents is free as schematically shown in (99d):

(99) a. Wiilki **moos** **buu** cunayaa.
         boy-the banana FM-SCL is-eating
      b. **Moos** **buu** cunayaa wiilki.
         banana FM-SCL is-eating boy-the
      c. **Moos** **buu** / **baa** wiilki cunayaa.
         banana FM-SCL / FM boy-the is-eating
         'The boy is eating **a banana**.'
      d. [cp XP [cp XP [c° bàa/ayàa] [ip XP [ip …]]]]
         (Svolacchia et al. 1995)

Such clauses deserve special attention, since they constitute the syntactic parallel to wh-questions in Somali. Lecarme (1999) assumes for this construction type a clausal structure with free constituent order and adjunction slots at the CP- and IP-level in which full NPs, DPs or APs appear. Pronominal elements occur inside the IP while elements with the discourse pragmatic functions such as focus appear in SpecCP (see 99d). Given the fact that only one constituent can be focused by *bàa/ayàa* (cf. 110a, b, c, d) and other full NPs can precede (cf. 99a), follow (cf. 99c) the focused element, and even appear in a clause

---

[45] The focus markers *bàa* and *ayàa* are phonological variants of the same category and are freely exchangeable (see Lamberti 1983 for discussion on their origins, Saeed 1984 and 1999 for their function).

final position (cf. 99b), I propose a modified structure for *bàa/ayàa*-clauses adopting Rizzi's (1997) detailed structure of the left periphery. As the structure in (100) indicates NPs, DPs or APs are located outside the IP in separate layers (TopP or FocP) where TopP is represented as a recursive projection (for further discussion see section 3.2.2.):

(100)

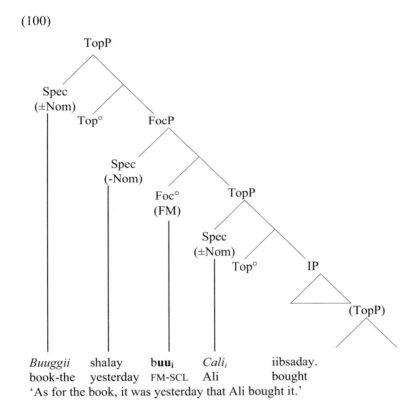

Buuggii	shalay	**buu**ᵢ	*Cali*ᵢ	iibsaday.
book-the	yesterday	FM-SCL	Ali	bought

'As for the book, it was yesterday that Ali bought it.'

A binary system of morphological ±Nom-case is available in topic positions. The morphological case of the topic position always corresponds to the case of the clause internal pronominal argument it is connected to. The element in the focus position bears an invariant -Nom-case (also called the *absolutive case*, which corresponds to the default case of the noun in citation form). This -Nom-case is independent of the case of the pronominal argument inside the clause (see also the discussion of anti-agreement effects in section 3.2.6.). The relation between topics or focused elements and the pronominal arguments at the IP level is coreference. However, a θ-theoretical problem emerges with this concept. Two elements seem to bear one and the same θ-role. Jelinek (1984) has proposed a linking rule in terms of case compatibility for non-configurational languages like Warlpiri. Typically for that language type full NPs are optional and always appear in non-argument positions. This mechanism describes how pronominal arguments are connected to full NPs in adjoined positions:

(101) Linking Rule:
     A clitic pronoun may be coindexed with a nominal, providing the case of the nominal and the case of the clitic pronoun are compatible.
     (Jelinek 1984)

Kayne (2002) promotes another idea in order to solve the problem of θ-role assignment to two apparently independent elements (an antecedent and a pronoun) in English (for a similar analysis of clitic left dislocation in Italian see also Cecchetto 2000 and Grewendorf 2002 for an analysis of the same phenomenon in German). He assumes that the antecedent and the coreferent pronoun are primarily base-generated as a complex DP. Subsequently the non-pronominal part of this complex item moves to a higher position. Nevertheless, a solution of that kind for the clausal structure in Somali faces the problem that neither focusing nor topicalisation obeys constraints typical of movement (see sections 3.2.3. and 3.2.4. for relevant examples). Thus it is not clear enough what kind of relation is established between full NPs in the A'-positions and pronouns in the A-positions in Somali. I will use the term of coreference in order to describe this relationship.

At the level of phrasal phonology the focus marker *bàa* is phrased together with its specifier. (102b) shows the decomposed structure of (102a):

(102) a. **Lacágtàan**   ku   síinayaa.   (surface structure)
     money-the-FM-SCL to-you will-give
     'I will give you the money.'
    b. **Lacág+ta+bàa+ann** ku   síinayaa.   (morphologically
     money+the+FM+SCL to-you will-give   decomposed structure)

The focus marker *ayàa* with identical function does not undergo coalescence with the preceding wh- or focused element as shown in (103) (for more examples with wh-phrases see section 3.2.3.):

(103) **Lacág-ta**   ayàa-aan ku   síinayaa.
     money-the   FM-SCL   to-you will-give
     'I will give you the money.'
     (Saeed 1999:38)

The focus markers *waa/bàa/ayàa* are argued to originate diachronically from a copular verb with an incorporated 3MSG-pronoun (see Lamberti 1983 and the discussion of the anti-agreement pattern in Somali in section 3.2.6.). In clauses involving nominal focalisation (the contemporary *bàa/ayàa*-constructions) the predicative noun phrase appeared to the left of the copula while in sentences with verbal predicates (the nowadays *waa*-constructions) the predicate remained in place. According to Lamberti *bàa* has now become a real focus particle and functions as a copula of *wáxa(a)*-clefts additionally (see next subsection 3.2.1.3.). Besides highlighting the verbal predicate, the particle *waa* functions as a copula in nominal clauses.

3.2.1.3 The wáxa(a)-Focus Construction. The so-called *cataphoric focalisation* (also called the *heraldic construction*) requires the element *wáxa(a)*:

(104) Cali **wúxuu**   ii   dhiibay **warqáddii**.
      Ali FM-SCL   me-to   passed letter-the
      'Ali passed me **the letter**.'
      (Saeed 2000)

Hetzron (1971) defines such constructions as *presentative structures* in which a semantically empty expletive *wáxa(a)* occurs before the verb while the focused elements appear after it (see also Andrzejewski 1975 for a similar point of view). Another analysis is proposed by Saeed (1984:42ff; 1999:194ff) who claims that *wáxa(a)*-sentences correspond in use to English *it*-clefts, pseudo wh-clefts or existential *there*-constructions. Therefore, he considers a cleft-like structure for *wáxa(a)*-sentences.[46] Thus, Saeed assumes that *wáxa(a)*-clefts are historically derived from verbless *waa*-sentences containing a relative clause headed by the semantically underspecified element *wáx* 'thing' and the dropping of *waa*. In addition the process is accompanied by total semantic bleaching of the word *wáx-a* which has been grammaticalised to an expletive focus element (see also Svolacchia et al. 1995 for discussion and Lamberti 1983 for a different proposal: *wax* 'thing' + *a* 'the' + *bàa* 'FM'= *waxà(a)*):

(105) [[REL. CLAUSE wax-a…]waa[PREDICATE…]]→[[CLEFT CLAUSE wáxa(a)…][FOCUS…]]

---

[46] Traditionally clefts are assumed to have a biclausal structure of the following type:

    (i) [CP It   is   John [CP who   came]].   (cleft)
         EXPL COP DP   RELATIVE CLAUSE
    (ii) [CP [CP Who   came] is   John].   (pseudo-cleft)
        FREE RELATIVE CLAUSE COP DP

However, recent investigations on the syntax of clefts have shown that clefts can be considered monoclausal structures as proposed by Meinunger (1998) and É. Kiss (1998a) for English and Sabel & Zeller (2004) for Nguni. I will stick to the monoclausal representation of clefts (cf. subsection 3.3.1.2. for monoclausal representation of clefts in Berber).

The following two constructions are available in contemporary Somali. (106b) is derived from (106a) through *waa*-deletion:[47]

(106) a. Wáxaan   dóonayaa   waa **shàah**.
        thing-the-SCL want-1SG FM   tea
        'The thing that I want is tea.'
    b. Wáxaan   dóonayaa   **shàah**.
        FM-SCL   want-1SG   tea
        'What I want is tea.'
        (Saeed 1999:196)

In general, *wáxa(a)*-clauses are preferred when heavy constituents have to be focused. In the following, I will gloss the *wáxa(a)*-element with 'FM'. But note that contrary to the *bàa/ayàa*-focusing strategy, the focused material in the *wáxa(a)*-constructions appears postverbally. This kind of syntactic structures are not used to focus adverbial expressions and wh-constituents in real questions (see Saeed 1984:154; 2000 and for further discussion section 3.2.2.):

(107) *Wáxay   sameeyeen **máxay**?
      FM-SCL   did   what
      'What they did was what?' or 'What did they do?'
      (Saeed 2000)

I will now turn to the specific properties of the *bàa/ayàa*-focus construction which constitutes the syntactic parallel to wh-questions in Somali.

---

[47] Strong evidence for the parallel existence of two syntactically different *wáxa(a)*-constructions is provided by agreement patterns. Since the noun *wax* 'thing' is marked for 3MSG it sometimes agrees with the verb (cf. i). But there are cases in which the verb agrees with the postverbal subject (cf. ii):
    (i) Waxa   yimi   annaga.
        thing-3MSG-the came-3MSG we
        'It was we who came.'
    (ii) Waxa nimi   annaga.
        FM   came-2PL we
        'It was we who came.'
        (Saeed 1984:56)

3.2.2 The Specific Properties of the bàa/ayàa-Focus Constructions

One important property of the focus markers *bàa* and *ayàa* is the fact that they are restricted to root clauses, and are in most cases obligatory there.[48] The ungrammaticality of (108) confirms the statement that focusing is a main clause phenomenon in Somali:

(108) **Cali** baa sheegay [in Muuse (***baa/*waa**) yimid].
    Ali   FM   said   that   Muuse   FM/ FM   came
    'Ali said that Muuse has come.'
    (Svolacchia et al. 1995)

There is a widespread opinion in the literature on Somali grammar that the language lacks embedded infinitival clauses and shows a remarkable limitation of clausal structures (Lecarme 1999, for a different point of view see Saeed 1999:226f and subchapter 3.5.). Beside root clauses there are only relative and complement clauses. Important for the current discussion is the fact that subordinated questions in Somali do not exist. Given the fact that focusing is a root clause phenomenon it follows that interrogatives, both wh- and yes/no-questions are only root syntactic phenomena as the contrast between (109a) and (109c) shows (cf. Saeed 1999:204). An embedded constituent question is usually expressed by means of a non-interrogative head noun that introduces a relative clause like in (109b):

(109) a. **Halkee**   buu   tegayaa?
       place-which FM-SCL go
       'Where is he going?'
    b. Weydii **halka**   [REL uu   tegayo].
       ask-IMP place   SCL go
       'Ask him where he is going.'
    c. *Weydii [**halkee**   uu   tegayo].
       ask-IMP   place-which SCL go
       'Ask him where he is going.'
       (Saeed 1984:140)

The focus position left-adjacent to *bàa/ayàa* is unique, i.e. a clause may contain only one focus marker of this type and there may be only one constituent in the sentence focused by *bàa/ayàa*.[49] Consider four examples (cf. 110a, b, c,

---

[48] Well-known exceptions are the short accented forms of the past independent, the past comparative, the imperative and the exclamative verbal forms. Common to all these paradigms is the absence of both focus markers and subject clitics.
[49] An exception to this rule occurs when there is a succession of two adverbial expressions. It is possible only in this case that a second *bàa* appears (see for discussion Hetzron 1965).

d) which show that a focused element and a wh-phrase cannot occur in the same clause and that two wh-elements are excluded as well. The situation in Somali resembles the observations on the information structure in Italian (see subchapter 3.1.):

(110) a. ***Yaa**   **Maryan** baa   arkay?
          who-FM   Maryan FM   saw
          'Who is it that Marian saw?'

      b. ***Maryan** baa   **yaa**   arkay?
          Maryan   FM   who-FM   saw
          'Who did Marian see?'

      c) ***Kuma maxaa** ayaa   cunay?
          who   what   FM   ate
          'Who ate what?'

      d) ***Kuma** ayaa   **maxaa**   cunay?
          who   FM   what   ate
          'Who ate what?'
          (Cabdelqadir Ruumi, p.c.)

Saeed (1999) reports that a combination of the *bàa/ayàa-* and the *wáxa(a)-* focusing strategy results in a multiple focus construction with restricted distribution. Consider a clause typically used as the beginning of a narrative:[50]

(111) **Waa** baa   waxaa   jirey   **nin   iyo   afa-diis**...
      time FM   FM   were man   and   wife-his
      'Once upon a time there was a man and his wife...'
      (Saeed 1999:247)

Nominal focus marked by *bàa/ayàa* cannot appear in one and the same clause with predicative focus which is marked through *waa* (see Frascarelli & Puglielli to appear, among others):

(112) ***Maryan** baa   Xamar   way   **tagtay**.
      Maryan   FM   Mogadishu FM-SCL go-PAST-3FSG
      'Maryan goes to Mogadishu.'

There can be multiple topics in a clause which are optional and typically unordered (cf. the structure in 100). Contrary to the distribution of focused constitu-

---

[50] The examples I know of show an initial adverbial followed by *bàa* and a succeeding *wáxa(a)-*cleft. The relation between the focused adverbial and the cleft clause is not clear. The possibility that they form two separate clauses structurally is not excluded.

ents, topics are possible in every clausal type (for discussion of topic constructions in Somali and references see Stoyanova to appear).

3.2.3 Wh-Questions and Focus Constructions

Consider first yes/no-interrogatives in Somali. They require a question particle
má (cf. 113a). Their appropriate answers are instances of the *waa*-construction
(cf. 113b). A sentence with nominal focus is an inappropriate answer to a
yes/no-question (cf. 113c):

> (113) a. Gabádhdhii **má**   seexatay?
>   girl-the   Q   slept
>   'Did the girl go to sleep?'
>   b. Hàa, (gabádhdhii) **wày**   **seexatay**.
>   yes, (girl-the)   FM-SCL slept
>   'Yes, (the girl) she went to sleep.'
>   c. #Hàa, **gabádhdhii** ayàa   seexatáy.
>   yes,   girl-the   FM-SCL slept
>   'Yes, the girl went to sleep.'
>   (Saeed 2000)

This observation indicates that the syntax of interrogatives in Somali is complex to the extent that it has different unrelated derivational patterns for yes/no-
questions and wh-questions (see the discussion in subchapter 4.3.).

As already mentioned the *wáxa(a)*-construction cannot be used to focus wh-
constituents in information questions. Consider the contrast between (114a)
and (114b):

> (114) a. *Wáxay   sameeyeen **máxay**?
>   FM-SCL   did   what
>   'What they did was what?' or
>   'What did they do?'
>   b. **Maxáy**   sameeyeen?
>   what-FM-SCL did
>   'What did they do?'
>   (Saeed 2000)

An unmarked wh-question is usually expressed by means of the *bàa/ayàa*-
focus construction (cf. 114b). The wh-element appears left-adjacent to the focus marker *bàa/ayàa*. The ungrammatical example (114a) shows a further important property of the wh-items in Somali: wh-phrases cannot be left in-situ

(for the same generalisation in Italian see the discussion of the previous sub-chapter 3.1.)

Wh-questions strictly pattern with *bàa/ayàa*-focus constructions. A single constituent question and its most appropriate answer show the same syntactic structure. This correlation is shown for subjects in (115), for direct objects in (116) and for adjuncts in (117):

(115) a. **Kuma** ayaa kalluunkii cunay?
　　　　who　　FM　　fish-the　　ate
　　　　'Who ate the fish?'
　　　b. **Cali** baa　kalluunkii cunay.
　　　　Ali　　FM　　fish-the　　ate
　　　　'Ali ate the fish.'
　　　c. #Kalluunkii baa　**Cali** cunay.
　　　　fish-the　　　FM　　Ali　ate
　　　　'Ali ate the fish.'

(116) a. Cali **muxuu**　　　cunay?
　　　　Ali　what-FM-SCL　eat
　　　　'What did Ali eat?'
　　　b. **Kalluunkii**baa　Cali　cunay.
　　　　fish-the　　　FM　　Ali　ate
　　　　'Ali ate the fish.'
　　　c. #Cali baa　**kalluunkii** cunay.
　　　　Ali　FM　　fish-the　　　ate
　　　　'Ali ate the fish.'
　　　　(Saeed 1984:25f)

(117) a. Wìilkii **hálkùu**　　　　　　joogaa?
　　　　boy-the place-which-FM-SCL　stays
　　　　'Where is the boy?'
　　　b. **Qólkáasùu**　　　　kú jiraa.
　　　　room-that-FM-SCL　in is
　　　　'He is in that room.'
　　　c. #Wìilkii　bàa　**qólkáas**　kú jirá.
　　　　boy-the　FM　room-that　in is
　　　　'The boy is in that room.'
　　　d. #Wìilkii　**qólkáas**　　wuu　kú jiraa.
　　　　boy-the　room-that　FM-SCL　in is
　　　　'The boy is in that room.'
　　　　(Saeed 2000)

The logical conclusion is that both wh-phrases and focused constituents in Somali are very similar to their Italian counterparts. They occur in the same syntactic position. Constituents focused by means of the focus marker *bàa/ayàa*
are interpreted in general as elements that bear new information as the ques-
tion-answer pairs in (115), (116) and (117) indicate. Depending on the context,
they can also have a contrastive interpretation (Lecarme 1999; Saeed 2000 and
Svolacchia et al. 1995):

(118) a. Maroodigu [NP   takarta   ku joogta] ma   arka   ee
         elephant-the   gadfly-the on is   not see-NEG but
         [NP   TAN   KALE   KU   JOOGT]UU   arkaa.
               the-one another on   is-FM-SCL   sees
         'The elephant does not see the gadfly which is on itself but sees
         THE ONE ON ANOTHER.'
      b. Libàax   yeedháy iyo   libàax   aammusáy,
         lion   roaring and   lion   silent
         LIBÀAX   AAMMUSÁY   bàa   xún.
         lion   silent   FM   bad
         'Of a roaring lion and a silent lion, A SILENT LION is worse.'
         (Saeed 2000)

In (118a) two complex NPs are contrasted to each other by means of the *bàa*-
focus construction. The constituent in the first clause is negated. The focus
marker *bàa* is attached to the end of the complex NP in the second clause,
which serves as a contrast.[51] Another instance of contrastive use of the
bàa/ayàa-construction is (118b). Here two NPs appear as hanging topics at the
beginning or rather outside of the clause (for discussion of semantically different topic types see Li 1976). Then one of the NPs is focused and thus contrasted to the other one.

As already discussed, the element *bàa* usually coalesces with the left-hand focused constituent or wh-element. Livnat (1984:111) points out that in some
cases the phonological structure of the interrogative word makes it difficult to
decide whether the nominal focus marker *bàa* occurs or not. The analogy between wh-questions and their answers (cf. 115, 116 and 117) leads me to assume that even wh-elements with unclear morphophonological structure like
yàa 'who' bear a coalesced focus marker *bàa*. Thus, (119a) has a segmented
structure as in (119b) (see Lamberti 1983):

---

[51] Note that the whole complex NP is focused. The focus marker *bàa* is attached to the last
constituent of the relative clause within the complex NP and undergoes the typical coalescence
process (see also subsection 3.2.1.2.).

(119) a. **Yàa**   keenáy?   (surface structure)
who-FM brought
'Who brought it?'
b. ayó+bàa keenáy   (morphologically decomposed structure)
who+FM brought

Verbless information questions are also available in Somali. They are formed
in the same way as verbless declaratives and involve the focus marker *waa* in
its function as a copula.[52] The following structures (120a, b and c) are actually
copular clauses in which the wh-phrase occupies the position of the predicative
noun:[53]

(120) a. Xisáabtu   waa   **immisa?**
bill-the   FM   how-much
'How much is the bill?'
b. Dukàankii waa   **xaggée?**
shop-the   FM   place-which
'Where is the shop?'
c. Máanta   waa   **ayáanma?**
today   FM   day-which
'What day is it today?'
(Saeed 1999:204)

Another type of wh-question with limited distribution is a construction that
may consist of a single wh-phrase without a focus marker like *mée* 'where',
wàayo 'why' or *iyàa* 'what' (the latter corresponding to English: 'What did you
say?' or 'Pardon?') (cf. 121a, b and c). The question word *mée* may be also
combined with a single NP (cf. 121d). Such structures resemble the verbless
wh-questions discussed above. What does not appear in the following examples is the element *waa*. I consider the following clauses to be nominal sentences in which the copular element is deleted:

---

[52] Recall that *waa* was classified as predicate focus marker in subsection (3.2.1.1.). Its function
as copula is not surprising since it originates from a copula (for more on this see Lamberti
1983). Together with the predicative NP, *waa* forms the copular predicate. It can be dropped as
well. *waa*-dropping results in a real nominal clause.
[53] Note that it is an old assumption of the Prague School and the traditional grammarians that
the notion of focus is inherent to predicates (see also Calabrese 1987). I will not discuss the
waa-construction extensively since it is rare in the syntax of wh-questions in Somali. Therefore, I do not provide an analysis of this construction (for more on the syntax of copula constructions and clefts see subchapters (3.3.) and (3.4)).

(121) a. **Méeyey**?
where-he
'Where is he?'
b. **Méeday**?
where-she
'Where is she?'
c. **Méeye**?
where-they
'Where are they?'
d. Áxmed **mée**?
Axmed where
'Where is Axmed?'
(Saeed 1999:203)

What is important for the syntax of wh-questions in Somali is the fact that in all sentences the wh-element appears in a focus position. They are usually focused by means of the *bàa/ayàa*-focus construction. Occasionally they may occur as focused predicative NPs. The latter process may be accompanied by deletion of *waa*. Given the observation that the focus markers *waa* and *bàa/ayàa* cannot occur in the same clause (see 112) both strategies of wh-questioning cannot be combined in order to derive a grammatical multiple wh-question.

3.2.4 The Derivation of Wh-questions
Unlike Italian, the focus position in Somali does not exhibit the properties of a quantificational operator (for operator tests and the structural distinctions between different elements in the left periphery see Rizzi 1997, see also Drubig 2000 for typological differences in focus constructions and the discussion of section 3.1.1.). Both topic and focus constructions require the insertion of pronominal clitics in all argument positions. Wh-, focused and relativised subjects in matrix clauses represent well-known exceptions from this rule (see for extensive discussion section 3.2.6. and 3.5.3). Compare a focused phrase originating in a root clause such as (122a) with a focused phrase originating in an embedded one such as (122b):

(122) a. **Adiga**$_i$ b-uu   *(ku$_i$)   dilay Cali.
you   FM-SCL   OCL   beat Ali
'Ali beat you.'
(Svolacchia & Puglielli 1999)

b. **Nimankii**ᵢ buu   Cali   rumaysanayay
men-the   FM-SCL   Ali   think-PAST3SG
[in*(**ay**ᵢ)   tageen]
COMP-SCL   leave-PAST3PL
'It was the men that Ali thought would leave.'
(Livnat 1984:80)

In (122a) the object is focused and the coreferent clitic is incorporated into the verb. In (122b) the subject is focused and the corresponding subject clitic is attached to the subordinating complementizer. Short and long focalisation does not show any difference with respect to the occurrence of coreferent clitics. The same pattern is documented by long distance wh-questions. Example (123) represents long subject extraction:

(123) **Ninkee**ᵢ   baad   sheegtay   in*(**uu**ᵢ)   ku   caayey?
man-which FM-SCL   report-2SG   that-SCL   you   insult
'Which man did you say insulted you?'

Note, however, that object 3SG/PL-clitics are invisible for the overt syntax because they are represented by Ø-forms in the paradigm of Somali clitic pronouns (Saeed 1999). Since object wh-phrases are always marked for the third person, we cannot find any substantial evidence against movement in these cases. Therefore, such examples are irrelevant and will not be discussed. As already mentioned I will come to the exceptional behaviour of focused and wh-subjects later.

The observation that the base positions of extracted elements are filled by pronominal elements is not predicted by standard approaches to wh-question formation as a result of A'-movement. Note that this behaviour of wh-elements is not expected by the classical analysis of polysynthetic languages as proposed by Baker (1996) either (see for discussion subchapter 2.3.). The fact that overt pronominal arguments cooccur with wh- or focused elements suggests that the latter are not initially base generated in argument positions and subsequently moved to SpecCP as in Baker's (1996) analysis of wh-questions in polysynthetic languages (see also Kayne 2002, Cecchetto 2000 and Grewendorf 2002 for alternative analyses of clitic doubling constructions in English, Italian and German, and Drubig 2000 for a crosslinguistic typology of focus constructions).

Let us turn to another property of wh-elements in Somali which also shows that wh-phrases are rather directly merged into their surface position. As a subcase of focus constructions wh-interrogatives in Somali do not display the properties of overt wh-movement as in English or Italian. Constituent questions and focus constructions lack wco-effects:

(124) a. **Yaa**$_i$ hooyádiis$_i$ jecéshahay?[54]
     who-FM mother-the-his loves
     'Who$_i$ does his$_i$ mother love?'
     (Lecarme 1999)

    b. **Isaga**$_i$ bay   hooyádiis$_i$ jecéshahay.
     him   FM-SCL mother-the-his love.
     'It is him that his mother loves.'
     (Cabdelqadir Ruumi, p.c.)

Next, the relation between the focused or wh-constituent and the pronominal argument is not sensitive to island constraints.

(125) a. **Qoraagée**$_i$ ayaad   jecéshahay búugga [$_{REL}$ Ø uu$_i$ qoray]?
     writer-which FM-SCL like-2SG   book-the   he   wrote
     'Which author do you like the book he wrote?'

    b. **Ardaygée**$_i$ ayaad$_j$ dóonayasaa[ínaad$_j$ lá   hadashid
     student-which FM+SCL   want-2SG   COMP-SCL to-him talk
     [íntuu$_i$san   tegin?]][55]
     part-the-SCL-NEG go-NEG
     'Which student do you want to talk to before goes?'
     (Lecarme 1999)

(125a) represents questioning out of a relative clause.[56] (125b) shows a wh-question out of an adjunct clause. I conclude that wh-questions in Somali do not show movement properties. The lack of wco-effects and the inactivity of island constraints in Somali suggest that some base generation account may be adopted to analyse the facts. Drubig (2000) proposes an account for the languages which do not show wco-effects and island effects (see also section 3.3.3. for discussion of wco-effects in Berber). He also claims that the absence of these phenomena is crosslinguistic evidence against movement analyses. In

---

[54] It is not clear if *yaa* 'who' bears a coalesced subject clitic. This is presumably due to its unclear morphological status (see section 3.2.3.). Note further that subject clitics on focus markers are for some reason optional when the full subject appears in a postfocal position (for more on this see Frascarelli & Puglielli 2004).

[55] Due to fact that that Somali allows embedded declaratives and relative clauses as subordinated structures only, an adjunct clause is formed by means of relativisation (for more on this see Saeed 1999:217ff). In this example a relative clause headed by the noun *inta* 'the amount, the extent, the part' communicates the meaning 'while' or 'until'.

[56] Relative clauses in Somali display neither an overt relative pronoun nor an invariant C° element like in English.

contrast to Frascarelli & Puglielli (2004, see also references cited there) I will assume that wh-elements, like their focal NP, DP, or AP counterparts, are directly merged into the specifier of a functional head which is endowed with a focus feature and occupied by the focus marker *bàa/ayàa* (see also the analysis proposed by Saeed 1984):[57]

(126) a. [FocP **Yáa**   [VP   fahmay]   [TopP su'áashayda]]?   (Subject)
            who-FM   understood   question-the-my
         'Who understood my question?'
     b. [FocP **Muxúu**   [TopP Bíibisiída] [VP   ká maqlay]]? (Object)
            what-FM-SCL   BBC-the   at heard
         'What did he hear at the BBC?'
     c. [SpecFocP **Xaggée** [Foc° bay]   [VP   ahayd]]?   (Adjunct)
            place-which   FM-SCL   COP
         'Where was it?'
         (Lecarme 1999)

The observations from this section allow the generalisation that crosslinguistically focusing does not obligatorily involve operator movement. In some languages focus constructions are the result of A'-movement, in others they are not. Somali belongs to the latter language type.

3.2.5 A Brief Typology of Wh-Phrases in Somali
Somali has three morphologically different types of wh-phrases. One kind of wh-word shows a combination of a prefixed interrogative morpheme *ma-* and an indefinite pronoun (Lecarme 1999). Thus contracted forms like *maxaa* 'what' (cf. 127a) consist of the following single elements (cf. 127b):

(127) a. maxaa   (surface structure)
         Q-thing-FM
         'what'
     b. ma+wax+bàa   (morphologically decomposed structure)
         Q+thing+FM

Another, similar, way of forming wh-phrases is by suffixing the interrogative morpheme *-ma* to a noun (cf. 128a and b), to an independent pronoun or to the indefinite word *ku/tu* 'one (masculine/feminine)' (cf. 129 a, b).

---

[57] Similar behaviour is attested for wh- and focus constructions in Akan. Both wh- and focused elements bind pronominal elements in the base positions. Such derivational patterns call for a base generation account (see for discussion Sabel 1998 and Drubig 2000 among many others).

(128) a. nín-ma
   man-Q
   'which man'
   b. góor-ma
   time-Q
   'which time' or 'when'

(129) a. kú-ma
   one(M)-Q
   'which one'
   b. tú-ma
   one(F)-Q
   'which one'

Somali also has wh-phrases with a suffixed interrogative determiner -*kée* for masculine and -*tée* for feminine.[58]

(130) a. ninkée
   man-M-QD
   'which man'
   b. naagtée
   woman-F-QD
   'which woman'

A third type is represented by wh-phrases like *yaa* 'who', *immisa, méeqa* 'how much, how many' which do not correspond to any of the above mentioned morphological patterns of building wh-phrases in Somali (see Saeed 1999:203 and section 3.2.3.).

In the next section I will turn to a rather surprising phenomenon that characterises both subject focusing and wh-question formation. In what follows, I discuss the so-called anti-agreement effect and examine its relationship to the grammar of two languages without multiple wh-questions: Somali and the Italian dialect Trentino (see section 3.1.4.).

---

[58] Interrogative determiners undergo the same rules of sandhi as other determiners which are also suffix elements, but they usually lower high tones in the noun to which they are attached (for more on the tonal structure of Somali see Saeed 1999:114f). Note also that the phenomenon of D-Linking in Somali, Berber and Irish has not been investigated until now. Therefore, I will not discuss its influence on the acceptability of multiple wh-questions. Following the observations from Italian, I predict that the presence of a D-Linked wh-phrase may improve the acceptability of a multiple wh-question in these languages.

3.2.6 The Anti-Agreement Effect

3.2.6.1 Anti-Agreement in Somali. The last property of Somali to be discussed is the anti-agreement effect (cf. Svolacchia & Puglielli 1999, Mereu 1999, Frascarelli 1999, 2000, among others). As already pointed out, free word order and obligatory pronominal clitics are key features of Somali. Object clitics are obligatory no matter if or where a coindexed full DP occurs.[59] In contrast, subject clitics cannot occur when the coindexed DP is focused, questioned or relativised. In what follows, I will concentrate on the parallelism between focused and wh-subjects.

According to Frascarelli (1999, 2000) the absence of the nominative case and φ-features of the verb are combined effects of the same syntactic phenomenon in Somali. First, the contrast between (131a) and (131b) shows that a focused subject in Somali cannot have nominative case. It has the unmarked absolutive case. Second, a subject clitic is not attached to the focus marker. Third, there is no full agreement of the verb, but a form of the so-called '*restricted paradigm*' instead (cf. 131a).[60] For contrast consider the behaviour of the subject in a clause in which the direct object is focused (cf. 131c):

(131) a. Hilib **nimankaas**   baa   cunayá   (focused subject)
          meat men-those-ABS   FM   eat-PROG-REST
      b. *Hilib nimankaas-u$_i$ bay$_i$ cunayaan.
          meat   men-those-NOM   FM-SCL   eat-3PL-PROG
          'Those men are eating meat.'
      c. Nimankaas-u$_i$ **hilib**   bay$_i$ cunayaan   (focused object)
          men-those-NOM   meat   FM-SCL   eat-3PL-PROG
          'Those men are eating meat.'
          (Frascarelli 1999)

---

[59] Recall that when the non-subject argument is in the third person singular, the object clitic is not visible because 3SG/PL-object clitics in Somali always have Ø-forms.

[60] In the restricted paradigm 2SG-, 2PL- and 3PL-forms of the verb are replaced by a default one which resembles the morphologically poorly marked 3MSG-form of the verb. The following paradigm represents a prefix verb (Svolacchia et al. 1995):

Normal paradigm:		Restricted paradigm:	
1 imid	pl. nimid	1 imid	pl. nimid
2 timid	pl. timaaddeen	2 yimid	pl. yimid
3 yimid	pl. yimaaddeen	3 yimid	pl. yimid
3f timid		3f timid	

Prefix verbs are not as common as suffix verbs. In general suffix verbs in Somali have a morphological structure which has the linear order: root - derivational suffix -AGR - TAM (Saeed 1999:79ff). I have partly modified the original glosses of the examples in order to indicate the detailed information on verbal inflexion whenever necessary for the analysis.

The same effect occurs with wh-subjects (cf. 132a). As constituents that obligatorily appear in a focus position, they behave like their non-interrogative counterparts (see 131a). Wh-objects and non-interrogative focused objects on the contrary do not show the anti-agreement effect (compare 131c with 132c):

(132) a. **Nimankee**   hilibka   cunay?   (wh-subject)
         which-men-FM   meat-the   eat-PERF-REST

     b. *****Nimankee**ᵢ bayᵢ   hilibka   cuneen?
         which men   FM-SCL meat-the   eat-3PL-PERF
         'Which men ate meat?'

     c. **Maxay**   cuneen   nimanku?   (wh-object)
         what-FM-SCL   eat-3PL-PERF men-those
         'What did the men eat?'
         (Cabdelqadir Ruumi, p.c.)

Additionally, this phenomenon verifies the hypothesis that focus constructions and wh-questions in Somali are instances of the same derivational pattern. Now I will come back to the two Italian dialects, which exhibit a similar phenomenon.

3.2.6.2 A Comparison between Somali and the Italian Dialects. Somali and Trentino show a remarkable similarity with respect to the anti-agreement effect (see Mereu 1999). Both questioned and focused objects pattern with subjects in Trentino with respect to the anti-agreement effect, as they do not allow object clitics in the third person to occur. But since third person object clitics in Somali are always null-pronouns, there is no visible distinction between the two languages in this case (compare the examples from Trentino in 133 with these from Somali in 134):

(133) a. (*L') ho   encontrà **la**   **Giovanna**.   (Trentino)
         OCL have-1SG   met-PP-FSG the   Giovanna
         'I have met Giovanna.'

     b. **Cosa** hala   portà   la   Maria?
         what have-3SG-SCL bring-PP-FSG the   Maria
         'What did Maria bring?'

(134) a. Naagi **libaax** bay   Ø   aragtay.   (Somali)
         woman lion   FM-SCL OCL   see-3FSG-PAST
         'A woman saw a lion.'

     b. (Adigu) **yaad**   Ø   aragtay?
         you   who-FM-SCL   OCL   see-2SG-PAST
         'Who did you see?'

Focus and wh-constructions in Trentino show the anti-agreement effect in long distance contexts too. In the grammatical examples (135a) and (136a) the subject clitic does not occur in the extraction site and the embedded verbal forms do not show agreement with the extracted subjects:

(135) a. LA   MARIA te   sai   che è   vegnù,
         the   Maria SCL know-2SG that COP come-PP-SG
         non   la   Carla.
         not   the   Carla

   b. *LA MARIA te   sai   che **la**   è   vegnù,
         the Maria SCL know-2SG that SCL-3FSG COP come-PP-SG
         non   la   Carla.
         not   the   Carla
         'MARY, you know that she came, not Carla.'

(136) a. **Quante   putele** te   pensi che abia   parlà?
         how many   girls   you   think that have-SUBJ-3SG speak-PP

   b. ***Quante   putele** te   pensi   che **le**
         how many   girls   SCL   think-2SG that SCL-3PL
         abia   parlà?
         have-SUBJ-3PL speak-PP
         'How many girls do you think spoke?'

However, when focused NPs and wh-phrases in Somali are related to a deeper embedded position, anti-agreement effects do not occur at all. The observed subject-object asymmetry in root contexts does not hold. As examples (137a, b and 138 a, b) show there is an obligatory presence of respectively subject or object clitics in the embedded clause:

(137) a. **Nimankii**$_i$ buu   Cali rumaysanayay
         men-the   FM-SCL Ali think-3MSG-PAST
         [inay$_i$ / *in   tageen]
         COMP-SCL/ COMP   leave-3PL-PAST
         'It was the men that Ali thought that they would leave.'
         (Mereu 1999)

   b. **Gabadhee**$_i$ ayay   walaalahay   akhristeen buuga$_j$
         girl-which FM-SCL brothers-my   read   book-the
         [$_{CP}$Ø$_j$ *(ay$_i$)[$_{IP}$t$_i$ t$_j$ keentay]]?
                      SCL   bring-3FSG-PAST
         'Which girl did my brothers read the book that (she) brought?'
         (Svolacchia et al. 1995)

(138) a. **Aniga**$_i$ baad   sheegtay[in-uu$_j$ Cali$_j$ **i**$_i$/*Ø sugay   t$_i$]
me   FM-SCL say-PAST COMP-SCL Ali   OCL wait-3MSG-PAST
'You said that Ali waited for ME.'
(Svolacchia and Puglielli 1999)
b. **Maxaad**$_i$ doonaysaa
what-FM-SCL think-PROG-2SG
[inay$_i$/   *in   dhacaan?]
COMP-SCL   COMP happen-PRES-3PL-SUB
'What do you think (that it) will happen?'
(Mereu 1999)

Many attempts to explain the peculiar behaviour of subjects in such contexts have been made within the generative framework. Brandi & Cordin (1989) have ascribed this property of Trentino to the *pro*-drop parameter (for discussion of Ouhalla's 1993 analysis based on the *pro*-drop property of languages see section 3.3.5.).Most importantly, the lack of agreement features on the verb is manifested not only in extraction environments such as wh-questions and focus constructions in Trentino. The same pattern is found with postverbal subjects as the contrast between (139a) and (139b) indicates:

(139) a. E'   vegnu   la   Maria.
COP   come-PP-SG the   Maria
b. *L'è   vegnuda   la Maria
SCL-COP   come-PP-FSG   the   Maria
'Maria has come.'

The simplified structure of (139a) is as follows (for details see Brandi & Cordin 1989):

(140) *pro*$_{3MSG}$ e'$_{3SG}$ vegnu   la   Maria.
COP   come-PP-SG   the   Maria
'Maria has come.'

The canonical subject in (140) is generated in a postverbal position while the structural subject position, SpecIP, is filled by an expletive *pro*. Brandi & Cordin (1989) assume that the expletive *pro* in this dialect shares the properties of the expletive element *il* 'it' in French as in (141):

(141) Il   est   arrivé   des   garçons.
EXPL-3MSG be-3SG   come-PP-MSG of-the   boys
'The boys came.'

As (141) indicates this kind of expletive elements require agreement with the verb (see Chomsky 1995:286ff for a classification of expletive elements). Thus, the expletive *pro* in Trentino has a set of default 3MSG-features and triggers agreement with the verb. The consequence is that the postverbal subject does not agree with the verb which is marked for 3MSG-features. It is argued that such agreement patterns show the extraction site of subjects. Focused and questioned subjects are extracted from a postverbal position (cf. Brandy & Cordin 1989, Ouhalla 1993 for discussion and Campos 1997 for a similar proposal). Within Brandi & Cordin's approach, Standard Italian is assumed to be a language with a featureless expletive *pro*. The verb in Standard Italian agrees with the postverbal subject in inversion constructions. These syntactic structures in Standard Italian parallel *there*-constructions in English. The expletive elements (*pro* in Standard Italian and *there* in English) are coindexed with the postverbal subjects, i.e. they are in the same thematic chain and inherit the person, gender and number features from the full postverbal subjects. As always, the verb agrees with the features of the preverbal element that inherits the features of the inverted subject.

The analysis Brandi & Cordin (1989) propose for Trentino cannot hold for Somali. First, Somali is not a *pro*-drop language. Second, Somali does not show an anti-agreement effect when subjects appear postverbally or elsewhere. The anti-agreement effect in Somali is restricted to subject focus constructions, wh-questions and relative clauses. Third, Somali also has a matrix vs. embedded subject asymmetry. Anti-agreement in Somali is a root phenomenon.

Brandi & Cordin have suggested that the anti-agreement effect emerges from the *pro*-drop property of some languages. Relying on the opposite generalization, Frascarelli & Puglielli (2004, to appear) account for the anti-agreement effect in Somali and several other Cushitic languages. They claim that the anti-agreement effect is related to non-*pro*-drop languages (see also Frascarelli 1999, 2000 who proposes an alternative analysis based on the idea of competition between nominative case and focus feature assignment). Given the fact that full NPs are licensed in A'-positions in Somali the presence of clitic pronouns that form the argument structure of a clause is obligatory. The authors implement Lamberti's (1983) theory for the origin of focus markers in Somali. Recall, the focus markers are assumed to have emerged diachronically from a copula incorporating a 3MSG-subject clitic (see also subsection 3.2.1.2.). Thus, *ayàa* and its phonological variant *bàa* are composed as follows:

(142) *ak+y+aa   > ayaa / awaa / waa /baa[61]
     be+3MSG+PRES
     'it is'

Nominal *bàa/ayàa*-focus constructions are analysed as complex structures in which an (original) matrix copula (the present focus marker) selects a subordinate small clause (for the details of this small clause analysis and predicate raising cf. Moro 1997). Thus, the syntactic derivation of *bàa/ayàa*-focus is reminiscent to that of a cleft construction:

(143) $[_{TopP}$ Hilib $[_{FocP}$ **nimankaas**$_i$ $[_{Foc^\circ}$ baa]$[_{SC}[_{DP}$ e_i cunayá   ] t_i]]]
     meat   men-those$_{ABS}$ FM-3MSG   eat-PRES-PROG-REST
     'Those men are eating meat.'

In (143) a headless relative clause and a predicative DP are merged as independent constituents within a small clause. Note that in this case the predicative NP, which in addition undergoes focus movement to SpecFocP, is not the subject of the relative clause. It is therefore marked for the absolute case. Frascarelli & Puglielli (2004, to appear) assume that the subject inside the headless relative clause is an empty element *e* identified by the default 3MSG-feature of the focus marker.[62] The presence of such a kind of empty element is the cause for the anti-agreement effect. How does it work exactly? The authors stipulate that an empty element that serves as the subject of the relative clause constitutes a contradiction to the polysynthetic structure of Somali. Somali requires overt pronouns in order to produce the proper clausal argument structure. Therefore, they argue that when the subject in a polysynthetic language is an empty element, agreement features on the verb cannot appear. The 3MSG-subject clitic incorporated into the focus marker controls and identifies the empty subject (*e*) of the relative clause as an element marked for the 3MSG-features (cf. 142). The verb inside the relative clause takes the 3MSG-form. They claim next that the predicative DP undergoes operator movement to SpecFocP for scope reasons. In this position it governs the whole structure and can reidentify the empty category (*e*) inside the relative clause. The focused constituent is therefore reinterpreted as the subject by virtue of its identificational role with respect to the empty element. The fact that the anti-agreement effect does not show up in long relativisation structures is traced back to the

---

[61] The different forms are due to regional differences (see Frascarelli & Puglielli 2004, for detailed information on diachronic development and regional variations cf. Lamberti 1983).

[62] It is not clear what kind of empty element serves as a subject of the relative clause: *pro*, PRO or an expletive *pro*. The authors do not refer to its syntactic status. They call it a *semantic variable*, i.e. 'a piece of information that we lack and that we are going to identify through the predicative DP' (cf. Frascarelli & Puglielli to appear).

observation that relativisation is a phenomenon restricted to matrix clauses (see Frascarelli & Puglielli to appear).

Although the analysis explains why the focused subject bears the absolutive case, it faces a serious derivational problem. As we have seen, focus constructions in Somali do not represent any piece of evidence in favour of a movement analysis (see section 3.2.4.). Moreover, the derivation of subject relatives remains obscured. It is not clear at all how anti-agreement effects are to be accounted for in subject relative clauses given the fact that the head noun is present in the structure. Moreover, Frascarelli & Puglielli (2004) assume a derivation for relative clauses as proposed by Kayne (1994) in which the nominal head of a relative clause is generated within the relative clause and additionally undergoes movement to SpecCP (see Frascarelli & Puglielli 2004:fn. 13). Following this proposal they also have to assume that in subject relatives in Somali the head noun is generated inside the relative clause.[63] But in a case like this, the subject should be able to trigger agreement features on the verb. This, however, does not happen as (144a) shows:

(144) a. nimánka   buugágga keená   (subject relative clause)
         men-the-ABS books-the bring-3MSG
         'the men who bring the books'
      b. buugágga nimanku   keenàan   (object relative clause)
         books-the men-the-NOM bring-3PL
         'the books which the men bring'
         (Saeed 1999:213)

Note also that the analysis of Frascarelli & Puglielli (2004, to appear) suggests that the 3MSG-clitic incorporated into the focus marker is still morphologically visible at the synchronic stage. This assumption causes a problem for instance with object focusing (cf. 131c and 132c). Provided this is true, the focus marker will incorporate two morphologically visible clitics: the default 3MSG-clitic and the subject clitic corresponding to the full subject. It is then not clear which clitic will induce agreement features on the verb.

---

[63] They assume the following derivation of relatives:
    (i)   the girl that I know
    (ii)   [DP the [CP [C° that   [IP I know girl]]]]
    (iii)   [DP the [CP girl_k   [C° that   [IP I know t_k]]]]
According to this approach, subject relatives in Somali should also be derived by a movement operation, which shifts the subject from its base position. Note that Somali does not exhibit that-trace effects, so movement of the subject across the complementizer will not cause a problem for a derivation analogous to the derivation of object relatives (see Saeed 1984 or Livnat 1984). Frascarelli & Puglielli (2004) fail to consider these facts.

To conclude the discussion of the anti-agreement effect in Somali and Trentino, the analyses I have discussed have related this phenomenon to the availability of empty elements in languages that can serve as structural subjects. The
pro-drop parameter seems not to be responsible for the occurrence of the anti-
agreement effect. As we have seen both *pro*-drop (Trentino) and non-*pro*-drop
languages (Somali) exhibit this behaviour. I will come back to these problems
in the discussion of the anti-agreement effects in Berber and Irish (both *pro*-
drop languages) in the next subchapters. I will also address another important
question: what kind of relation exists between languages that exhibit an anti-
agreement effect and languages that do not allow multiple wh-questions (see
section 3.5.3.)? For the time being the anti-agreement effect provides additional evidence that in Somali wh-questions are instances of structurally
marked focus constructions (cf. 131a and 132a).

3.2.7 *Concluding Remarks on the Syntax of wh-questions in Somali*

Before turning to the next language without multiple wh-questions, let me
summarise the observations about the syntax of wh-questions in Somali. In this
subchapter I have discussed three syntactic structures typical of the syntax of
Somali. We have seen that wh-elements are licensed in a focus position marked
by the focus marker *bàa/ayàa* (see section 3.2.3.). Crucially, *bàa/ayàa*-focus is
a manifestation of unique focus (see section 3.2.2.). Like in Italian, the FocP in
Somali cannot host more than one element, i.e. either a phrase bearing new
information, a contrasted element or a wh-item can appear in this structurally
marked position. Unique focus is typical of languages with structural focus
assignment. In other words, Somali represents a language in which a focused
element is licensed in a spec-head configuration with a functional head that
bears a focus feature. Wh-phrases as instances of *bàa/ayàa*-focus constructions
show exactly the same distributional pattern as focused constituents:

(145) $[_{\text{SpecFocP}}$ wh-phrase / DP $[_{\text{Foc}°}$ bàa]...$[_{\text{VP}}$...]]

The syntactic structure in (145) is the only environment in which a wh-phrase
is properly licensed. Given that the *bàa/ayàa*-construction is an instance of
unique focus it follows that it is impossible for more than one wh-element to
appear per clause and multiple wh-questions are therefore excluded (see for
discussion and analysis chapter 4.).

3.3   Berber

3.3.1 Preliminaries to the Syntax of Berber

Before we start with the overview and the discussion of wh-questions and related syntactic phenomena of Berber it is worth briefly reviewing the properties
of the Berber language family. Berber varieties are considered to be *pro*-drop
languages with a VSO basic word order (cf. Calabrese 1987 among others).
They allow for alternations to the basic word order which I will come to in
subsections (3.3.1.1.) and (3.3.1.2.). As it is not desirable to consider all Berber
varieties for the current purposes of the investigation, I will concentrate on the
subvariety of Ait Seghrouchen, which belongs to the group of Tamazight (spoken in the Middle Atlas, in central Morocco), on Tarifit (spoken in North Morocco) and partly on Ait Hassan (spoken in northern Marrakech). I will indicate
the variety only in cases when needed.

3.3.1.1 Left Dislocation.

Consider first a syntactic construction in Berber re-
ferred to as *left dislocation* (LD) (for discussion see Shlonsky 1987).[64] LD
shows the typical properties of the topic constructions discussed in the Italian
examples (see subchapter 3.1. for discussion):

(146) a. y-xdl   uhamosh   /   *ahamosh.
        3MSG-arrived CS-boy   FS-boy
        'The boy has arrived.'

    b. ahamosh$_i$ /   *uhamosh y-xdl   *pro$_i$*.
        FS-boy   CS-boy   3MSG-arrived
        'The boy, he has arrived.'

    c. ahamosh-a$_i$ zri-gh-t$_i$ idnnat.[65]
        FS-boy-this   saw-1SG-him yesterday
        'This boy, I saw him yesterday.'
        (Ouhalla 1991:121)

    d. ssen-x   litub$_i$ is-t$_i$ y-uzn   Mohand.
        know-1SG   book   that-it   3MSG-sent Mohand
        'I know that as for the book, Mohand sent it.'
        (Shlonsky 1987)

---

[64] Shlonsky (1987) uses the term of *left dislocation* in order to describe a XVX- structure which
differs from semantically neutral structures with the basic VSO-word order. It merely reflects
the observation that a constituent may appear preverbally (for theoretical implications of the
term *left dislocation* and its relation to *topicalisation* see Grewendorf 2002, among others).

[65] Note that -t$_i$ in the examples is a clitic resumptive pronoun, not just the usual notation for a
coindexed trace.

(146a) represents the common unmarked VSO-word order for Berber. In this case the postverbal subject appears in a special morphological form, the so-called *construct state* (CS). Left dislocated subjects require the morphological form of the *free state* (FS) as in (146b) (for more on these differences see Ou-halla 1988). The next difference from the unmarked VSO-word order is clearly exemplified by (146c and d). LD in Berber requires a resumptive pronoun in the base position of the left dislocated element, which is a significant property of this construction type across languages.[66] (146c) shows LD of an object phrase out of a matrix clause while in (146d) an object phrase is left dislocated out of an embedded one. Note that in the latter example the left dislocated element appears to the left of the subordinating complementizer.

Long distance LD is also possible and shows the same properties as LD in root clauses, i.e. resumption of the left dislocated element by a pronoun:

(147) a. Mohand$_i$ssen-x   [is-t$_i$ t-essudem   Tifa].
      Mohand knew-1SG   that-him 3FSG-kissed   Tifa
      'As for Mohand, I knew that Tifa kissed him.'
      (Guerssel 1984)
   b. Tifa$_i$ y-nna   Bassu   [is   y-ssen   Mohand
      Tifa 3MSG-said   Bassu   that   3MSG-know   Mohand
      [is   t-udf *pro$_i$*   taddart]].
      that   3FSG-entered   house
      'As for Tifa, Bassu said that Mohand knows that she entered the house.'
      (Shlonsky 1987)

The left dislocated object crosses one clausal boundary in (147a). The left dislocated subject in (147b) emerges in the second subordinated clause.

Another property of left dislocated elements is the fact that they are not sensitive to wh- (cf. 148a) and complex NP-islands (cf. 148b):

(148) a. Aysum$_i$ sal-x   wi-t$_i$ yttcin.
      meat   asked-1SG   who-it   ate
      'As for the meat, I asked who ate it.'

---

[66] Left dislocated subjects are en exception to the rule, as they are associated with a null pronoun due to the fact that the Berber varieties are null subject languages (see Shlonsky 1987 and Rizzi 1997 for Italian).

b. Litub$_i$ ssen-x   araz din-t$_i$ yurin.
book   know-1SG man that-it   wrote
'As for the book, I know the man who wrote it.'
(Shlonsky 1987)

The characteristic properties of LD structures, i.e. the presence of clitic pronoun resumption and the lack of island sensitivity, suggest that a movement
process is not involved in their derivation. Rather, they are instances of base
generation into a topic-like position of the left periphery as described by Rizzi
(1997). I will therefore assume that left dislocated elements in Berber are inserted by the operation merge into a left-peripheral TopP:

(149) [$_{TopP}$ ahamosha$_i$ [$_{IP}$ zri-gh-t$_i$ idnnat]]
            FS-boy-this   saw-1SG-him   yesterday
'This boy, I saw him yesterday.'
(Ouhalla 1991:121)

Next, I examine cleft constructions in Berber which constitute the relevant syntactic parallel to wh-questions.

3.3.1.2 Focus Clefts. Focus constructions in Berber appear in the form of
clefts. Root clefts show a highly grammaticalised structure that has often been
referred to as a *reduced cleft* (see Calabrese 1987). Optional omission of the
copula in matrix clefts results in a reduced cleft construction (cf. 150a).[67]
(150a) shows that a focused constituent appears to the left of an invariant cleft
marker *ay*. Syntactically, the cleft marker has the status of a head element. Its
function is merely to signal that the constituent preceding it is focused and it
does not have any semantic content:

(150) a. (d) **tabratt** ay y-uzn   wraz gher Fas idennatt.
              COP letter CM 3MSG-sent man to   Fes yesterday
'It is a letter that the man sent to Fes yesterday.'
      b. *(d) **tabratt**$_i$ ay tt$_i$ y-uri   Mohand.
              COP letter CM-it 3MSG-wrote Mohand
'It is a letter that Mohand wrote (it).'

The contrast between (150a) and (150b) indicates that a clefted constituent
cannot be resumed by a clitic element inside the clause.

---

[67] I propose the following monoclausal structure for focus clefts in Berber using the split C-
system as a basis (see also Meinunger 1998 and É. Kiss 1998a):
    (i) [$_{SpecFocP}$ XP [$_{Foc°}$ CM]   …   [$_{IP}$ …]]

Shlonsky (1987) summarises the structural properties of cleft constructions in Berber as follows:

i)   Any [-V]-element can be clefted while only NPs can be left dislocated.

ii)   Clefts in Berber do not allow resumptive pronouns (cf. 150a) in contrast to left dislocated elements indicated by example (149).

iii)   The clefted constituents appear to the left of a complementizer-like element *ay/a* (cf. 150a) while left dislocated elements in root clauses appear without any complementizer-like element separating them from the rest of the clause (see 149).

iv)   In embedded LD constructions the left dislocated NP appears to the left of the subordinating complementizer *is* (cf. 146d). In subordinated clauses the clefted element appears to the right of the subordinating complementizer *is* and is obligatory preceded by the copula *d* (cf. 151).[68]

(151) y-fhem   Bassu is   (*d) **Tifa** ay   yjnin.
      3MSG-understood Bassu that COP Tifa CM   slept-PART
      'Bassu understood that it is Tifa that is sleeping.'

v)   When the subject is clefted, the verb appears in the participial form which is unmarked for φ-features. This phenomenon is referred to as the anti-agreement effect as already discussed for Somali and the Italian dialect Trentino (see section 3.3.5. for discussion).

vi)   Long distance clefting is also possible in Berber. As pointed out by Guerssel (1984) it consists of a twofold operation, i.e. left dislocation followed by short-distance clefting (see section 3.3.3.).

I have discussed two possible alternatives to the unmarked word order in Berber: topic constructions (cf. subsection 3.3.1.1.) and focus clefts (cf. subsection 3.3.1.2.). In the next section (3.3.2.) I will show that wh-questions are instances of focus clefts in Berber.

3.3.2 Wh-Questions and Focus Constructions
The diagnostics for determining the syntactic properties of the wh-position used in the previous sections are also applicable to Berber. It has been pointed out that wh-constituent questions pattern with cleft focus constructions in these languages (Calabrese 1987, Guerssel 1984 and subchapter 2.2.). Thus, the in-

---

[68] Recall that the appearance of the copula is optional in matrix clauses (see 150a).

vestigation into the properties of wh-questions goes hand in hand with the investigation into focus clefts.

Now compare wh-questions in Berber with the cleft constructions discussed in subsection (3.3.1.2.). As argued by Calabrese (1987) an interrogative wh-phrase must be in a focus position in Berber and real wh-questions are parasitic on cleft focus constructions. The expectation that both focus clefts and wh-questions are identical with respect to their syntactic properties is borne out. Furthermore, the appropriate answer to a wh-question is a clause containing a clefted phrase (cf. 152a, b). In this respect Berber patterns exactly with Somali:

(152) a. **May**   t-sghu   terbatt?
        what-CM   3FSG-bought girl
        'What did the girl buy?'
      b. **Adil**   ay   t-sghu   terbatt.
        grapes   CM   3FSG-buy   girl
        'It is grapes that the girl bought.'

(152a) and (152b) show that a wh-phrase and a focused element respectively appear left-adjacent to the cleft marker.

Consider next the following two examples:

(153) a. Adlis,   **Idir** ay-t ysghin.
        Book   Idir   CM-it bought-PART
        'As for the book, it is Idir that bought it.'
      b. Idir,   **adlis** aggsghu.[69]
        Idir   book CM-3MSG-bought
        'As for Idir, it is a book that he bought.'
        (Guerssel 1984)

As the translation of (153a and b) indicates, two constituents in the left periphery (two elements located to the left of the cleft marker) can never be interpreted as focused phrases. The extreme left item is always a topic phrase, i.e. an element referring to a set of presupposed elements or to already contextually activated information. The second element immediately adjacent to the cleft marker is, according to its semantic function, an item providing new, not presupposed information. Since wh-interrogatives are instances of clefting, the

---

[69] Berber has very complex phonology rules of contraction that sometimes lead more than two lexically independent items to conflate (see Guerssel 1984).

same pattern should also apply to wh-clauses. As (154a and b) show, this prediction is born out:

(154) a. Adlis,   **wi**   t   ysghin?
        book   who-CM it   bought-PART
        'The book, who bought it?'
   b. Mohand,   **m**aggsghu?
       Mohand   what-CM-3MSG-bought
       'Mohand, what did he buy?
       (Guerssel 1984)

As we can see, the information structure in Berber is very similar to that of
Italian and Somali. The cleft focus construction usually expresses new information as the question and answer pairs (cf. 152a and b) indicate. In certain
contexts it can also be interpreted as contrastive focus (Calabrese 1987). Consider the following example:

(155) TIFA i(g)   ywsan   rfrus (, wa   dzi   d   Ali).
     Tifa CM   stolen-PART money NEG have-ASP COP Ali
     'It was Tifa who stole the money, (not Ali).'
     (Noureddine Elouazizi, p.c.)

In this section I have shown that wh-questions in Berber are instances of focus
clefts. Following the observations in (153a, b) and (154a, b) I conclude that the
cleft focus position in Berber is unique since it cannot host more than one element (for discussion and more supporting evidence see chapter 4.). The focusing mechanism in Berber is also unique in the sense that both information and
contrastive focus are expressed by clefts (cf. 152b and 155).

3.3.3 The Derivation of Wh-Questions
Consider next some properties of focus and wh-constituents in Berber that are
generally related to topic constructions (see for discussion Rizzi 1997). Wh-
questions do not show wco-effects when a resumptive pronoun correlating with
the wh-object is present in the Tamazight variety:

(156) **Wi**$_i$ *(t_i)   t-utu   ymma-s$_i$?
     who-CM him   3FSG-hit mother-his
     'Who did his mother hit?'
     (Choe 1987)

Also note that according to the intuitions of native speakers, wco-effects are
absent in clefts in the Tarifit variety:

(157) a. **W(g)-i**   t-xis   yama-s$_i$?
        who-CM 3FSG-love   mother-his$_i$
        'Who does his mother love?
   b. (d) **Muhand**$_i$ i   t-xis   yama-s$_i$.
        COP Muhand   CM   3FSG-love mother-his
        'It is Muhand that his mother loves.'
        (Noureddine Elouazizi, p.c.)

The observations in (156, 157a, b) suggest that wco-effects are probably not crosslinguistically prototypical of focusing as Rizzi (1997) proposes (see also Drubig 2000 for discussion of similar phenomena in other languages, and for discussion of wco-effects in Somali and Irish section 3.2.4. and 3.4.2. respectively).

Wh-elements seem not to be sensitive to certain syntactic islands. Wh-extraction out of an embedded interrogative clause is possible:

(158) **May**$_i$ t-ssen-t   **wi**-t$_i$ ysghin?
        what-CM   2SG-know who-CM-it bought-PART
        'What do you know who bought?'

This behaviour of wh-elements is paralleled by focus clefts. Thus, clefting out of an embedded cleft is also acceptable:

(159) **Tajmartu**$_i$ ay   ssen-x   is   d   **Mohand**   ay-tt$_i$
        this-mare   CM   know-1SG that COP Mohand   CM-her
        ysghin.
        bought-PART
        'It is this mare that I know that it is Mohand that bought it.'
        (Choe 1987)

Note, however, that clefts are still sensitive to some islands. First, clefting across a left dislocated element is ungrammatical, as (160b) shows (see Shlonsky 1987). Example (160a) is the starting point for the derivation of (160b).

(160) a. zri-x   Mohand$_i$ is   t$_i$ t-essudm   Tifa.
        saw-1SG Mohand that him 3FSG-kissed   Tifa
        'I saw that, as for Mohand, it was Tifa who kissed him.'
   b. *(d) **Tifa** ay   zri-x   Mohand$_i$ is   t$_i$ t-essudm.
        COP Tifa CM   saw-1SG Mohand   that him 3FSG-kissed
        'I saw that, as for Mohand, it was Tifa who kissed him.'

Second, clefting obeys the Complex NP Constraint:

(161) *(d) **Tifa**$_i$ ay   zri-x   aryaz din-tt$_i$ yssudmen.
      COP Tifa CM   saw-1SG man   that-her kissed-PART
      'It is Tifa that I saw the man that kissed her.'
      (Shlonsky 1987)

How can these puzzling facts about extraction out of syntactic islands be accounted for? Now it is time to come back to the property of cleft constructions
pointed out in section (3.3.2.). Recall, clefting across clause boundaries is considered to be a twofold operation consisting of base generation into the topic-
like position of the embedded clause and subsequent short movement to the
matrix clause (see also Guerssel's 1984 analysis).[70] The fact that the left periphery of embedded structures is different from that of root clauses has, since
Rizzi 1997, been often recognised and discussed in many subsequent develop-

---

[70] First, evidence in favour of this analysis is provided by the obligatory insertion of a resumptive pronoun in the embedded position of the direct object phrase. Compare (i) and (ii):

  (i) (d) **tabratt**$_i$ ay t-enna   Tifa is-**tt**$_i$ y-uri   Mohand.
     COP letter   CM 3FSG-thought Tifa that-it 3MSG-wrote Mohand
     'It is a letter that Tifa thought that Mohand wrote.'

  (ii) *(d) **tabratt** ay t-enna   Tifa is e$_i$ y-uri   Mohand.
     COP letter   CM 3FSG-thought Tifa that   3MSG-wrote Mohand
     'It is a letter that Tifa thought that Mohand wrote.'

Second, clefting across a clause boundary can affect only elements that allow LD i.e. long
distance clefting of adverbs and anaphors is excluded in Berber, as they do not undergo LD at
all. Thus, unlike English, wh-adjuncts in Berber may have scope only over the closest verb, i.e.
the wh-adjunct in (iii) cannot be interpreted in the embedded clause. It can only be related to
the matrix verb. The contrast between (iv) and (v) shows that anaphors may be clefted but not
left dislocated. Example (iv) shows that long distance clefting of anaphors is not an available
option in Berber. The interpretation of adjuncts and the distribution of anaphors serve as independent support for the analysis of long clefting proposed by Guerssel (1984) (for discussion
see Shlonsky 1987):

  (iii) **maymi** t-ennit   is   xf-i   y-isu?
     why   2SG-think that   on-me 3MSG-laughed
     'Why do you think that he laughed at me?'

  (iv) (d) **ixf-nns** ay y-wtu   Mohand.
     COP self-his   CM 3MSG-hit Mohand
     'It is himself that Mohand hit'

  (v) ***ixf-nns** y-wtu-t   Mohand.
     self-him 3MSG-hit-him Mohand
     'Himself, Mohand hit him.'

  (vi) ***ixf-nns** ay zri-x   is   t/Ø   y-wtu   Mohand.
     self-him CM saw-1S   that   him   3MSG-him Mohand
     'It is himself that I saw Mohand that hit him.'

ments of his theoretical proposal. The following discussion provides supporting evidence in favour of this claim.[71]

I will account for both apparent island violations pointed out by Shlonsky (1987) in terms of constituent ordering constraints that are active in Berber. Both focusing and topicalisation can apply in the same sentence if the topic phrase appears first. Consider the following examples:

(162) a. Mohand,   d   **Amazigh**   aggju.   (Ait Seghrouchen)
         Mohand   COP   Berber   CM-3MSG-be
         'As for Mohand, it is Berber what he is.'
         (Guerssel 1984)
     b. Aysum$_i$ **wi-t$_i$**   yttcin?
         meat   who-CM-it eaten-PART
         'As for the meat, who ate it?'
         (Cole & Tenny 1987)

(163) a. ḥmad,   **tabrat** a i-ara.   (Ait Hassan)
         Ahmed   letter CM   3MSG-wrote
         'As for Ahmed, it is a letter that he wrote.'
     b. *__Lktab__ a   ḥmad   i-sRa.
         book   CM   Ahmed 3MSG-bought
         'It is a book, Ahmed, he bought.'
         (Ennaji & Sadiqi 1986)

The examples (162a, b) and (163a) show that topics have to precede focused constituents and that it is not possible for a topic phrase to appear to the right of a focused element (cf. 163b). I conclude that, contrary to what we have observed in Italian and Somali, topic phrases in Berber are not recursive. For the ease of representation I propose a sentence structure of Berber following Rizzi's (1997) theory about the clausal left periphery:

(164) $[_{TopP} [_{SpecForceP/FinP} [_{Force°/Fin°} \textit{is}]] [_{SpecFocP} [_{Foc°} \textit{ay/i}]] [_{VP} \dots]]$[72]

---

[71] In the following I use the term 'topic position or topic-like position' merely as a descriptive term without intending to make strong theoretical implications. One must not understand the claim that the focused phrase merges into a topic or topic-like position of the embedded left periphery in such a way that this phrase first checks a topic feature and additionally a focus feature in the matrix clause. A focused phrase in Berber firstly merges into an embedded left-peripheral position which seems to share the syntactic properties of topic positions.

[72] This structure resembles the already proposed analyses of clefts (see É. Kiss 1998a and Meinunger 1998). I have not discussed the distinction between ForceP and FinP Berber, since the empirical material used in the book does not contain any piece of evidence in favour of a positional differentiation between ForceP and FinP in the sense of Rizzi (1997). Additional

Now it becomes clear that the potential transmitting site for movement to the target position in the matrix clause is already occupied by a topic phrase in the case of (160b) and by an empty relative operator (*Op*) in (161), repeated here as (165a) and (165b) respectively:[73]

(165) a. *(d) **Tifa**$_j$ ay   zri-x
         COP Tifa CM   saw-1SG
         [$_{TopP}$ Mohand$_i$[$_{ForceP/FinP}$ is   t$_i$ *pro*$_j$ t-essudm]].
         Mohand   that him   3FSG-kissed
         'I saw that, as for Mohand, it was Tifa who kissed him.'

      b. *(d) **Tifa**$_i$ ay   zri-x   aryaz
         COP Tifa CM   saw-1SG man
         [$_{TopP}$ *Op* [$_{Top°}$ din]-tt$_i$ yssudmen].
                         that-her kissed-PART
         'It is Tifa that I saw the man that kissed her.'
         (Shlonsky 1987)

Tifa in (165a) and in (165b) cannot be merged into SpecTopP because a topic phrase and a relative operator respectively already occupy this position. Long distance clefting can therefore not apply, hence the ungrammaticality of clefting across topicalised elements and clefting out of relative clauses. The grammaticality of extraction out of a focus cleft and an embedded wh-question is then straightforward. Consider again (158) and (159) repeated as (166a) and (166b) respectively:

(166) a. **May**$_i$ t-ssen-t   [$_{TopP}$ e$_i$ [$_{FocP}$ **wi**-t$_i$ ysghin]]?
         what-CM   2SG-know   who-CM-it   bought-PART
         'What do you know who bought?'

---

research is necessary in order to verify the hypothesis that there is no need to assume the existence of both ForceP and FinP for Berber. Given the crosslinguistic observation that matrix predicates select clausal complements of certain sentence type, it is not a usual assumption that a matrix verb can optionally select a TopP. For computational reasons it is more logical that the highest clausal projection is always ForceP, i.e. the projection where clausal type information is encoded. The problem can be avoided if we assume more than one position for complementizers in Berber following Rizzi (1999) who proposes a second complementizer position for embedded interrogatives in Italian or, Roussou (2000), who argues for different complementizer positions in Modern Greek. If these lines of argumentation are on the right track ForceP in Berber remains empty, and *is* 'that' is located deeper in the structure between TopP and FocP. I leave this issue unsolved for future research (see also Stoyanova to appear).

[73] I assume that relatives are connected with a topic feature crosslinguistically (cf. Kuno 1976, Sabel 2000, Frascarelli & Puglielli 2004 among others for discussion). Thus, a TopP in the sense of Rizzi's split C-system is involved in the syntactic structure of relative clauses in Berber.

b. **Tajmartu**$_i$ ay   ssen-x
  this-mare   CM   know-1SG
  [$_{TopP}$ e$_i$ [$_{ForceP/FinP}$ is   d [$_{FocP}$ **Mohand**   ay-tt$_i$ ysghin]]].
            that   COP   Mohand   CM-he   bought-PART
  'It is this mare that I know that it is Mohand that bought it.'
  (Choe 1987)

The presence of a clefted item in FocP does not prevent other phrases to be base generated in the available TopP. Thus, focused elements (cf. 166a) and wh-phrases (cf. 166b) may use the topic position as a transmitting site in order to undergo additional short movement into the matrix clause.[74] To summarise, LD in Berber as an instance of a topic construction results from base generation. Clefting is always a short movement operation. In the surface structure wh-phrases and their non-interrogative focused counterparts appear left-adjacent to a specific cleft marker and thus establish a spec-head relationship with this element. The head-adjacency configuration counts as an obligatory licensing environment for focused elements and wh-phrases in Berber.

3.3.4 The Dialectal Variation of Wh-Questions

There are some inconsistencies in the literature concerning wh-questions in different Berber varieties which I will discuss briefly. Contrary to Calabrese (1987), Cole & Tenny (1987:fn. 7) mention that the variety of Ait Seghrouchen allows for multiple questions like the following one:

(167) **Wiy** yzrin   **mit**?
     who seen-PART what

In (167) the regular object wh-phrase *may* is replaced by 'a special wh-word' *mit*. The authors stipulate further that *ay* is an operator and as part of the canonical wh-phrases it cannot stay in-situ. The example above represents the only way of expressing multiple wh-questions that the authors point out. Cole & Tenny (1987) do not give any information about the interpretation of this kind of multiple questions, i.e. they do not say if such multiple wh-questions have the reading of a real information question, which requires answers to both interrogative items, or perhaps of an echo question.[75] Since this is not clear, I will assume that there are no true multiple wh-questions in Berber.

---

[74] See Shlonsky (1987) for a similar anlysis in terms of CP-recursion.

[75] Noureddine Elouazizi (p.c.) reports a special form of an echo wh-argument in the variety of Tarifit:

  (i)   w-i   (animate subject / direct object)
        'who'

Furthermore, Ennaji & Sadiqi (1986) claim that question words in Ait Hassan can never be clefted:

(168) a. ***ma**   a   t-zri-t   g ssug?
        what CM   saw-2SG at market
        'What did you see at the market?'
  b. <u>***manza dida**</u> a   g i-zdR   ḥmad?
        which place CM   in 3MSG-live Ahmed
        'Where does Ahmed live?'

Note, however, that the wh-phrases in both examples end with an 'a', i.e. an element which resembles the cleft marker a in this variety. Therefore, sentences like (168a and b) might be ungrammatical because of a doubling of the cleft marker. Like in (167) the morphosyntactic structure of the examples (168a, b) is not clear at all. Therefore, I will follow Choe (1987) in assuming that even when the cleft marker is morphologically not recoverable, wh-questions in every Berber variety involve a combination of a wh-element and a cleft marker.[76] I will further assume, contrary to Calabrese (1987) that wh-adjuncts in Berber do not differ from wh-arguments. In both cases, an adjacent cleft marker is present (see for discussion of Calabrese's proposal subchapter 2.2. and Guerssel 1984).

As already mentioned at the beginning of subchapter (3.3.), Berber constitutes a language family with many different varieties. As it is not possible to show the phenomenon of wh-question formation for every single variety in the cur-

---

    (ii)   min   (inanimate subject / direct object)
           'what'
    (iii)   manayn   (emphatic, in echo questions)
           'what'

[76] Guerssel (1984) observes that certain clitic prepositions in the Ait Seghrouchen variety have different forms in clefts (compare i and ii):
    (i)   wci-x   adlis **i** Mohand
          gave-1SG book to Mohand
          'I gave a book to Mohand.'
    (ii)   Mohand a **mu**wci-x   adlis.
          Mohand CM to gave-1SG book
          'It is Mohand that I gave a book to.'
Consider now an indirect object wh-question:
    (iii)   **mu**mi   y-wcu   Mohand adlis
          to-whom 3MSG-gave Mohand book
          'Whom did Mohand give a book to?'
The same form of the preposition *mu* 'to' appears as a part of the wh-phrase in (iii). This fact clearly indicates that even if cleft markers are not visible in the morphological structure of wh-questions they are still there. Such complex clitisation phenomena in Berber are not sufficiently documented in the language literature.

rent investigation, I will briefly draw a parallel between the wh-questions in Ait Seghrouchen, a subvariety of Tamazight (see 169a-d) and Tarifit (see 170.a-d).

(169) a. **May**   t-sghu   terbatt?   (Ait Seghrouchen)
   what-CM   3FSG-bought girl
   'What did the girl buy?'

    b. **Adil**   ay   t-sghu   terbatt.
   grapes CM   3FSG-bought girl
   'It is grapes that the girl bought.'

    c. **Melmi** aggsghu   wrba adlis?
   when   CM-3MSG-bought boy book
   'When did the boy buy the book?'

    d. **Idennatt** aggsghu   wrba adlis?
   yesterday CM-3MSG-bought boy   book
   'It was yesterday that the boy bought the book?'
   (Guerssel 1984)

(170) a. **W(g)-i** i-zw   Ali?   (Tarifit)
   who-CM 3MSG-kiss Ali
   'Who did Ali kiss?'

    b. **Tifa** i   i-zw   Ali.
   Tifa CM   3MSG-kissed Ali
   'It is Tifa who Ali kissed.'

    c. **W(g)-i**   yzwn   Tifa?
   who-CM   kissed-PART Tifa
   'Who kissed Tifa?'

    d. **Muhand**   i(g)   yzwn   Tifa.
   Muhand   CM   kissed-PART Tifa
   'It was Muhand who kissed Tifa'
   (Noureddine Elouazizi, p.c.)

The examples from Ait Seghrouchen and Tarifit parallel each other exactly: Both the wh-questions and their answers appear as cleft constructions. Multiple wh-questions are impossible in both varieties:

(171) a. *__Maymi__   **may**   t-sghu   terbatt?   (Ait Seghrouchen)
   why   what-CM   3FSG-bought girl
   'Why did the girl buy what?'
   (Calabrese 1987)

      b. ***Wiy**   yzrin   **may**?
         who-CM   seen-PART what-CM
         'Who saw what?'
         (Cole, J & C. Tenny 1987)

(172) a. ***W** **manwn** i(g) yzwn?   (Tarifit)
         who whom   CM   kissed-PART
         'Who kissed whom?'
      b. ***W(g)i**   yzwn   **manwn** i?
         who-CM   kissed-PART   whom   CM
         'Who kissed whom?'
         (Noureddine Elouazizi, p.c.)

Based on the identical behaviour of the Tamazight and Tarifit varieties, I conclude that the grammar of Berber is invariant. All wh-questions are clefts and
multiple wh-questions do not occur.

3.3.5 The Anti-Agreement Effect
Anti-agreement effects are also attested for Berber. According to Ouhalla's
(1993) generalisation, anti-agreement in Berber refers to the obligatory lack of
agreement between the verb and the subject triggered by local extraction of the
latter. In this respect Berber behaves more like Somali because only short subject extraction, i.e. clefting, relativisation and wh-interrogation trigger anti-
agreement effects. All these contexts require a special form of the verb known
by traditional grammarians as the participle. The most significant property of
this form is that it does not contain an AgrS-element (for discussion cf. Ouhalla
1993). As examples (173b), (174b) and (175b) show, agreement between a
questioned, relativised or focused subject and the verb gives rise to ungrammaticality. A participial verbal form is required instead as (173a), (174a) and
(175a) illustrate.

(173) a. **Man tamghart** ay yzrin   Mohand?   (subject wh-questions)
         which woman   CM seen-PART Mohand
      b. ***Man tamghart** ay   t-zra   Mohand?
         which woman   CM   3FSG-saw Mohand
         'Which woman saw Mohand?'

(174) a. tamghart   nni   yzrin   Mohand   (subject relatives)
         woman   that-REL seen-PART Mohand
      b. *tamghart nni   t-zra   Mohand
         woman   that-REL 3FSG-saw Mohand
         'the woman that saw Mohand...'

(175) a. **Tamghart-a** ay   yzrin   Mohand.   (subject clefts)
   woman-this CM   seen-PART Mohand
  b. *****Tamghart-a** ay   t-zra   Mohand.
   woman-this CM   3FSG-saw Mohand
   'It was this woman who saw Mohand.'
   (Ouhalla 1993)

In long distance dependencies involving subjects the anti-agreement effect does not arise:

(176) a. **Man   tamghart** ay   nna-n   qa   t-zra   Mohand?
   which   woman   CM   said-3PL that 3FSG-saw Mohand
   'Which woman did they said saw Mohand?'
  b. tamghart nni   nna-n   qa   t-zra   Mohand
   woman   that-REL said-3PL that 3FSG-saw Mohand
   'the woman that they said saw Mohand...'
  c. **Tamghart-a** ay   nna-n   qa   t-zra   Mohand.
   woman-this CM   said-3PL that 3FSG-saw Mohand
   'It was this woman that they said saw Mohand.'

In Ouhalla's (1993) compositional approach the nature of the anti-agreement effect is referred to as a strategy used by some *pro*-drop languages to prevent the licensing of a resumptive *pro* in a subject position (SpecAgrSP) which is accessible to binding by an A'-moved antecedent. A resumptive *pro* in this position will give rise to violation of the A'-disjointness requirement on the distribution of pronominal elements.[77] Therefore, an AgrS-element incapable of licensing *pro* is inserted into the derivation, instead of one that is capable. Adopting Chomsky's (1986) assumption that *pro* may function as a variable, Ouhalla (1993) claims that operator A'-movement may leave a variable trace or a variable *pro*. These two empty categories have to obey different rules. Traces have to satisfy the ECP.[78] Being a pronominal element, *pro* has to obey

---

[77] Ouhalla (1993) reformulates the A'-disjointness requirement as follows:
  (i) A pronoun must be free from the most local A'-binder in the smallest Complete Functional Complex which contains the pronoun.
The 'most local A'-binder' is defined as follows:
  (ii) A is the most local A'-binder of B if there is no C such that C is an A'-binder and A c-commands C. C c-commands B.
[78] Ouhalla (1993) adopts the definition of the ECP provided by Rizzi (1990) who reduces proper government to head-government:
  (i) The Empty Category Principle (ECP)
   An empty category must be properly head-governed. A category YP is properly governed by a head category X° if YP is contained inside the immediate projection X' of X°.

the A'-disjointness requirement. Hence, variable traces and variable *pro*s are not found in the same environment.

Let us now consider the derivation of short subject extraction in Berber as proposed by Ouhalla (1993):

(177) [$_{\text{SpecCP}}$ **Man** **tamghart**$_i$ [$_{\text{C}^\circ}$ ay$_i$] [$_{\text{SpecIP}}$ t_i yzrin   Mohand]]?
          which   woman   CM   seen-PART Mohand
     'Which woman saw Mohand?'

Following Rizzi (1990) Ouhalla stipulates that wh-questions, relatives and clefts in the Berber and the Celtic languages have a special C-element which is considered to incorporate an agreement element triggered by the presence of an A'-moved operator in SpecCP (see Rizzi 1990 for details, for discussion of the agreement pattern in Irish see section 3.4.3.). This complex C-element bears an AgrS-element and is assumed to be a proper head-governor of the subject trace in SpecIP in (177).

Consider now long distance dependencies involving subjects:

(178) [$_{\text{SpecCP}}$ **Man** **tamghart** [$_{\text{C}^\circ}$ ay]   nna-n
          which   woman   CM   said-3PL
     [$_{\text{CP}}$ qa [$_{\text{IP}}$ *pro* t-zra   Mohand]]]?
          that   3FSG-saw Mohand
     'Which woman did they say saw Mohand?'

In long distance dependencies involving subjects the embedded position related to the subject is filled by *pro*, which does not have to satisfy the ECP (for discussion of subject extraction out of complement clauses see Rizzi 1986). The A'-disjointness requirement is satisfied because the antecedent is sufficiently far removed from *pro*. Ouhalla (1993) assumes that subject extraction in Berber takes place from a preverbal position. A variable trace in that position will rise to an ECP-violation or a *that*-trace effect because a *that*-complementizer is incapable of properly governing a trace in SpecIP (see Rizzi 1990). Rich verb morphology and, consequently, subject agreement occur exactly in those cases, i.e. anti-agreement is not found in long distance dependencies involving subjects. Note that this account for long dependencies involving subjects is consistent with the syntactic derivation proposed in section (3.3.3.). I have argued, based on Guerssel (1984) and Shlonsky (1987), that extraction out of embedded clauses is a twofold operation consisting of topicalisation and focus movement, i.e. base generation into TopP of the embedded clause and subsequent movement to FocP in the matrix clause. Contrary to Ouhalla (1993), I have assumed that short distance extraction in Berber takes place from a post-verbal position. The reason for doing so was the unmarked VSO-word order in these languages. Recall also that a SVO-structure has a more marked reading, which has been referred to as a topic construction. Finally, representational ECP-accounts for subject vs. object asymmetries seem not to be compatible with minimalist derivational economy approaches, which dispense with the theoretical notions of government and binding (see e.g., Pesetsky & Torrego 2000 for minimalist approaches to movement of wh-subjects, T-to-C movement and the EPP). It is therefore not clear if Ouhalla's ideas about the occurrence of anti-agreement effects can be represented in minimalist terms. [79]

I will briefly summarise the observations about the anti-agreement phenomenon made so far. Ouhalla (1993) has come to different conclusions from those of Brandi & Cordin (1989) and Frascarelli & Puglielli (2004, to appear) about the nature of anti-agreement. Ouhalla (1993) has accounted for the anti-agreement effect in terms of interaction of licensing requirements on the empty categories: variable trace vs. variable *pro*. The empty category in the subject position of Fiorentino and Trentino identified by Brandi & Cordin (1989) is an expletive *pro* with full 3MSG-feature set that triggers agreement with the verb. Tracing back the historical development of focus markers to an invariant copular element Frascarelli and Puglielli have argued for the occurrence of a 3MSG-form of the verb induced by the 3MSG-pronominal element inside the decomposed focus marker in Somali (see subsection 3.2.6.1.). The common aspect of all approaches is the fact that they all have to do with the nature and distribution of different kinds of empty elements. Most probably, the phenomenon of anti-agreement cannot be accounted for uniformly (see for a further difference of agreement patterns among languages section 3.4.3. and for an alternative analysis section 3.5.3.). The exact answer of this question requires a careful examination of all languages which exhibit any kind of anti-agreement. Such investigation is, however, not the central aim of the current work. For the current purposes, anti-agreement effects found in Berber can serve as an additional test showing that wh-questions and focus constructions are instances of the

---

[79] Ouhalla (1993) also tries to capture the anti-agreement phenomena in the Italian dialects I have discussed by the example of Trentino in section (3.1.4.) and subsection (3.2.6.2.). Recall that the anti-agreement effect appears when subjects are extracted out of embedded clauses as well (for examples see subsection 3.2.6.2.). Consequently, a matrix/embedded asymmetry is not observed in Trentino. Ouhalla (1993) argues that the empty category which A'-moved subjects leave is identified for both matrix and long distance contexts as a trace in this dialect. The trace is properly head-governed by the lexical head $V°$, which further implies that subject extraction in the Italian dialect takes place from a postverbal position. Recall that subjects in Fiorentino and Trentino originate in a postverbal position in Brandi & Cordin's (1989) approach either.

same derivational pattern. They are both instances of a cleft construction (cf. 173 with 175 and 176a with 176c).

3.3.6 Concluding Remarks on the Syntax of Wh-Questions in Berber

As we have seen, wh-questions in Berber are instances of cleft focus constructions. Like the NP-focus construction in Somali, clefts in Berber are instances of unique focus as they are used to represent new information in wh-interrogatives and their answers or contrastively focused material. The cleft construction in Berber is the only way of expressing any kind of focus (see also chapter 4.). Like in the other languages without multiple wh-questions, Italian (cf. subchapter 3.1.) and Somali (cf. subchapter 3.2.), focused and wh-phrases cannot be realised in-situ. In a language like Berber, focused elements and wh-items are licensed only in the following syntactic structure:

(179) $[_{\text{SpecFocP}}$ wh-phrase / XP $[_{\text{Foc}^\circ}$ CM]...$[_{\text{VP}}$ ...]]

(179) represents a head-adjacency configuration for wh- and focused elements.

3.4 Irish

Modern Irish is, like the Berber languages, a *pro*-drop verb initial language which does not allow multiple wh-interrogatives. Although both Irish and Berber exemplify the VSO surface word order there are still a lot of differences between them. I will concentrate on the relevant differences when I discuss the anti-agreement pattern in Irish (cf. section 3.4.3.). Typical of Irish is the complementary distribution between lexical subjects and inflection morphology on verbs. Irish verbs therefore have a form that encodes information about tense and mood but is not specified for agreement with the subject. This morphological form is referred to as the *analytic* form. Inflected verb forms in Irish are referred to as *synthetic* forms (see McCloskey & Hale 1984, among others). These forms involve a single inflectional ending that encodes information about tense, mood and agreement with the subject.[80]

---

[80] Consider the present tense forms of the verb *tógaim* 'to raise' (Russell 1995: 93):

Synthetic:	Analytic:	Relative form:	thgógas
1. tógaim	1. –		
2. tógair	2. tógann tú		
3. –	3. tógann sé/sí		
1. tógaimid	1. tógann muid		
2. –	2. tógann (sibh)		
3. tógaid	3. tógann said		

I will explicitly indicate the form of the verbs in the examples only when needed.

3.4.1 Wh-Questions and Related Syntactic Constructions

As pointed out by McCloskey (1979, 1990, 2001, and 2003) wh-questions are similar to relatives as they make use of the same syntactic mechanism. Both constructions involve the insertion of the same complementizer-like element (henceforth glossed as COMP). In wh-interrogatives the complementizer appears right adjacent to the wh-phrase. In relatives the same element directly follows the relativised NP. The so-called *reduced clefts* in Irish show the same syntactic pattern (see McCloskey 1979:90ff). It therefore seems reasonable to analyse wh-questions in Irish in the same way as the wh-questions in Berber. Consider a wh-question (180a), a relative clause (180b) and a reduced cleft (180c):

(180) a. **Cé**   *aL*   dhíol an   domhan?   (wh-question)
     who COMP sold the   world
     'Who sold the world?'
   b. **an** **fear**   *aL*   dhíol an   domhan   (relative clause)
     the   man   COMP sold the   world
     'the man that sold the world'
   c. **Seán Bán** *aL*   d'inis   an   scéal dom.   (reduced cleft)
     Seán Bán COMP told   the   story to-me
     'It was Seán Bán who told me the story.'
     (McCloskey 1979:52, 91f)

The complementizer *aL* is characteristic of all these examples. Such clauses are argued to be the consequence of a movement operation. The element moved to the left of the complementizer *aL* leaves a gap in its base position.

A base generation derivation is also possible in the Irish grammar. In this case the questioned, relativised or clefted phrase is resumed by a pronoun in the position where it is interpreted. Note that in these constructions a different complementizer appears: *aN*. Consider again a wh-question (181a), a relative clause (181b) and a reduced cleft (181c) (for more on similarities and differences of the movement and base generation construction see section 3.4.2):[81]

---

[81] The examples illustrate this phenomenon with prepositional phrases. But note that the *aN*-construction is not restricted to prepositional phrases only. It alternates freely with the *aL*-construction in direct object relatives, wh-questions and clefts (for more examples see McCloskey 1979:53 and section 3.4.2.).

(181) a. **Cén fear**$_i$ *aN* bhfaigheann tú an t-airgead uaidh$_i$?
which man COMP get you the money from-him
'Which man do you get the money from?'

b. **an fear**$_i$ *aN* bhfaigheann tú an t-airgead uaidh$_i$
the man COMP get you the money from-him
'the man from whom you get the money'

c. **Teach beag seascair**$_i$ *aN-r* mhair muid ann$_i$.[82]
house little snug COMP-PAST lived we in-it
'It was a snug little house that we lived in.'
(McCloskey 1979:52; 2003)

The examples discussed support the claim that constituent questions, relative and cleft clauses show the same surface pattern. McCloskey (1979, 1990, 2001, and 2003) argues that these three sentence types in Irish are instances of an identical syntactic derivation. The differences between relative and interrogative clauses with a gap and those with a resumptive pronoun are marked formally in a particularly clear way. There are different complementizers and, as a consequence, different verbal morphology depending on whether the bound element in a relative clause or a constituent question is a gap or a resumptive pronoun. The complementizer associated with the binding of a gap is represented above as *aL* ('L' being a symbol for the fact that it induces the *Lenition* mutation on the initial consonant of a following verb). The complementizer associated with the binding of a resumptive pronoun is represented as *aN* ('N' indicates that the particle induces a different mutation effect, namely *Nasalization*, on the initial consonant of the following verb).

As far their surface structure properties are concerned, the syntactic unit headed by a wh-phrase with the associated clause is indistinguishable from the unit formed by a head NP with its relative clause (or respectively a reduced cleft clause). Thus, given any relative clause (or respectively a reduced cleft clause), it is possible to form a corresponding constituent question by replacing the head NP with the appropriate interrogative phrase (compare again 180 and 181).

---

[82] Note that '*r*' in *aN-r* is a morpheme for past tense that becomes attached to the complementizer.

3.4.2   The Derivational Properties of Wh-Questions, Relative Clauses and Clefts[83]

3.4.2.1 Wh-Questions and Relative Clauses. Let us consider some similarities between these constructions in detail. Pronouns are deleted or retained at the questioned or relativised site, being subject to the same conditions and constraints. Deletion is only obligatory in a subject position. This rule is referred to as the *Highest Subject Restriction* (HSR) (see McCloskey 1990 and the discussion of the anti-agreement effect in Irish in section 3.4.3.). Consider the difference between (182a, b) and (183a, b):

(182) a. **an   fear**$_i$ aL   thiteann t$_i$ go talamh
          the   man   COMP falls   to earth
          'the man who falls to earth'
       b. **Cén   fear**$_i$ aL   thiteann t$_i$ go talamh
          which   man   COMP falls   to earth
          'Which man falls to earth?'

(183) a. *__an   fear__$_i$ aN   thiteann **sé**$_i$ go talamh
          the man   COMP falls   he to earth
          'the man who falls to earth'
       b. *__Cén   fear__$_i$ aN   thiteann **sé**$_i$ go talamh
          which   man   COMP falls   he to earth
          'Which man falls to earth?'
          (McCloskey 1979:53)

(183a) and (183b) are instances of the *aN*-construction, which usually requires a pronominal element in the site the questioned or relativised element is reconstructed to (see the discussion in section 3.4.1.). The sentences are nevertheless ungrammatical. Regardless of the derivational strategy involved (*aL*- vs. *aN*-constructions), subject pronouns are illicit when their antecedent is in the next higher A'-position.

Pronouns are optional in direct object positions. Thus, both derivational patterns, the *aL*- (cf. 184a and b) and the *aN*-construction (cf. 185 a and b), are possible in Irish:

---

[83] Since relative clauses and (reduced) clefts in Irish exhibit the same structural pattern, the conclusions derived for relative clauses will also be valid for (reduced) clefts and visa versa (see subsection 3.4.2.2.).

(184) a. **an**   **t-údar**$_i$ aL   mholann   na   léirmheastóirí t$_i$
the   author   COMP praise   the   critics
'the author that the critics praise'

     b. **cén**   **t-údar**$_i$ aL   mholann   na   léirmheastóirí t$_i$
which   author   COMP praise   the   critics
'Which author did the critics praise?'

(185) a. **an**   **t-údar**$_i$ aN   mholann   na   léirmheastóirí é$_i$
the   author   COMP   praise   the   critics   him
'the author that the critics praise'

     b. **cén**   **t-údar**$_i$ aN   mholann   na   léirmheastóirí é$_i$
which   author   COMP   praise   the   critics   him
'Which author did the critics praise?'
(McCloskey 1979:53)

Relativisation or questioning of PPs is an instance of the *aN*-strategy. Questioning of PPs shows an exceptional behaviour still not convincingly explained in the language literature. PPs optionally show piped piping of the preposition and the pronoun, which appear to the right of the wh-phrase (cf. 186 a and b) (see McCloskey 1990, 2003 for discussion and more examples):

(186) a. **Cé**   aN   raibh tú   ag caint   leis?
who   COMP were you   at talking   with-him
'Who were you talking to?'

     b. **Cé**   **leis**   aN   raibh tú   ag caint?
who   with-him   COMP were you   at talking
'Who were you talking to?'
(McCloskey 2003)

Wh-adjuncts often trigger the appearance of *aN*. An optionality of *aL* and *aN* is restricted to certain cases such as locative, manner and temporal adverbials. Duratives and frequency adverbials only take *aL*. Reason adverbials by contrast are only followed by *aN*. In the following I will not discuss the behaviour of adjuncts and PPs since they are irrelevant for the purposes of my investigation (for more on this and certain dialectal differences see McCloskey 2003 and references cited there).

In long distance relatives and questions the situation is more complex. There are two basic patterns of long distance dependencies. If a gap appears in the relativisation or question site then the complementizer *aL* must head every hierarchically higher subordinate clause that contains the deepest embedded clause with the gap. This derivational mechanism is illustrated in (187a and b) for relatives and wh-questions respectively.

(187) a. **an   fear$_i$ aL** deir said [**aL** shíleann an   t-athair
the   man COMP say they COMP thinks the   father
[**aL**   phósfaidh Síle t$_i$]]
COMP   will-marry Sheila
'the man that they say the father thinks Sheila will marry'

b. **Cén   fear$_i$ aL** deir said [**aL** shíleann an   t-athair
which man COMP say they COMP thinks the   father
[**aL** phósfaidh Síle t$_i$]]?
COMP will-marry Sheila
'Which man do they say the father think Sheila will marry?'
(McCloskey 1979:55)

The syntactic structure of (187a and b) can be diagrammed as follows:

(188) ...[$_{CP}$ aL... [$_{CP}$ aL... [$_{CP}$ aL... t ...]]]

McCloskey (1990, 2001) assumes that the appearance of *aL* in every embedded clause is associated with an application of successive-cyclic wh-movement which leaves a trace in every intermediate SpecCP-position. In McCloskey (2003) the derivation is analysed according to the theoretical model proposed by Chomsky (2001). Thus, *aL* is an instance of C endowed with both an operator and an EPP-feature. The operator feature on *aL* enters into an agreement relationship with an empty operator (in the case of relatives) or a wh-operator (in the case of wh-questions) within its c-command domain. The EPP-feature on *aL* forces the empty operator or the wh-operator to rise to SpecCP, thus yielding clauses like (187a and b).

In the case of long distance relatives or wh-questions, in which a resumptive pronoun is used to mark position that is more deeply bound, *aN* is the highest complementizer. All hierarchically deeper clauses are headed by the particle *go/gur*. The latter is in fact the subordinating complementizer in ordinary declarative complements:

(189) a. **an   rud** [**arN**   dhúirt sé [**go**   gcoinneodh sé ceilte é]]
the   thing COMP-PAST said he COMP keep-COND he hidden it
'the thing that he said he would keep hidden'

b. **Cén   t-oifigeach** [ar**N**   shíl   tú
which   officer   COMP-PAST   thought you
[**go**   mbeadh   sé i láthair]]?
COMP   be-COND   he present
'Which officer did you think would be present?'
(McCloskey 1990)

This distributional pattern is diagrammed as follows:

(190)...[$_{CP}$ aN... [$_{CP}$ go... [$_{CP}$ go ... pronoun ...]]]

McCloskey (1990) assumes the presence of an operator in the highest SpecCP position for cases like (189a, b), which binds the resumptive pronoun in the deeper position. Since the relationship between the operator and the resumptive pronoun is established by means of A'-binding and not by the way of movement, the intermediate specifier positions are irrelevant for the structure. Since they are not occupied the associated C-head is realised as the default complementizer *go*. In McCloskey (2003) this syntactic pattern is analysed as follows: In the case of *aN*, C bears only the EPP-feature which means that its specifier must be filled. This requirement is satisfied by the operation merge. An empty relative operator or a wh-operator merges into the specifier position of *aN*. This theoretical assumption captures the fact that *aN* is associated with the absence of movement properties.[84]

Island constraints force the insertion of resumptive pronouns in both constructions. In these structures the distinction between *aL* and *aN* clauses is not relevant. The following examples illustrate that extraction out of an interrogative clause is ungrammatical when the resumptive pronoun in the extraction site is absent (for similar syntactic patterns in Somali and Berber see subchapters 3.2. and 3.3. respectively). Example (191a) shows clefting out of a wh-island, (191b) relativisation out of a wh-island, (191c) questioning out of a wh-island and (191d) questioning out of embedded yes/no-questions:

---

[84] Note that there are three further syntactic patterns attested for long distance A'-dependencies, which are very rare (see for discussion McCloskey 2003):

(i)   [$_{CP}$ aN... [$_{CP}$ aL...t...   ]]
(ii)   [$_{CP}$ aL... [$_{CP}$ aN... pronoun   ...]]
(iii)   [$_{CP}$ aN... [$_{CP}$ aN... pronoun...   ]]

(191) a. **Sin fear**ᵢ nachN   bhfuil   fhios   agam
     that man NEG-COMP COP   knowledge at-me
     [**cén   cineál   mná**ⱼ
     what   sort   woman-GEN
     aL   phósfadh   tⱼ *(**é**ᵢ)].
     COMP would-marry   him
     'That's a man that I don't know what sort of woman would marry
     him.'
     (McCloskey 1979:33)

    b. **an   píobaire**ᵢ aN   mbíonn fhios   agat   i gcónai
     the   piper   COMP   COP   knowledge at-you always
     [**caidé**ⱼ aL   bhuailfidh *(**sé**ᵢ) tⱼ]
     what   COMP will-play   he
     'the piper that you always know what he's going to play'

    c. **cén   píobaire**ᵢ aN   mbíonn fhios   agat   i gcónai
     which   piper   COMP   COP   knowledge at-you always
     [**caidé**ⱼ aL   bhuailfidh *(**sé**ᵢ) tⱼ]
     what   COMP will-play   he
     'Which piper do you always know what he is going to play?'
     (McCloskey 1979:54)

    d. ***Cén   sagart**ᵢ aL   d′fhiafraigh Seán   díot
     which   priest   COMP asked   John   of-you
     [**arL** bhuail   tú **t**ᵢ]?
     if   hit   you
     'Which priest did John ask if you hit?'
     (McCloskey 1979:32)

Extraction out of complex NPs also requires the insertion of a resumptive pronoun. Otherwise, the clauses are unacceptable (cf. 192a and b):

(192) a. **an   fear**ᵢ aL   phóg   mé
     the   man COMP kissed   I
     [**an   bhean**ⱼ aL   phós   *(**sé**ᵢ) tⱼ]
     the   woman COMP married   he
     'the man that I kissed the woman he married'

    b. **Cén   fear**ᵢ aL   phóg   tú
     which   man COMP kissed   you
     [**an   bhean**ⱼ aL   phós *(**sé**ᵢ) tⱼ]
     the   woman COMP married he
     'Which man did you kiss the woman he married?'
     (McCloskey 1979:30)

Wco-effects arise when the resumptive pronoun is dropped. This fact confirms the conclusions reached from the analysis of the Somali and Berber data. The absence of a wco-effect does not automatically lead to the conclusion that the examined syntactic structure is not a focus construction. This means that the presence of a wco-effect cannot be taken as a reliable crossliguistical diagnostic for focus constructions as Rizzi (1997) suggests.[85]

(193) a. **fear**$_i$ aL   d`fhág   a$_i$ bhean   *(**é**$_i$)
      man COMP left   his   wife   him
      'a man that his wife left'

    b. **Cén**   **fear**$_i$ aL d`fhág   a$_i$ bhean   *(**é**$_i$)?
      which   man COMP left   his   wife   him
      'Which man did his wife leave?'
      (McCloskey 1990)

To conclude the observations of the current section, wh-questions and relative clauses obey the same derivational rules. They are either instance of movement or base generation derivations.

3.4.2.2 Wh-Questions and Reduced Clefts. Due to the striking parallels between the wh-questions and relative clauses I have just reviewed, wh-questions in Irish are very similar to those in Berber as they are instances of grammaticalised syntactic structures which can be represented as reduced clefts (see Stenson 1981:107ff and subsection 3.3.1.2.). There are several arguments in favour of this assumption. First, McCloskey (1979:91) points out that indefinite NPs may not appear in the focus position of full clefts:

(194) *Is   **capall** **mór bán** aL   chonaic mé.
     COP horse   big   white COMP saw   I
     'It was a big white horse that I saw.'

Similarly, given the nature of wh-elements as indefinites, wh-questions are not attested in the form of full clefts either (see also Stenson 1981:107). The wh-

---

[85] Note also that German does not exhibit wco-effects either; nevertheless Sabel (2004) proposes a convincing focus movement analysis of German wh-questions. Another well-known exception is Hungarian. É. Kiss (1998a), among many others, proposes a movement analysis of focus constructions in Hungarian (see also Drubig 2000 for more on the absence of wco-effects in focus constructions). I believe that the nature of the wco-effect needs to be re-examined carefully. Using my observations as a basis, I propose that the wco-effect is merely a semantic fact, which can be observed in certain constructions in some languages. It does not provide strong evidence for the type of the construction that it occurs in.

questions I have mentioned in this subchapter (3.4.) never exhibit an initial copula.

Second, Noonan (1997) refers to examples discussed by Duffield (1995:196f) and points out that the following syntactic structures are ambiguous. They could be seen as a relative clause or a focus cleft:

(195) a. **an   sagart** aL   thug an   leabhar dom
        the   priest   COMP gave the   book   to-me
        i) 'the priest who gave me the book'
        ii) 'It is the priest who gave me the book.'
   b. **ar maidin Déardaoin** aL   thoisigh mé
        on morning Thursday   COMP began   I
        i) 'on the Thursday morning that I began…'
        ii) 'Thursday morning was when I started.'

Third, Noonan (1997) points out that the clauses in (195a) and (195b) with the interpretations outlined in (195a, ii) and (195b, ii) are the proper answers to the corresponding wh-questions. Stenson (1981:107f) also discusses question and answer pairs (cf. 196a, b):[86]

(196) a. **Cé**   aL   bhaineanns an   féar?
        who   COMP cut-REL   the   grass
        'Who cuts the grass?'
   b. **M'uncail**   aL   bhaineanns an   féar.
        my-uncle   COMP cut-REL   the   grass
        'It's my uncle who cuts the grass.'

Minimal pairs like (195b) and (196b) clearly show that the structure of relatives and answers to wh-questions is identical. The structural parallelism between wh-questions and their answers (cf. 196a and b) unambiguously indicates that wh-questions in Irish make use of the syntactic mechanism for the expression of information focus. In other words, clefting in Irish is the syntactic structure used to express information focus.

However, a subtype of wh-questions in Irish does not show this typical reduced cleft structure, i.e. the complementizer *aL/aN* is missing. This is the case in nominal wh-questions like (198a, b). How can we explain this exceptional be-

---

[86] Note that the verb in examples 196a and b appears in the so-called *relative form*, which was the only indication of relativisation in the earlier stages of Irish. In modern Irish relative clauses are marked by the complementizers *aL* and *aN*, and the relative forms of the verb are more restricted (Stenson 1981:29).

haviour? I assume that when wh-questions and their answers have a nominal clause structure, the wh-item and the element in the answer corresponding to it also appear in one and same position. This position is the canonical position of predicative NPs in Irish.[87] Carnie (1995: Chapter 4.-6.) argues for two structurally distinct copular clauses in Irish: the equative and the predicative copular clause. Only the predicative copular clause is of interest here because it parallels wh-questions as the structures in (197a, b, c and d) show:

(197) a. (COP) NP$_{PREDICATIVE}$ (pronoun)   NP$_{SUBJECT}$ (predicative copular clause)
  b. Ø   wh-phrase   (pronoun)   NP$_{SUBJECT}$ (nominal wh-question)
  c. Ø   wh-phrase$_i$ [aL...t$_i$...]
  d. Ø   wh-phrase$_i$ [aN...pro$_i$...]

Nominal wh-questions (197b) and the predicative copular construction (197a) have an identical structure in Irish: A pronoun preceding the subject NP (cf. 197a, b and 198a, b) is optional in both constructions (see also Stenson 1981:97, 107):

(198) a. **Cén sort dochtúra** (é)   McCoy?
   what kind doctor-GEN he   McCoy
   'What kind of doctor is McCoy?'
  b. Is   **dochtúir   capall**   (é)   McCoy.
   COP   doctor   horses-GEN he   McCoy
   'McCoy is a doctor of horses.'
   (Carnie 1995:194)

Next, I claim that clefts in Irish emerge from predicative copular constructions.[88] This means that nominal clauses like (197a, b) and clefts like (197c, d) emerge from a common underlying syntactic structure. I propose a uniform account for the four constructions in (197), assuming that structures referred to as reduced clefts in Irish are originally predicative copular clauses. The simplified structure in (199) shows an analysis of clefts in Irish as nominal clauses. The wh- or the clefted phrase occupies the position of the predicative noun. A more complex nominal category, represented below as a free relative clause headed by a zero noun, is the subject of the copular clause (see also Oda 2005).

---

[87] I use the terms nominal clause and copular clauses as synonyms, assuming that a nominal clause is a clause in which the copula is dropped.
[88] Note that there are still differences between clefts and the predicative copular construction as the HSR (see subsection 3.4.2.1.) holds for the former but not for the latter (for more on this see Carnie 1995: chapter 5.)

(199) [[wh-phrase/DP] [$_{DP}$ Ø [aL/aN ....]]]
      PREDICATE   SUBJECT

It is a wide-spread assumption that the predicative noun in a copular clause functions as the element expressing new information (for discussion of Irish copular sentences see Stenson 1981:92-102, see also subchapter 3.2. for Somali and 3.3. for Berber). The predicative element is the focus of new information. This fact supports the proposed analysis of clefts as structures that are histori-cally identical to predicative copular clauses. If the four apparently different clauses in (197) can be reduced to a single underlying one as in (199) we can explain the absence of the complementizer *aL/aN* in sentences like (198a, b). Recall, only in copular wh-questions the complementizer *aL/aN* may not ap-pear (cf. again 198a, b). It follows directly that when the subject in a copular clause is not a complex noun (i.e. not a free relative clause as represented in 199 schematically), the complementizer *aL/aN* is not present. Evidence is also provided by the following examples in which the complementizer *aL/aN* does not appear:

(200) a. **Céard**   é   sin?
         what   it that
         'What is that?'
    b. Is   **currach** é   sin.
        COP currach it that
        'That's a currach.'
        (Stenson 1981:108f)

I will now come back to the argument that wh-questions are cleft structures in Irish addressing a further pragmatic use of clefts. Another piece of evidence for the assumption of the thesis that wh-questions correlate crosslinguistically with the syntactic representation of new information is the fact that cleft construc-tions are typical for the beginning of a narrative. A cleft construction highlights what the story is about (for the same use of a NP-focus construction cf. the discussion of Somali in subchapter 3.2.):

(201) **Fear** aL   bhí   thíos in Anagaire   aN   raibh triúr mac aige.
      man COMP was down in Annagry   COMP was three sons at-him
      'There was a man in Annagry who had three sons.'
      (McCloskey 2001)

McCloskey (2001) claims that the *aL*- and *aN*-constructions do not show any detectable pragmatic distinction. The *aL/aN*-structures are also used in order to express contrastive focus:

(202) Ní   ABHAILE aL   chuaigh sé
      NEG-COPhome   COMPwent   he
      achisteach h go lár   na   cathrach.
      but-in   to centre the   city-GEN
      'It wasn't home he went, but (rather) into the city-centre.'

McCloskey (2001) concludes from the pragmatic use of the *aL/aN*-construction that the complementizers *aL* and *aN* can be described as syncretic expressions of the two obligatory heads in Rizzi's (1997) split-C system. Like the complementizer *that* in English, the *aL/aN*-complementizer in Irish combines finiteness (*aL* signals, among its other functions, embedding of a finite clause) and force features (shown by its use in relative clauses) (see also McCloskey 2003). Following Noonan's (1997) analysis of wh-questions as derivations involving checking of a focus feature, I will expand McCloskey's claim with the proposal that these C-elements can serve as the lexicalisation of a functional head which bears a focus feature. Thus, wh-questions as instances of focus clefts in contemporary Irish can be represented as FocPs. I assume that the structure in (199) has been reanalysed into the structure represented in (203). The wh-phrase or the focused element moves into the specifier position of Foc° in the presence of *aL* or is base generated into the same position in the presence of *aN*:[89]

(203) ...[$_\text{SpecFocP}$ wh-phrase / NP [$_\text{Foc°}$ *aL/aN*] [$_\text{VP}$ ...]]

Like in the other three languages without multiple wh-questions, wh- and focused phrases in Irish are not licensed in-situ, i.e. not in an IP-internal position or in a position usually referred to as an argument position (cf. also subchapter 3.2. for the same observation in Somali and chapter 4.). They target a left-peripheral position marked through head-adjacency to a functional head endowed with a focus feature, lexicalised by the element *aL/aN*.

3.4.3 The Anti-Agreement Effect

In Irish, when the subject is phonologically specified the verb does not carry person-number inflection, i.e. the presence of an overt subject forces the use of the analytic verb form (McCloskey & Hale 1984). There is an absolute com-

---

[89] Predicative copular clauses may also easily be represented as FocPs. I will not pursue this issue here, because it is not relevant for the discussion of the absence of multiple wh-questions in Irish. There is no reason to believe that the information structure of nominal wh-questions differs from that of wh-clefts in this respect. As a double constituent construction with only one slot for new information, the same as the slot for the predicative noun, a nominal clause does not offer any other position where an additional element bearing new information can be hosted.

plementarity between the appearance of person-number morphology of the verb and the appearance of an independent phonologically expressed subject (compare 204a and b):

(204) a. Chuirfeadh   Eoghan isteach ar an   phost sin.
         put-COND-ANALYTIC Owen   in   on the job   that
         'Owen would apply for that job.'
      b. *Chuirfinn   mé   isteach ar an   phost sin.
         put-COND-1SG   I   in   on the job   that
         'I would apply for that job.'
         (McCloskey & Hale 1984)

Wh-questions, relatives and clefts in Irish pattern in two respects. On the one hand, subject relatives, wh-questions and clefts in Irish illustrate the use of the analytic verb form which is not specified for AgrS-features, as for example, in (205):

(205) Chan   **mise** a   chuirfeadh   isteach ar an phos sin.
      COP-NEG   me   COMP put-COND-ANALYTIC in   on the job that
      'It's not me that would apply for that job.'
      (McCloskey & Hale 1984)

On the other hand, in A'-dependencies involving local subjects similar effects to those in Somali and Berber also occur in Irish (cf. the HSR in section 3.4.2. and McCloskey 1990). Resumptive subject pronouns are excluded from the subject position regardless of the derivational strategy used. Consider two instances of the *aN*-construction. Recall that this is the base generation strategy according to which resumptive pronouns have to appear in the base positions of A'-dependencies:

(206) a. *an   **fear**$_i$ aN   raibh   sé$_i$ breoite
         the   man   COMP be-PAST-ANALYTIC he ill
         'the man that was ill'
      b. *Cén   **fear**$_i$ aN   raibh   sé$_i$ breoite?
         which man   COMP be-PAST-ANALYTIC he ill
         'Which man was ill?'

By contrast, in long distance A'-dependencies involving subjects a resumptive pronoun may appear in the embedded position:

(207) a. **an**   **t-ór**$_i$ arN   chreid   corr-dhuine
       this   gold   COMP believed a-few-people
       go   raibh   **sé**$_i$ ann
       COMP be-PAST-ANALYTIC   it   there
       'this gold that a few people believed that it was there'
    b. **Cé**$_i$ arN   shil   tú   gur dhuúirt **sé**$_i$
       who   COMP   thought you COMP said   he
       go   bpósfadh   Máire **é**?
       COMP marry-COND-ANALYTIC Mary   him
       'Who did you think that he said that Mary would marry?'
       (McCloskey 1990)

McCloskey (1990) accounts for these facts in terms of the disjoint reference effect (see for discussion of anti-agreement in Berber according to Ouhalla 1993 section 3.3.5.): A pronominal category cannot be bound by a local A'-antecedent. Therefore subject resumptive pronouns are illicit in root clauses involving A'-binding. In long distance dependencies the A'-antecedent is separated from the resumptive pronoun by the intervention of at least one maximal projection boundary. The resumptive subject pronoun can therefore appear.

However, the agreement pattern in Irish still differs from those found in Somali and Berber. The use of the synthetic verb form, which is specified for φ-features, is ungrammatical whenever the subject is realised overtly, i.e. verbs that do not agree with their subjects are not restricted to local A'-dependencies. Consider (208a and b):

(208) a. *Chuirfinn   mé   isteach ar an   phost sin.
        put-COND-1SG I   in   on the   job   that.
        'I would apply for that job.'
    b. Dá   gcuirfeá   Ø isteach ar   an   phost sin
       if   put-COND-2SG in   on   the job   that
       gheobhfá   Ø é.
       get-COND-2SG   it
       'If you apply for that job, you would get it.'
       (McCloskey & Hale 1984)

Ouhalla (1991:128ff) analyses this property of Celtic languages using the so-called *AGR/TNS-parameter*. According to his analysis the surface VSO word order is derived through verb movement to AgrSP.[90] I will adopt his clausal

---

[90] There are many different accounts for the syntax of Irish (see Chung & McCloskey 1987, Carnie 1995, among others). Given the fact that Irish does not allow free alternation between the VSO and SVO order in contrast to Berber, Ouhalla assumes that AGR selects TNS. In his

structure for the purposes of the current discussion. Both agreement patterns in Irish can be derived in the following way:

(209)

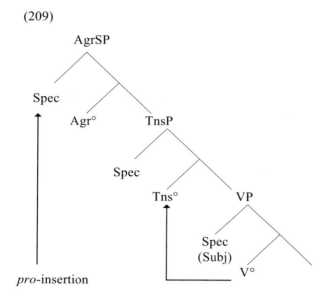

pro-insertion

The structure in (209) shows that a lexical subject can be assigned nominative case in SpecVP. This option is available in some languages and constitutes a language specific parameter which is also valid for Irish. Since Irish is a *pro-drop* language, the possibility that the subject position is filled by an expletive *pro* can be considered as an option as well.

Keeping in mind the simplified syntactic structure of Irish represented in (209), consider first the derivation of examples like (204a) which involve the analytic verb form. An expletive *pro*-element is inserted into the structural subject position (AgrSP) presumably for EPP reasons. Given the lack of agreement features of the verb in this case, I assume that the expletive *pro* inserted in SpecAgrSP is in accordance with Chomsky's classification an expletive element specified for default features (Chomsky 1995:286ff, see for discussion of Trentino subsection 3.2.6.2.). This explains why the analytic form of the verb, i.e. the kind of default form which does not agree with the lexical subject but cor-

---

system, declaratives are IP-structures and the CP projection is involved only in wh-constructions. Alternatively, the language has also been assumed to be a VP-movement language (see Doherty 1997, Legate 1997, Lee 2000, Massam 2000, Rackowsky and Travis 2000 and for discussion McCloskey 2005).

responds to the default features of the expletive *pro*, occurs in such cases. Since the lexical subject is already assigned nominative case in its base position and the clausal EPP-feature is satisfied, there is no reason for the subject to enter any further checking relations. Hence, no visible subject movement applies (see for another account based on the position of adverbs, which suggest that the subject moves out of the VP Rackowsky & Travis 2000).

Second, let us turn to the derivation of clauses like (204b) which involve the synthetic verb form. What is wrong with sentences like (204b) is the simultaneous presence of an overt subject and inflectional morphology of the verb. If the overt subject in (204b) were not present, the clause would be grammatical. For the grammatical variant of (204b), I assume a structure in which an argumental *pro* is licensed in SpecAgrSP. A verbal form specified for φ-features is compulsory. This is exactly the situation in which the inflected verbal form, i.e. the synthetic form, has to appear. Thus, the existence of both syntactic patterns, I have discussed above, accounts for the complementary distribution of lexical subjects and φ-features on the verb (see also Ouhalla 1991:132f):

(210) a. $[_{AgrSP}$ pro$_{expl}$ $[_{AgrS°}$ V$^{°}_{analytic}]$ $[_{TP}$ t_v $[_{VP}$ Subj t_v]]]
      b. $[_{AgrSP}$ pro$_{arg}$ $[_{AgrS°}$ V$^{°}_{synthetic}]$ $[_{TP}$ t_v $[_{VP}$ t_v]]]

It is clear from the latter discussion, that anti-agreement effects in Irish are not directly related to the derivation of wh-questions. In this respect, Irish patterns more strictly with Trentino than with Somali and Berber (see also the analysis of anti-agreement effects in section 3.5.3.).

3.4.4 Concluding Remarks on the Syntax of Wh-Questions in Irish
Wh-questions in Irish are expressed by cleft sentences similar to those in Berber. I therefore conclude that wh-phrases in Irish are licensed in a structurally marked focus position. This focus position is used in order to realise both information and contrastive focus. In this sense focus is a unique category in the grammar of Irish, just like in Italian, Somali and Berber. There is no evidence that focal information can be expressed by any other means but clefting. I assume that Irish belongs to the languages which exhibit unique focus. Thus, only one wh-phrase may appear in an interrogative clause followed by an adjacent head element endowed with a focus feature:

(211) $[_{SpecFocP}$ wh-phrase /NP $[_{Foc°}$ aL/aN] ... $[_{VP}$]]

3.5 Generalisations and Working Hypotheses
I have discussed the internal structural properties of Italian, Somali, Berber and Irish in relation to the syntax of wh-questions. The investigation has shown

some important similarities between the four languages. The most important descriptive generalizations that call for a uniform analysis of languages that do not admit multiple wh-questions are illustrated in the Table (3.):

Table 3. The Common Properties of the Languages without Multiple Wh-
Questions

Phenomenon Language	Multiple wh-questions	Head-adjacency	Wh-questions = Focus constructions	Anti-agreement
Italian	-	+	+	-Standard Italian +Dialects
Somali	-	+	+	+
Berber	-	+	+	+
Irish	-	+	+	+

The phenomenon this investigation attempts to explain is the unavailability of multiple wh-questions in the grammars of Italian, Somali, Berber and Irish (see the second column of Table 3.). At the beginning of chapter (3.) I formulated five important questions connected with the central issue under investigation. Now we can answer these questions:

Q1   Are there specific syntactic phenomena that correlate with the unavailable option to build multiple wh-questions and which are they?

A1   In the languages without multiple wh-questions the wh-question for-
mation shows a strict correlation with the available focusing strategies (see the fourth column of Table 3.). I have reached the conclusion that wh-question formation in languages in which multiple wh-questions do not occur is an instance of focusing into a designated position. This focus position is located in the clausal left periphery. A wh-phrase or a focused element appears left-adjacent to a functional head endowed with a focus feature (see the third column of Table 3.). A further, rather inconsistent, correlation between the syntactic properties of wh-questions and focus constructions in languages without multiple wh-questions is the anti-agreement effect which accompanies subject con-stituent questions and focus constructions in three of the examined languages, i.e. Somali, Berber and Irish. Standard Italian does not ex-hibit anti-agreement effects but certain varieties discussed on the

Trentino example do show an anti-agreement effect in wh-questions and focus constructions (see the fifth column of Table 3.).

Q2 How do the relevant syntactic phenomena interact with each other?

A2 The relevant correlation for the account of the ungrammaticality of multiple wh-questions in Italian, Somali, Berber and Irish is the identity between focusing and wh-question formation. Because the focusing devices in these languages are restricted to a single syntactically marked configuration, the distribution of wh-phrases is also extremely restricted (see also Q3 and A3 below). The anti-agreement effects did not turn out to correlate exactly with the fact that multiple wh-questions in Italian, Somali, Berber and Irish are not allowed. The nature of anti-agreement has remained more or less mysterious so far since the investigation has revealed different reasons for its appearance. I will propose a tentative solution in section (3.5.3.).

Q3 Which properties of language block the formation of multiple wh-questions?

A3 The fact that the occurrence of wh-elements in Italian, Somali, Berber and Irish is limited to a specifier of a head element endowed with a focus feature, combined with the observation that more than one focused element cannot appear in a single clause, unambiguously suggests that multiple wh-phrases per clause are not allowed for the same reasons as multiple focusing is not. The relevant hypothesis will be proposed in section (3.5.2.) and will be elaborated in detail throughout chapter (4.).

Q4 Are there similarities between Italian, Somali, Berber and Irish and which are they?

A4 The answer of this question is clearly positive (see A1, A2 and A3 above).

Q5 Is a uniform analysis of the phenomenon possible?

A5 A uniform analysis is the only right solution since the grammar of wh-interrogatives in Italian, Somali, Berber and Irish shows striking similarities (see subchapter 4.6.).

3.5.1 The Head-Adjacency Generalisation

Since in all languages that do not allow multiple wh-questions the licensing of a wh-word takes place in a head-adjacency relation, I have assumed the following structural positions for each of them:

(212) a. [$_{SpecFocP}$ ma + wax / NP [$_{Foc°}$ baa]...[$_{VP}$ ...]] (Somali)
                        Q   thing   FM
      b. [$_{SpecFocP}$ m / NP   [$_{Foc°}$ ay]...[$_{VP}$...]] (Berber)
                        what   CM

c. [SpecFocP caidé / NP   [Foc° aL/aN   ]...[VP]]   (Irish)
        what   COMP
d. [SpecFocP che   cosa / NP [Foc° V°/ Ø]...[VP ...]] (Italian)
        which thing

In Somali wh-phrases are built up with the nominal focus marker *bàa/ayàa*. In Berber wh-words appear left-adjacent to a special cleft marker *a/ay* and show up as contracted forms in most cases. Wh-questions in Irish are also instances of cleft constructions and therefore wh-items are followed by the complementizer *aL/aN*. Italian does not show a straightforward coherency in all contexts. In matrix wh-questions the wh-phrase is followed by the inflected verb, in embedded clauses, however, wh-elements show much more freedom with respect to their licensing properties. Most of the Italian varieties considered here support the claim that head-adjacency is a relevant licensing requirement for wh-phrases. I have proposed that the minor differences can be accounted for by assuming that certain morphological properties of Foc° in root wh-questions require its lexicalisation (see subchapter 3.1.). This property of root interrogatives has often been referred to as a residual V2-phenomenon (cf. Poletto 2000:76 and Rizzi 1991, 1999). Therefore the adjacent Foc° is sometimes lexicalised, mostly by verb movement to Foc° (cf. a root wh-question in 213a), sometimes not (cf. a contrastive focus construction 213b).

(213) a. **Dove**   è   andato Gianni?
         where   be-3SG gone   Gianni
         'Where did Gianni go?'
     b. QUESTO Gianni ti   dirà
         this   Gianni to-you say-3SG-FUT
         (, non quello che pensavi).
            not   that   what you-thought
         'THIS Gianni will say to you (, not what you thought).'
         (Rizzi 1997)

Wh-phrases in languages that do not allow multiple wh-interrogatives cannot appear in-situ, or more precisely, they cannot appear in argument positions. There is a specific morphological requirement on the licensing of wh-items in the above mentioned language type. I will refer to this language specific requirement as the Head-Adjacency Generalisation (see also Stoyanova 2004):

(214) The Head-Adjacency Generalisation
Languages that do not allow multiple wh-questions are languages that
license wh-phrases only through an overtly established spec-head relationship with a head element endowed with a focus feature:
[$_{\text{SpecFocP}}$ wh-phrase [$_{\text{Foc}°}$ X°] [...]][91]

3.5.2 The Uniqueness Hypothesis

Another common property of the languages without multiple wh-questions is
the striking similarity between wh-questions and the available focus constructions. There is a clear parallel between the *bàa/ayàa* focus strategy and wh-
interrogatives in Somali. Irish and Berber make use of a cleft focusing strategy
in order to build a wh-question. Furthermore, Somali, Berber and Irish do not
show a structural distinction between the expression of information and contrastive focus. Wh-questions in Italian share common properties with both contrastive and information focus constructions. Important in this respect is the
structural correlation between wh-items and contrastively focused constituents,
as both involve fronting to a left-peripheral FocP. I have argued that there is no
difference with respect to the licensing position of contrastive and information
focus in Italian. There cannot be more than one phrase per single clause in both
information and contrastive focus constructions. Therefore, these two semantically different types of focus are licensed in the left-peripheral FocP. What
may differ in structures involving contrastive or information focus is the presence of strong ground- or topic-like features which trigger (remnant) IP-
movement to a higher position of the left periphery (see for extensive discussion of Italian subchapter 3.1.). Since both focus constructions and wh-
questions in languages without multiple wh-questions reveal the same syntactic
properties, I assume that both are subject to the same licensing requirements.
Hence, wh-items and focused constituents in languages without multiple wh-
questions appear in the same structural position. The fact that there is a unique
focusing device in languages without multiple wh-questions is expressed by the
following hypothesis (see also Stoyanova 2004):

---

[91] Note that the opposite generalisation is not necessarily true (see the discussion in chapter 4.)

(215) The Uniqueness Hypothesis
Languages that license wh-phrases only in a unique structural focus position are languages without multiple wh-questions. The notion of uniqueness has to be understood as the interaction of the following three parameters:
a. no focus in-situ
b. no multiple specifiers of a FocP or alternatively no clustering of focused constituents
c. no FocP-recursion

3.5.3 The Relation between Anti-Agreement and Multiple Wh-Questions

The third generalisation about languages without multiple wh-questions is the fact that three of them (Somali, Berber, Irish) and some subvarieties of Italian show anti-agreement effects in subject extraction contexts. Consider now, when and where anti-agreement effects occur in languages without multiple wh-questions:

Table 4. Where and When Anti-Agreement Effects Occur

When \ Where	Berber	Irish	Somali	Trentino
pro-drop parameter	+	+	-	+(?)
A'-constructions	+	+	+	+
basic word order	-	+	-	+
long A'-dependencies	-	+	-	+

The anti-agreement patterns found in the languages without multiple wh-questions are not consistent in three aspects. First, the anti-agreement effect cannot be attributed to the *pro*-drop parameter as Ouhalla (1993) and Frascarelli & Puglielli (2004, to appear) stipulate (cf. the second row of Table 4.). As we can see, the languages do not behave consistently with respect to the possibility of licensing *pro*-subjects. Second, Standard Italian does not show the anti-agreement effect at all. Turkish for instance exhibits anti-agreement effects in relative clauses but not in wh-questions (cf. for details Ouhalla 1993 and references cited there). Consider the following examples:[92]

---

[92] Note that the structures in (216a, b) referred to as 'relative clauses' are in fact participial constructions. Note also that wh-question formation in Turkish is sometimes analysed as wh-in-situ, sometimes as focus movement. I will not discuss the grammar of Turkish here, since it goes far beyond the topic of this book. The interested reader is referred to Kornfilt (1997).

(216) a. [REL tᵢ okul - a   gid-en -Ø]   *adam*ᵢ   (subject relative)
         school DAT go-SUBJECT-PART   man
     'the man who goes to school'
   b. [REL *adam*-in tᵢ git-tiğ   -i]   okulᵢ   (object relative)
         man-GEN   go-OBJECT-PART-3SG   school
     'the school the man goes to'

In the subject relative clause (216a), the verbal element does not have an agreement morpheme corresponding to the φ-features of the relativised subject (*adam*ᵢ). This is shown through the character '-Ø' in the example. By contrast, in the object relative clause (216b), the subject (*adam*) does agree with the verbal element. Agreement is indicated by the presence of the agreement morpheme '-*i*'.

Furthermore, Turkish allows multiple wh-questions (see Kornfilt 1997):

(217) Hasan **kim-e**   **ne-yi**   ver-di?
     Hasan   whom-DAT what-ACC give
     'What did Hasan give to whom?'

The observations from Turkish imply that anti-agreement effects are related closer to the nature of relativisation as an instance of noun modification than to the nature of wh-questions. Hence, there is no strict correlation between the anti-agreement effects and the absence of multiple wh-questions.

Third, the lack of agreement features of the verb in Irish as well as in the considered variety of Trentino is not restricted to subject extraction contexts only (cf. the third and the fourth row of Table 4.). On the grounds of these three generalisations, I conclude that the anti-agreement effect does not belong to the specific language properties that block multiple wh-question formation. I have used the anti-agreement effect merely as an additional test in order to support the thesis that wh-questions are instances of focus constructions especially in Somali and Berber. The connection between the anti-agreement effects and the ungrammaticality of multiple wh-questions is indirect. It is found in three of the languages without multiple wh-questions. What these three languages have in common is the fact that wh-questions are instances of clefts in Berber and Irish. Somali exhibits highly grammaticalised focus constructions.[93] This means in general that anti-agreement effects can occur in languages in which

---

[93] Heine & Reh (1983) observe that focus constructions emerge from clefts crosslinguistically. Typical of clefts is the striking similarity between the clause out-of-focus and the restrictive relative clause. This indicates that clefting and relativisation are derivationally connected with each other (see also Schachter 1973 and Drubig 2000).

wh-questions are formed by means of clefting which in turn is related to rela-tivisation.

How can the anti-agreement effect be analysed independently from the analysis of the absence of multiple wh-questions in Somali, Berber, Trentino and Irish?

I will first address the anti-agreement pattern in Berber. This effect is mani-fested in subject relatives, wh-questions and focus clefts. The three phenomena are best accounted for if we assume that cleft constructions depend on relativi-sation. I will begin with the derivation of subject relativisation:

(218) [$_{CP}$ Ssen-x   aryaz$_i$[$_{CP}$ [$_{C°}$ din] PRO$_i$ y-ffgh-en]].
      knew-1SG man   that   gone-out-PART
'I know the man who went out.'

I assume that (218) involves a participial modifier clause.[94] Typical of non-finite verbal forms, the participle in (218) cannot assign nominative case to its subject. Therefore, subjects of non-finite verbs are crosslinguistically argued to be PRO-elements which are identified from outside of their own CP through control.[95] The participial clause is adjoined to the NP it modifies (see also the following analysis of anti-agreement in Somali).

The postulation that clefting originates from relativisation is additionally sup-ported by the existence of the so-called *neutral pronouns* which are not marked for gender, number and person. Guerssel (1984) claims that these morphologi-cal forms behave like nouns since they exhibit the free/construct state alterna-

---

[94] Participial modifier clausal structures have often been referred to as *reduced relative clauses*. Probably the structure of (218) is a later development of structures like (i):
    (i) [$_{CP}$ Ssen-x   aryaz-din$_i$ [$_{CP}$ PRO$_i$ y-ffgh-en]]
         knew-1SG man-that   gone-out-PART
    'I know the man gone out.'
The emergence of relative complementizers from demonstratives is attested for many lan-guages. E.g., *that* in English may be both a complementizer and a demonstrative. The morpho-logical form –*din*, which usually introduces relatives in Berber, is still available as a demon-strative with the meaning 'that (close to hearer, away from speaker)'. As a demonstrative and a relative complementizer *din* alternates with other elements with deictic semantics, e.g., *u* 'this' and *inn* 'that (away from hearer and speaker)' (see Guerssel 1984). It is plausible to assume that the structure in (i) has been reanalysed as (218). The difference is that in (218) *din* is grammaticalised as the neutral relative complementizer.

[95] Milsark (1988) e.g., assumes an independent CP status with a controlled PRO-subject for postnominal modifier constructions in English (cf. i). Additional evidence for an independent CP-status is provided among others by the fact that such participial constructions constitute barriers for syntactic movement.
    (i) A man$_i$ [$_{CP}$ PRO$_i$ knowing the system] can usually cheat easily.

tion that full nouns usually do. The morphological forms such as (219a, b and c) consist of semantically neutral nouns with an arbitrary reference such as e.g., *person, somebody, something* and an attached demonstrative pronoun like *this, that*:

(219) a. a-yu
      one-this
      'this one'
   b. a-din
      one-that
      'that one (close to hearer, away from speaker)'
   c. a-yinn
      one-that
      'that one (away from hearer and speaker)'

Compare now the form of the so-called cleft marker (220a) and the relative complementizers (220b, c, d) in the same Berber variety:

(220) a. a/ay
      CM
   b. din
      COMP$_{REL}$
      'that (neutral, close to hearer, away from speaker)'
   c. u
      COMP$_{REL}$
      'this (close to speaker)'
   d. inn
      COMP$_{REL}$
      'that (away from hearer and speaker)'

The morphological element referred to as the cleft marker (cf. 220a) is in fact the semantically neutral noun *a/ay* 'the one, the person, somebody, something' which we also find in the morphological units (219a, b and c). Given the observation that the deictic elements in (219) and relative complementizer in (220) have the same form, it now becomes clear that the two phenomena, subject clefting and relativisation, have to be analysed uniformly. Thus, using the analysis of subject relativisation I have proposed as a basis, I assume the following underlying structure for reduced subject clefts in Berber:

(221) [$_{ForceP}$ d [$_{FocP}$ **tamgharta**$_{PRED-DP}$
          COP   woman-this
       [$_{SC}$[$_{SUBJECT-DP}$ay$_i$[PRO$_i$ yzrin   Mohand]] t$_{PRED-DP}$]]]
              the-one see-PART   Mohand
'It is this woman who saw Mohand.'

I adopt a small clause analysis of clefts as copular structures with predicate raising (see Moro 1997 for details of this analysis and Frascarelli & Puglielli 2004, to appear for its application for Somali). According to this analysis a matrix copula selects a small clause as its complement. The subject of this small clause is a complex DP headed by the semantically neutral noun *ay/a* 'the-one' and an adjoined modifier participial clause: *[$_{SUBJECT-DP}$ ay$_i$ [PRO$_i$ yzrin Mohand]]* 'the one seeing Mohand'. Similarly to structures like (218), usually referred to as 'subject relativisation', what we find in (221) is a participial modifier clause adjoined to the noun *ay* 'the one'.[96] Therefore, the verbal form inside the complex subject DP is marked neither for gender nor for number. The predicative DP *tamgharta*$_{PRED}$ 'this woman' additionally undergoes focus movement. Thus, we get surface structures with initial predicative NPs. The syntactic structure in (221) is the input for a grammaticalised focus construction with the semantically neutral noun *a/ay* being reanalysed as the cleft marker, a semantically empty element. Thus, sentences referred to as reduced cleft constructions (see e.g., Calabrese 1987) have the following structure:

(222) [$_{FocP}$ **tamgharta**$_i$[$_{Foc°}$ ay] [$_{SC}$[PRO$_i$ yzrin   Mohand] t$_i$]]
          woman-this   CM   see-PART Mohand
'It is this woman who saw Mohand.'

The derivation of (222) is identical to that of (221). The DP *[PRO yzrin Mohand]* 'the one seeing Mohand' and the DP *tamgharta* 'this woman' are generated within a small clause as the subject and the predicative DP respectively.[97] Additionally the predicative DP *tamgharta* 'this woman' undergoes focus movement to the specifier of *ay* which acts as a purely functional element lexicalising a functional head endowed with a focus feature. After movement to

---

[96] Since clefts in Berber are in fact reduced clefts in the sense that the initial copula is usually omitted, I assume that the relative complementizer *din* 'that', which we normally find in relative clauses, is deleted as well.

[97] Note that clefted DPs in Berber appear in the free state. This fact presents an additional piece of evidence that they do not move from the canonical postverbal subject position, i.e. the position where subjects appear in the construct state. Hence, focused DPs as in (222) are not subjects at all.

SpecFocP, *tamgharta* 'this woman' identifies the PRO-subject inside the participial clause under control. To simplify the derivation is represented in (223).[98]

(223)

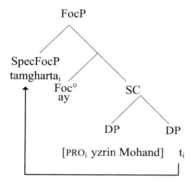

Next, I provide an analysis for the anti-agreement phenomenon in Somali. Although Frascarelli & Puglielli (to appear) do not make use of the assumption, they suggest that the verbal form in subject relatives, wh-questions and focus constructions in Somali is in fact a '*sort of participial verbal form*'. Taking up this idea, I will propose the same analysis of relatives and focus constructions in Somali as I did for Berber. Focus constructions in Somali evolved from the following underlying structure:

---

[98]I will not discuss in detail the internal structure of the participial clause [PRO$_i$ yzrin Mohand]. It can be analysed as free infinite relative clause acting as a subject in (222). It is traditionally assumed that infinite relatives are structures involving empty operators (see e.g., Clark 1990:147). The presence of an empty operator is not relevant for the purposes of my analysis. The subject clause of (222) may also have a simplified structure as *[Ø$_{N°}$ [Op$_i$ [t$_i$ yzrin Mohand]]]* 'the one seeing Mohand'. I think the analysis I propose here is compatible with the analysis proposed by Clark (1990) of PRO itself acting as a non-overt operator. He discusses structures like (i), which are, in my opinion, similar to (222). In (i), an example adapted from Clark (1990:142) the controller (the wh-object phrase) is obviously located in an A'-position and PRO is inside a sentential subject (for more discussion on PRO see also Vanden Wyngaerd 1994 and for a discussion of control as a grammatical phenomenon see Davies & Dubinsky 2004):

    (i) [$_{CP}$ Who$_i$ does [PRO$_i$ kissing Mary] bother t$_i$]?

(224) [TopP hilib [FocP **nimankaas**PRED-DP b- [SC[SUBJECT-DP-aai [PROi
       meat   men-those-ABS COP-   -the-one
       cunayá]]   tPRED-DP]]]
       eat-PART
       'Those men are eating meat.'

The structure in (224) is derived as follows: As in Berber, a matrix copula selects a small clause as its complement in Somali. Recall that the nominal focus
marker *bàa* developed from a copular verb with an adjoined 3MSG-pronoun
(see Lamberti 1983, Frascarelli & Puglielli 2004, to appear and for discussion
subchapter 3.2.). I propose that this pronominal element together with its modifier, actually an adjoined participial clause *[-aa [PRO cunayá]]* 'the one eat-
ing', acts as the subject of the small clause.[99] The predicative DP *nimankaas*
'those men' has undergone focus movement as in Berber. Case marking represents an additional support for the assumption that *nimankaas* 'those men' is
not the subject of the clause, as it is not marked for the nominative case (see
also the discussion of subchapter 3.2. and Frascarelli & Puglielli 2004, to appear). For simplification, the structure of (224) can be represented as follows:

(225)

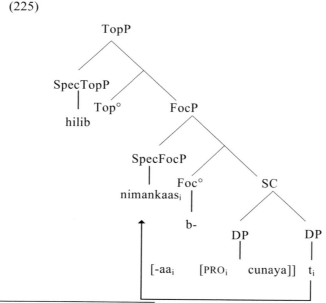

---

[99] Contrary to what has been generally proposed concerning the properties of Somali syntax, I
assume that non-finite clauses are limited in that language but nevertheless exist (see also
Saeed 1999:226). The subject relative construction belongs to these rare cases.

In contemporary Somali (224) is grammaticalised into a focus construction like (226):

(226) [TopP hilib [FocP **nimankaas**i   [Foc° baa] [PROi cunayá]   ]]
      meat   those men   FM   eat-PART
    'THOSE MEN are eating meat.'

The object *hilib* 'meat' in (226) is base generated into the topic position. In order to capture the observation that focusing in Somali does not show movement properties I have assumed throughout the investigation that focused elements in contemporary Somali are base generated in SpecFocP. Thus, after being base generated into SpecFocP, the focused PD *nimankaas* 'those men' controls and identifies the PRO-subject inside the participial clause.

One advantage of this analysis of focus constructions in Somali and Berber is the fact that the proposal is related neither to *pro*-drop nor to non-*pro*-drop languages. It correctly predicts that anti-agreement effects may occur in both *pro*-drop (e.g., Berber) and non-*pro*-drop languages (e.g., Somali). The second advantage is that this analysis correctly explains the asymmetries between short and long A'-dependencies in Somali and Berber. As we have seen anti-agreement effects in both languages are not found with long distance wh-questions and focus constructions. Long distance clefts in Berber were analysed as base generation into the TopP of the embedded clause with subsequent short focus movement (see subchapter 3.3. for discussion). The motivation for this analysis was the presence of a pronoun in the embedded subject position, which represents a property generally attributed to topicalisation. This pronominal element triggers agreement on the verb. In Somali the focused phrase is base generated into the matrix FocP. The embedded subject position related to that of the focused element in the main clause is filled by a clitic pronoun which triggers subject agreement on the verb. This pronoun and the focused element are coindexed in Somali (see subchapter 3.2.). Long distance A'-dependencies with relativised or focused embedded subjects, which have been additionally extracted to a position inside the matrix clause, will constitute the syntactic environment where anti-agreement effects are supposed to appear.[100] In subchapter (3.2.), I discussed the fact that focusing and relativisation in Somali are matrix phenomena only and structures like (i) or (ii) outlined in the latter footnote are not expected to appear at all. Such constructions are illicit in Berber as well. As we have seen in subchapter (3.3.) any long distance A'-

---

[100] Clauses like (i) are crosslinguistically impossible:
    (i) *Which man does Peter believe that I met [ti [who bought a book / buying a book]]?
    (ii) Who does Peter believe that it was [ti [that bought a book / buying a book]]?
A clause like (ii) is not judged to be as bad as (i) is.

dependencies in Berber are formed by base generation into a left-peripheral position of the embedded clause followed by movement to the matrix clause. Thus in both Somali and Berber the phenomenon of anti-agreement is only found in short distance A'-dependencies.

As for Trentino and Irish, anti-agreement effects occur not only in contexts involving A'-dependencies but also in sentences with an unmarked word order. The clauses representing the anti-agreement effect for Trentino and Irish respectively are (227a) and (228a):

(227) a. E'   vegnu   la   Maria.   (Trentino)
         be-3MSG come-PP   the   Maria
      b. *L'è   vegnuda Maria
         SCL-be-3MSG come-PP-F Maria
         'Maria has come.'

(228) a. Chuirfeadh Eoghan isteach ar an   phost   sin.   (Irish)
         put-COND   Owen   in   on the job   that
         'Owen would apply for that job.'
      b. *Chuirfinn   mé   isteach ar an   phost sin
         put-COND-1SG   I   in   on the job   that
         'I would apply for that job.'

I adopt the idea of an expletive *pro* with formal 3MSG-features for Trentino originally expressed by Brandi & Cordin (1989) (see 229a). For Irish I assume that an expletive *pro* with some default features triggers the appearance of the analytic verbal form, which correspondingly also has default features (see 229b):

(229) a. [IP *pro*-expl3MSG   e'   vegnu   [VP la   Maria]] (Trentino)
                              be-3MSG come-PP   the   Maria
         'Maria has come.'
      b. [IP *pro*-explDEFAULT chuirfeadh   (Irish)
                              put-CONDDEFAULT
         [VP Eoghan isteach   ar an   phost sin]]
              Owen   in   on the job   that
         'Owen would apply for that job.'

Given the observation that these structures represent the basic word order for Trentino and Irish, we expect to find the anti-agreement effect in focus constructions as well as in wh-questions. This is exactly what happens in both languages. Another correct prediction of my proposal is the fact that the anti-agreement effect occurs in both long and short A'-dependencies (for more data see section 3.1.4. and subsection 3.2.6.2. for Trentino and section 3.4.3. for Irish).

To conclude the discussion of the phenomenon anti-agreement in languages without multiple wh-questions: The exact examination of the environments where anti-agreement effects occur has shown that this phenomenon is not directly related to the syntax of wh-questions. Although the coexistence of anti-agreement effects and the ungrammaticality of multiple wh-questions initially seemed to be a causal one, this investigation has falsified the hypothesis. Anti-agreement phenomena do not belong to the language-specific properties that block multiple wh-question formation.

CHAPTER 4
ANALYSIS

In this chapter, I will verify the generalisation (cf. section 3.5.1.) and the working hypothesis (cf. section 3.5.2.) directly related to the languages without multiple wh-questions. The Head-Adjacency Generalisation describes the structural environment in which a wh-phrase in Somali, Italian, Berber and Irish is properly licensed. Wh-phrases in languages without multiple wh-questions appear in a designated focus position. The Uniqueness Hypothesis refers to the parametric properties of this structurally marked focus position. First, it articulates the observation that there is only one way of expressing focus in languages without multiple wh-questions. Languages without multiple wh-questions can realise focus only in a structurally marked focus position, this means that languages without multiple wh-questions do not licence focus and wh-phrases in-situ, i.e. in argument positions. Second, the Uniqueness Hypothesis entails that in languages without multiple wh-questions there is only one focus position per clause. Given the fact that wh-phrases in languages without multiple wh-questions are focused elements that have to be in a focus position, the Uniqueness Hypothesis renders multiple wh-questions ungrammatical.

4.1 The Head-Adjacency Generalisation and the Uniqueness Hypothesis Revisited

As stated in the introduction of this work, Somali, Italian, Berber and Irish are languages which constitute a separate language type with respect to the possibility to build multiple wh-questions. I claim that they belong to a different language type that cannot apply any of the three basic strategies of multiple wh-question formation. Consider the relevant examples again:

(230) a. **Maxáy** sameeyeen? (Somali)
   what-FM-SCL did
   'What did they do?'

   b. ***yaa- goormuu** yimid?
   who-FM time-which-FM-SCL came
   'Who came when?'

c. *__yaa__   yimid   __xaggee__?
who-FM   came   place-which
'Who came where?'
(Svolacchia & Puglielli 1999)

(231) a. __May__   t-sghu   terbatt?   (Berber)
what-CM3FSG-bought girl
'What did the girl buy?'
(Calabrese 1987)

b. *__W   manwn__ i(g)   yzwn?
who whom   CM   kissed-PART
'Who kissed whom?'
(Noureddine Elouazizi, p.c.)

c. *__Wiy__   yzrin   __may__?
who-CM   seen-PART what-CM
'Who saw what?'
(Cole & Tenny 1987)

(232) a. __Che cosa__   ha   fatto, Carlo?   (Italian)
what   have-3SG done Carlo
'What did Carlo do?'

b. *__Chi che cosa__   ha   fatto?
who what   have-3SG done
'Who did what?'
(Rizzi 1997)

c. *__Che cosa__ hai   dato __a chi__?
what   have-2SG given to whom
'What did you give to whom?'
(Calabrese 1987)

(233) a. __Caidé__   aL   thug tú   dó?   (Irish)
what   COMP give you to-him
'What did you give him?'

b. *__Cé caidé__   aL   rinne?
who what   COMP did
'Who did what?'

c. *__Cé__ aL   rinne __caidé__?
who COMP did   what
'Who did what?'
(McCloskey 1979:61,71)

[Handwritten margin notes:] Interestingly, this does not apply to: when?

Not interested in adjunct w* 8 PPs → (113); but only when does not have it/ not wh-q but argument wh-q

The grammatical examples show the only position in which wh-phrases in Somali, Berber, Irish and Italian are licensed properly. This is a position left-adjacent to a focus marker in Somali (cf. 230a) and left-adjacent to a cleft marker in Berber (cf. 231a). In Italian wh-phrases are licensed in a left-peripheral focus position that has been identified by Rizzi (1997) as FocP in the clausal left periphery (cf. 232a). In Irish the wh-phrase appears left-adjacent to the head elements *aL/aN* which serve as the lexicalisation of a functional head endowed with a focus feature (cf. 233a). The ungrammatical examples (230b, 231b, 232b, 233b) prove that multiple wh-fronting is not possible. The observation that a wh-phrase cannot be left in-situ is represented in (230c, 231c, 232c, 233c). Hence, the mixed strategy cannot be applied in Somali, Berber, Italian and Irish. In chapter (3.) I argued that wh-formation in Somali, Berber, Italian and Irish is an instance of a focus construction. I reached the conclusion that there is a specific morphosyntactic licensing configuration for wh-items in languages that do not allow multiple wh-interrogatives. I referred to this language specific licensing mechanism as the Head-Adjacency Generalisation repeated here:

(234) The Head-Adjacency Generalisation
    Languages that do not allow multiple wh-questions are languages that license wh-phrases only through an overtly established spec-head relationship with a head element endowed with a focus feature:
    $[_{SpecFocP}$ wh-phrase $[_{Foc°}$ X°$]$ $[$ ... $]]$

However, using a head-adjacency environment as a licensing position for wh-phrases is not a new proposal (see e.g., the wh-Criterion by Rizzi 1990 or the Clausal Typing Hypothesis by Cheng 1997). This generalisation reflects merely the observation that languages that do not allow multiple wh-questions are not languages traditionally referred to as wh-in-situ languages. I have therefore proposed the Uniqueness Hypothesis in order to account for the ungrammaticality of multiple wh-questions in Somali, Berber, Italian and Irish:

(235) The Uniqueness Hypothesis
    Languages that license wh-phrases only in a unique structural focus position are languages without multiple wh-questions. The notion of uniqueness has to be understood as the interaction of the following three parameters:
    a. no focus in-situ
    b. no multiple specifiers of a FocP or alternatively no clustering of focused constituents
    c. no FocP-recursion

According to my hypothesis the wh-interrogative mechanisms in languages without multiple wh-questions parallel their focusing systems exactly. Now, a better crosslinguistic survey is necessary in order to confirm the Uniqueness Hypothesis and to account for the language variation with respect to differences within focusing mechanisms and the corresponding syntactic devices of multiple wh-question formation.

4.2   Wh-Questions in Languages without Multiple Wh-Questions and their Answers as Focus Constructions

Let us now turn to the focusing strategy and its relationship with wh-questions in Somali, Berber, Italian and Irish in order to make the licensing requirements for wh-phrases in languages without multiple wh-questions more precise. In general, wh-phrases crosslinguistically possess a focus feature. Therefore, wh-questions are closely related to the linguistic mechanisms for the expression of focus (see e.g., Horvath 1986, among others and the discussion in chapter 2.). According to this standard view, wh-questions in Somali and Italian exactly parallel declarative focus constructions. Wh-questions in Berber and Irish correspond to focus clefts. I have reached the conclusion that wh-questions and focus constructions in Italian are the result of a movement operation into the left-peripheral FocP. Wh-questions and focus constructions in Somali are emerge from a base generation of a wh- or focus phrase into a designated focus position, which was represented as FocP. As for Berber, I have argued that short wh-questions and focus constructions show the properties of a movement operation. Long distance wh-questions and focus constructions arise from a complex operation. This consists of a base generation into a left-peripheral position of the embedded clause, which I have referred to as a topic position (TopP) merely descriptively, and subsequent movement to the designated focus position (FocP) of the matrix clause. We have seen that wh- and focus constructions in Irish reflect either a base generation process, or movement of a wh- or respectively a focus phrase into a designated left-peripheral focus position (FocP). What is important for the current argumentation is the fact that wh-questions and their answers show the same structural properties. Consider again the following wh-question and answer pairs. The only appropriate answer to a wh-question is a clause in which the constituent bearing the new information is focused:

(236) a. **Kuma**   ayaa kalluunkii cunay?   (Somali)
          who   FM   fish-the   ate
          'Who ate the fish?'

      b. **Cali** baa   kalluunkii cunay.
          Ali   FM   fish-the   ate
          'Ali ate the fish.'

c. #Kalluunkii   baa   **Cali**   cunay.
   fish-the   FM   Ali   ate
   'Ali ate the fish.'
   (Saeed 1984:25)

In Somali a wh-subject appears to the left of a focus marker (cf. 236a). In the
appropriate answer the subject NP is focused (cf. 236b) and shows the same
structure as the wh-interrogative. Focusing of the object (cf. 236c) is not a
compatible answer in this context. Consider Berber now:

(237) a. **May**   t-sghu   terbatt?   (Berber)
         what-CM3FSG-bought   girl
         'What did the girl buy?'
      b. **Adil**   ay   t-sghu   terbatt
         grapes   CM   3FSG-buy   girl
         'It is grapes that the girl bought.'
      c. #t-sghu   terbatt   **adil**.
         3FSG-bought girl   grapes
         'The girl bought grapes.'
         (Calabrese 1987)

The same rule is true for Berber. The wh-question (237a) and the correct answer (237b) are structurally identical. The wh-word and the corresponding NP
in the answer are focused by a cleft construction. A clause with an unmarked
VSO word order (cf. 237c) is, as expected, not a suitable answer to (237a). The
next examples show the information structure of wh-questions and their answers in Italian:

(238) a. **Che cosa**$_i$ hai   letto t$_i$?   (Italian)
         what   have-2SG   read
         'What have you read?'
      b. [$_{GroundP}$ [$_{IP}$ Ho   letto t$_i$]$_j$ [$_{FocP}$ **il**   **libro**$_i$... t$_j$]].
         have-1SG   read   the   book
         'I have read a book.'
      c. [$_{FocP}$ **Il**   **libro**$_i$... [$_{IP}$ ho ———— letto t$_i$]].
         the   book   [have-1SG read]
         '[I have read]the book.'
      d. #[$_{FocP}$ IL LIBRO$_i$ ... [$_{IP}$ ho   letto t$_i$]] (non il   giornale)
         the   book   have-1SG   read   not the   magazine
         'THE BOOK I have read, not the magazine.'

I have argued that answers to wh-questions in Italian have two alternating structures (cf. 238b and 238c). The structure represented in (238b) involves the activation of a strong ground feature which is checked via remnant IP-movement to SpecGroundP. In (238c) a weak ground feature is selected from the lexicon. Therefore, remnant IP-movement does not take place here. Since the IP represents old information, it is deleted in the phonological part of the derivation. In both (238b and c) the element corresponding to the wh-phrase in the wh-question is in FocP (see for arguments subsection 3.1.1.4.). Contrastive focus is inappropriate as an answer (cf. 238d). Finally consider Irish:

(239) a. **Cad** arL   cheann Máire?   (Irish)
         what COMP-PAST bought Mary
         'What did Mary buy?'
     b. (Is) **Leabhar** arL   cheann Máire.
         COP book   COMP-PAST bought Mary
         'It was a book that Mary bought.'
     c. #Cheann   Máire   **leabhar**.
         bought   Mary   book
         'Mary bought a book.'
         (Patricia Ronan, p.c.)

The examples from Irish reflect the situation in Somali, Berber and Italian. As instances of clefts, wh-questions (cf. 239a) structurally correspond to their answers (cf. 239b). A clause with the unmarked VSO word order (cf. 239c) is judged as a less appropriate answer to wh-questions like (239a).

Since both wh-questions and their answers reveal identical syntactic properties, I assume that both are subject to the same licensing requirement.[101] In other words, since wh- and focus in-situ do not occur in languages without multiple wh-questions, the Head-Adjacency Generalisation holds for declarative focus constructions and for wh-constructions. The formation of wh-questions in Somali, Berber Irish and Italian is a derivation driven by the need to satisfy a focus feature. Wh-questions in many other languages have been analysed as focus constructions (e.g., Hungarian among many others). Therefore, we have to discuss the particular properties of the focusing strategies in the languages without multiple wh-questions that distinguish them from the focusing mechanisms found in languages with multiple wh-questions.

---

[101] For additional syntactic tests such as the wco-effect, extraction and anti-agreement phenomena supporting the claim that wh-questions in languages without multiple wh-questions are instances of focus constructions see chapter (3.).

I have argued that the head-adjacency environment is the only distributional pattern for both wh-phrases and focused constituents in Somali, Berber, Irish and Italian. According to the Uniqueness Hypothesis the focusing strategy in Somali, Berber, Irish and Italian is unique in that it can affect only one constituent per clause. I have proposed that this syntactic condition constitutes a special parametric property of the languages that do not allow multiple wh-questions. In order to confirm the Uniqueness Hypothesis I will present evidence that the parameters (a), (b) and (c) in (235) are valid for languages without multiple wh-questions. In the following I will compare other languages in which the wh-question formation is an instance of structurally marked focusing with Somali, Berber, Italian and Irish. The languages I will consider for the current purposes are Hungarian and Malagasy. By this comparison I will draw an exact picture of the syntactic properties that exclude the possibility of deriving multiple wh-questions in Somali, Berber, Italian and Irish. I will address the question why wh-phrases cannot be licensed in-situ (see parameter (a) of 235). Next, I will show that the focus projection in these languages is not recursive. I also provide evidence that the appearance of a second focus marker causes ungrammaticality in Somali. Similarly, I will show that it is not possible to cleft two constituents in the same clause in Berber and Irish and that focusing of two constituents in Italian is also ungrammatical (see parameter (b) of 235). Finally, I will prove that the option to form a cluster of focused constituents (Grewendorf 2001, Sabel 2001, 2003) or alternatively to realise focused elements in multiple specifiers of a head endowed with a focus feature (Richards 1997) is not available in Somali, Berber, Italian and Irish (see parameter (c) of 235).

4.3 Wh-in-situ and Optional Licensing of Wh-Phrases in a Focus Position

First, I will examine a wh-in-situ language like Malagasy (cf. Sabel 2003). As the examples show, wh-phrases usually appear in their base position (cf. 240a), but the language also has an option to license wh-words in a focus position marked by a special focus particle: *no* (cf. 240b). Thus, a combination of both strategies results in a grammatical multiple wh-question (cf. 241a and b). For the ease of representation I will call this variant of multiple wh-question formation 'Malagasy strategy I'.

(240) a. Nividy   **inona** Rabe?   (Malagasy)
         PAST-AT-buy what   Rabe
      b. **Inona**   no   novidin-d   Rabe?
         what   FM   PAST-TT-buy   Rabe
         'What has Rabe bought?'

(241) a. **Iza**$_i$ no   nividy   **inona** t$_i$?
       who FM   PAST-AT-buy   what
    b. **Inona**$_i$ no   novidin   **iza**   t$_i$?
       what   FM   PAST-TT-buy   who
       'Who bought what?'

Recall now the most important prediction of the Clausal Typing Hypothesis. A language exhibiting yes/no-particles is a wh-in-situ language (Cheng 1997:16f, see for discussion section 1.3.2.). Somali and Berber have yes/no-particles (cf. 242a for Somali, 243a for Berber and 244a for Irish), nevertheless, wh-phrases are excluded in-situ, i.e. in canonical argument positions (cf. 242b for Somali, 243b for Berber and 244b for Irish):

(242) a. **Muu** kúu   dhiibay?   (Somali)
       Q-he you-to hand
       'Did he hand it to you?'
       (Saeed 1999:197)
    b. *Maryan   baa   **kuma**   arkay?
       Maryan   FM   who   saw
       'Who did Maryan see?'
       (Cabdelqadir Ruumi, p.c.)
    c. **Yaa**   Maryan arkay?
       who-FM Maryan saw
       'Who saw Maryan?'
       (Svolacchia & Puglielli 1999)
    d. *****Kuma** ayaa **maxaa** cunay?
       who   FM   what   ate
       'Who ate what?'
       (Cabdelqadir Ruumi, p.c.)

(243) a. **Is** y-sghu   Mohand adlis?   (Berber)
       Q 3MSG-bought Mohand book
       'Did Mohand buy a book?'
       (Guerssel 1984)
    b. *t-sga   tarbat   **min**?
       3FSG-bought girl   what
       'What did the girl buy?'
    c. **W(g)i**   yzwn   Tifa?
       who-CM   kissed-PART Tifa
       'Who kissed Tifa?'

d. ***Manwan** i(g) ysgin **manyn**?
who CM bought-PART what
'Who is it that bought what?'
(Noureddine Elouazizi, p.c.)

(244) a. **An** bhfaca tú an fear sin? (Irish)
Q saw you the man that
'Did you see that man?'
(Stenson 1981:25)

b. *Bhuail Cathal **cad**?
hit Charles what
'What did Charles hit?'
(Carnie 1995:194)

c. **Caidé** aL thug tú dó?
what COMP give you to-him
'What did you give him?'

d. *Cé aL rinne **caidé**?
who COMP did what
'Who did what?'
(McCloskey 1979:61,71)

Since Somali (cf. 242a), Berber (cf. 243a) and Irish (cf. 244a) do have question particles, wh-fronting to SpecCP obviously cannot apply for clausal typing purposes. Recall, it is generally assumed for languages like English that they type interrogative clauses through spec-head agreement in the C-system. Consequently, wh-fronting in Somali, Berber and Irish does not have to take place for clausal typing purposes. But why do these languages use overt fronting strategies for wh-question formation? In other words, why are Somali, Berber and Irish not wh-in-situ languages with optional fronting of wh-elements? Recall that the languages make use of specific focusing strategies for the representation of wh-items. Wh-phrases in Somali appear left-adjacent to a focus marker and wh-words in Berber precede a cleft marker. In Irish the wh-phrase is followed by the complementizer elements *aL/aN*. These items have been identified as the lexicalisation of the functional head Foc°. It follows that head-adjacency (cf. 234) as a language specific licensing pattern for wh-phrases is fully independent of clausal typing. Note further that the Clausal Typing Hypothesis still holds because the head elements, which enter into a spec-head relation with the wh-phrases in Somali, Berber and Irish, are different in nature from the question particles (cf. 242a and b for Somali, 243 a and b for Berber, and 244 a and b for Irish).[102] I therefore propose that another rule is crucial for the distribution of wh-phrases in Somali, Berber and Irish. This rule has been referred to as the Uniqueness Hypothesis. Unique focus is a subtype of structurally marked focus into a designated position. This position is the specifier of a functional head that bears a focus feature. In other words, a wh-phrase as an instance of a focused element cannot stay in-situ in languages without multiple wh-questions because they lack an in-situ focusing strategy. This restriction is obviously not necessary for wh-in-situ languages like Malagasy. Somali, Berber and Irish obligatorily license wh-phrases in a structurally marked focus position, while Malagasy makes use of this possibility optionally (see subchapter 4.6. for theoretical arguments that account for this typological variation). As expected, the Malagasy strategy I of deriving multiple wh-questions is, not available in Somali, Berber, and Irish (cf. 242d for Somali, 243d for Berber and 244d for Irish).

Consider finally Standard Italian. Italian does not exhibit an overt yes/no-particle. Yes/no-questions do not differ from declaratives with respect to word order (cf. 245a and b). The only way to distinguish them is by means of intonation. The same pattern applies to French yes/no-questions. Given this observation and the fact that French is an optional wh-fronting language, Cheng & Rooryck (2000) have argued that yes/no-intonation is a yes/no-question morpheme in the overt syntax with a PF spell-out in the form of a rising yes/no-intonation (see for more on the derivation of optional wh-ex-situ Cheng & Rooryck 2000). I suggest that intonation plays the same role in Italian yes/no-interrogatives (see 245a and b), i.e. intonation counts as an overt question morpheme. This fact implies that Italian may be an optional wh-fronting language. This is, however, not true, as example (245c) shows:

(245) a. La   macchina gli   si   è   rotta.   (declarative)
         the   car   him REFL be-3SG broken
         'His car broke down.'
      b. La   macchina gli   si   è   rotta?   (yes/no-question)
         the   car   him REFL be-3SG broken
         'Did his car break down?'
      (Giorgio Banti, p.c.)

---

[102] To my knowledge, the languages Cheng (1997) identifies as wh-in-situ languages exhibit clause final yes/no-particles. Somali, Irish and Berber have clause initial yes/no-particles. The differences between languages with clause initial yes/no-particles and the languages with clause final yes/no-particles has not been examined in detail so far, which in turn may also have some negative consequences for Cheng's generalisation about wh-in-situ languages.

c. *Gianni ha   fatto **che cosa?**[103]
   Gianni have-3SG   done what
   'What did Gianni do?'

d. **Che cosa**   ha   fatto Gianni?
   what   have-3SG   done Gianni
   'What did Gianni do?'

e. ***Chi** ha   fatto **che cosa?**
   who have-3SG   done what
   'Who did what?'

I suggest that Italian behaves like Somali, Berber and Irish and wh-fronting is for reasons different from clausal typing. Wh-fronting is, as we have seen, for focusing reasons (see subchapter 3.1.). Wh-in-situ is not available in Italian because wh-phrases have to be in a focus position (cf. 245c). The language has only one focus position located in the left periphery (cf. 245d). Focus in-situ is not an available option for Italian; hence, wh-in-situ and multiple wh-questions with one fronted wh-phrase and another one in-situ do not appear in Italian (cf. 245e). The Malagasy strategy I is not possible in Italian for the same reasons as in Somali, Berber and Irish. Thus, the focusing strategy in Somali, Berber, Italian and Irish is unique in the sense that focus is licensed only in a designated position and cannot appear in-situ. As we have already seen (cf. subchapter 4.2.), their interrogative systems reflect the situation in declarative focus constructions. Consequently, wh-phrases are licensed in the structurally marked unique focus position and cannot appear in-situ. Parameter (a) of the Uniqueness Hypothesis (cf. 235) holds. This is represented below by the example of an ungrammatical multiple wh-question involving wh-in-situ from Italian:

---

[103] I have excluded the possibility of remnant IP-movement to GroundP in root wh-questions in section (3.1.2.).

(246) a.

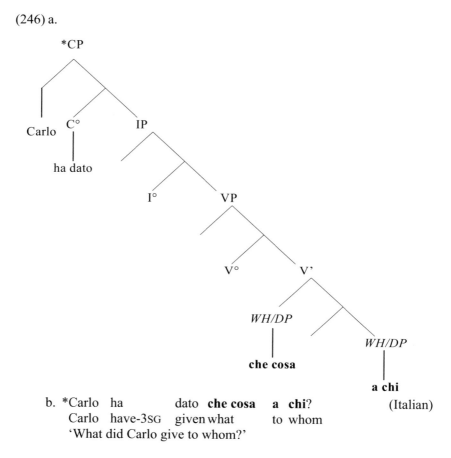

b. *Carlo   ha   dato **che cosa**   **a chi**?   (Italian)
   Carlo   have-3SG   given what   to whom
   'What did Carlo give to whom?'

I will return to the impossibility to front one wh-item and leave other wh-elements in-situ in the discussion of the phenomenon of focus recursion in the following subchapter.

4.4   Multiple Wh-Questions as Focus Recursion

Consider now another way of deriving multiple wh-questions. As argued by É. Kiss (1998b), Hungarian allows a multiple focus construction in which more than one focus phrase of the same type, i.e. 'more than one operator introducing a set and exhaustively identifying a proper subset of it' (É. Kiss 1998b) can appear in a single clause. Hungarian is therefore considered a language that allows for focus recursion (cf. 247a). The licensing head of focused elements in Hungarian is V°. It licenses both items in (247a) through successive movement from the lower to the higher focus projection. This construction syntactically corresponds to multiple wh-questions in Hungarian (cf. 247a and b).

(247) a. $[_{TopP} ... [_{TopP} ... [_{FocP} [_{Foc°} \quad V_i] ... PRT ... [_{FocP} [_{Foc°} \quad t_i] [_{VP} ... t_i ...]]]]]$

     b. $[_{FocP} \textbf{ Ki} [_{Foc°} \text{ vert}_i] ... \text{meg} ... [_{FocP} \textbf{ kit} \quad [_{Foc°} \quad t_i] ... [_{VP} ... t_i ...]]]$?
        who   beat   PRT   whom
        'Who beat somebody, and who was the person beaten by him?'

Now compare Hungarian with Somali, Berber, Italian and Irish. Recall that Somali, Berber and Irish exhibit overt focusing particles. So, if focus recursion were possible, these special markings would be expected to appear after every focused element. The following ungrammatical examples show that more than one focus phrases per clause in Somali (cf. 248b), Berber (cf. 249b), Italian (cf. 250b) and Irish (cf. 251b) as well as multiple wh-phrases are impossible (cf. 248a for Somali, 249a for Berber, 250a for Italian and 251a for Irish):

(248) a. ***yaa**   yimid**goorma**   baa?   (Somali)
        who-FM   came time-which FM
        'Who came when?'

     b. ***Cali**baa yimid   **shalay**   baa.
        Ali FM   came   yesterday FM
        'Ali came yesterday.'
        (Cabdelqadir Ruumi, p.c.)

(249) a. ***W(g)i**   yzwn   **manwn** i?   (Berber)
        who-CM kissed-PART whom CM
        'Who kissed whom?'

     b. ***Muhand** i(g) yzwn   **Tifa** i.
        Muhand CM   kissed-PART Tifa CM
        'Muhand kissed Tifa.'
        (Noureddine Elouazizi, p.c.)

(250) a. ***Chi** ha   scritto   **che cosa**?   (Italian)
        who have-3SG written what
        'Who wrote what?'

     b. ***Mario** ha   scritto una **lettera**.
        Mario have-3SG written a   letter
        'Mario has written a letter.'

(251) a. ***Cé** aL   rinne **caidé** aL?   (Irish)
        who COMP   did   what COMP
        'Who did what?'

b. *Is   í   **Máire** arL   cheann **leabhair**   aL.
   COP she Mary   COMP-PAST bought book   COMP
   'It is Mary who bought a book.'
   (Patricia Ronan and Robert Plaice, p.c.)

Note that it is not possible for the focus marker in Somali (cf. 242d), for the cleft marker in Berber (cf. 243d), for the complementizer *aL/aN* in Irish (cf. 244d) and for the verb in Italian (cf. 245e) to move upwards from FocP to FocP like the finite verb in Hungarian. These observations allow me to conclude that focus recursion is a language specific parameter, which does not exist in Somali, Berber, Italian and Irish. Considering the fact that wh-phrases can only occur in a focus position, which is unique in Somali, Berber, Italian and Irish, it follows that no other position in the clause is capable of licensing wh-phrases. Hence, it is impossible to derive a multiple wh-question as it is derived in Hungarian. The focusing strategy in Somali, Berber, Italian and Irish is unique in the sense that there is one focus projection (FocP) that cannot occur recursively. We have seen that wh-phrases do not occur recursively either and parallel the situation with focus in declaratives. Multiple wh-questions cannot appear as FocP-recursion and therefore do not exist. Parameter (c) of the Uniqueness Hypothesis (cf. 235) holds. This is shown in the following example from Irish:

(252) a.

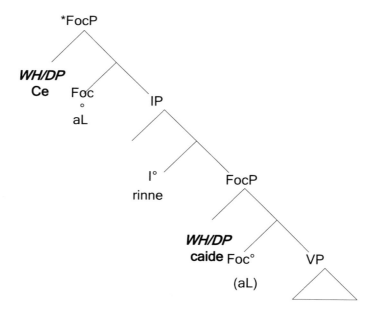

b. *Cé aL   rinne **caidé** aL?   (Irish)
   who COMP   did   what COMP
   'Who did what?'

4.5 Multiple Wh-Fronting as Focus Cluster

It has been argued in the minimalist literature that overt multiple wh-fronting languages like Bulgarian use a strategy which consists of moving a wh-cluster to SpecCP. The formation of a wh-cluster is motivated by the assumption that wh-elements can act as landing sites for wh-movement due to certain language-specific morphological properties. The clustering proceeds prior to wh-movement to SpecCP (see for details Grewendorf 2001 and Sabel 2001; for alternative analyses of multiple wh-fronting in Bulgarian see Richards 1997 and Bošković 1998, 1999 and 2003).[104]

As we have seen (cf. subchapter 4.2.) Malagasy is a wh-in-situ language, which usually exhibits multiple wh-in-situ questions (cf. 253a).[105] It has been considered to be an optional multiple wh-fronting language as well (cf. Sabel 2003). In order to distinguish the two options of multiple wh-question formation in Malagasy, I call this strategy 'Malagasy strategy II'. In this case, Malagasy behaves like Bulgarian, a language that obligatorily fronts all wh-items in a multiple wh-question (cf. 253b and c).

(253) a. Anasan'   **iza   inona** ny   savony?   (Malagasy)
          PRES-CT-wash who   what   the   soap
          'Who washes what with the soap?'
      b. **Aiza**   **iza**   no mividy   ny   vary?
          where   who   FM PRES-AT-buy   the   rice
          'Where does who buy the rice?'
      c. **Aiza**   (ny) **inona**   no   vidinao?
          where   (the) what   FM   PRES-TT-buy-you
          'Where do you buy what?'
          (Sabel 2003)

---

[104] Grewendorf (2001) and Sabel (2001) argue that the feature that triggers displacement of wh-elements in Bulgarian is the +EPP-feature or respectively the strong wh-feature of C°. This +EPP- or alternatively strong wh-feature of wh-phrases is responsible for the wh-cluster formation. Bošković (1998, 1999, and 2003) assumes that the first wh-phrase in multiple wh-questions in Bulgarian is attracted by the strong wh-feature in C°. Movement triggered by C° is called wh-movement. Other wh-elements move to C° in order to check their strong focus features. This movement is different from the first one and is therefore referred to as focus movement.

[105] I will not discuss multiple wh-in-situ questions in Malagasy (for discussion of several restrictions and more examples see Sabel 2003).

The feature that triggers displacement of wh-items in Malagasy is the strong focus feature of the clause (cf. the Malagasy Strategy I discussed in subchapter 4.2.). The most important part of this analysis is that wh-phrases can optionally be endowed with a strong focus feature (see also Cheng 1997 for a proposal of a null determiner endowed with an interrogative force in Bulgarian or alternatively Grewendorf 2001 and Sabel 2001 for an +EPP-feature and a strong wh-feature respectively). Therefore, the strong focus feature of a wh-phrase can attract other wh-elements. In (253b) the strong focus feature of *iza* 'who' and in (253c) the strong focus feature of *inona* 'what' attracts the wh-adjunct *aiza* 'where'. This intermediate derivational operation results in a cluster formation. Finally, the strong focus feature in C° attracts the whole wh-cluster. The derivational steps of a cluster formation are sketched as follows:[106]

(254)

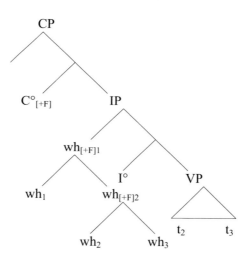

To summarize, there are two different focus features involved in the derivation of a multiple wh-question in Malagasy, namely the strong focus feature of the wh-phrase which makes the wh-phrase itself a target for wh-movement and the strong focus feature of the clause in C° (for further details of the analysis see Sabel 2003). The option of forming a wh-cluster prior to movement into a focus position, which is the canonical position of wh-phrases in Somali (cf.

---

[106] For the ease of representation, I ignore the fact that Malagasy is a subject final language which implies that INFL projects to the right. For detailed analysis of sentences like (253b, c) see Sabel (2003).

255a), Berber (cf. 255b), Italian (cf. 255c) and Irish (cf. 255d), is prohibited because the available focusing strategy is unique.

(255) a. ***yaa goormuu**   yimid?   (Somali)
who time-which-FM-SCL came
'Who came when?'
(Svolacchia & Puglielli 1999)

     b. ***W manwn** i(g) yzwn   (Berber)
who whom CM kissed-PART
'Who kissed whom?'
(Noureddine Elouazizi, p.c.)

     c. ***Chi che cosa** ha   fatto?   (Italian)
who what   have-3SG done
'Who did what?'
(Rizzi 1997)

     d. ***Cé caidé** aL rinne?   (Irish)
who what COMP did
'Who did what?'
(McCloskey 1979:71)

Since multiple wh-fronting and thereby forming a sequence of adjacent wh-elements in a left-peripheral position does not occur in Somali, Berber, Irish and Italian (cf. 255a, b, c and d), their wh-elements obviously lack the morphological properties of Bulgarian- and Malagasy-like wh-elements. I conclude that the Malagasy Strategy II does not exist in languages without multiple wh-questions. Thus, the focusing strategy in these languages is unique in that wh-phrases themselves cannot act as hosts for other wh-elements; i.e. wh-cluster formation is prohibited in languages without multiple wh-questions. This impossible option is schematically illustrated with an example from Somali:

(256) a.

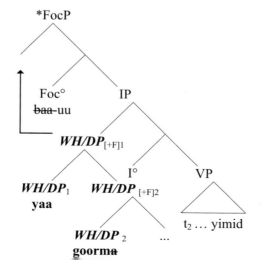

b. *yaa   **goormuu**   yimid?   (Somali)
   who   time-which-FM-SCL came
   'Who came when?'

I also want to address an alternative theoretical proposal for multiple fronting languages. Richards 1997 analyses multiple wh-fronting as wh-raising to multiple specifiers of the CP. This alternative can be sketched as follows:[107]

(257)

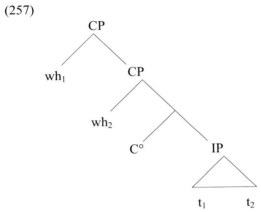

The possibility of wh-movement to multiple specifiers is not present in the grammars of Somali, Berber, Italian and Irish for the same reason wh-cluster formation is not manifested in languages without multiple wh-questions. Structures like (253a, b, c and d) are not attested in these languages. Let us present this observation for concreteness on the following example from Berber:

---

[107] Which analysis is correct is not relevant for this investigation. For discussion of both analyses see Stoyanova (2001).

(258) a.

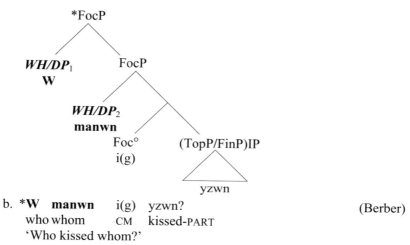

b. ***W manwn**   i(g)   yzwn?   (Berber)
   who whom   CM   kissed-PART
   'Who kissed whom?'

Since Somali, Berber, Irish and Italian do not allow focus and wh-clustering or alternatively focus and wh-movement to multiple specifiers, both focusing and wh-question formation are unique syntactic phenomena. Thus, parameter (b) of the Uniqueness Hypothesis (cf. 235) holds.

4.6 A Feature Checking Analysis for Languages without Multiple Wh-Questions

I will propose a feature checking analysis of wh-questions in languages without multiple wh-questions using Chomsky's (1995) system of syntactic derivations. According to this terminology, uninterpretable strong features of lexical items trigger overt movement. The analysis can also be translated in the terminology of a more recent version of his theoretical model, the probe-goal system. According to this theoretical system the notion of an additional +EPP-feature on a functional head replaces the notion of 'feature strength'.

How do we derive a wh-question in a language which does not allow multiple wh-questions? Since languages without multiple wh-questions show an obligatory spec-head configuration as a licensing mechanism for wh-phrases (i.e. wh-items may not stay in-situ), I assume that the derivation of wh-questions in these languages is a syntactic process driven by the need to satisfy an uninterpretable focus feature of the wh-elements. Furthermore the focus feature of wh-elements is strong and needs to be checked and eliminated before spell-out. Therefore, overt wh-raising applies. I propose that the focus feature on a functional head Foc° in the languages under investigation is interpretable.[108] The wh-element moves to (or merges into) the specifier of Foc°, checks and elimi-nates its uninterpretable strong feature against the interpretable focus feature of Foc°.

I will go through the parameters of the Uniqueness Hypothesis now and show what theoretical implications they have. First, suppose the syntactic derivation begins with a numeration containing more than one wh-phrase. One wh-element targets the specifier position of the functional head Foc° and checks its strong feature. What prevents a wh-element to stay in-situ is its uninterpretable strong focus feature. Therefore multiple wh-questions with wh-phrases in-situ are not allowed in languages without multiple wh-questions (see parameter (a) of the Uniqueness Hypothesis in 235).

Consider a second option. Wh-phrases in languages without multiple wh-questions possess an uninterpretable strong focus feature that triggers move-ment of the wh-elements to a functional head endowed with a corresponding interpretable feature, i.e. Foc°. If the numeration contains more than one wh-phrase the second and additional ones should be able to establish a spec-head relationship with a head bearing an interpretable focus feature. This is, how-ever, not the case because Foc° does not allow multiple specifiers in Somali, Berber, Italian and Irish. Whether a functional head allows multiple specifiers or not is a matter of language parameterisation.

A theoretical alternative to the latter derivational pattern that needs to be ex-cluded is the possibility of wh-cluster formation. The languages without multi-ple wh-questions lack the specific morphological property of wh-elements in certain languages that enables them to be the target of wh-movement. This fact can be accounted for if we assume that in these languages the D-head of the wh-phrases themselves does not bear an +EPP-feature.[109] This proposal re-

---

[108] It is a standard assumption that wh-phrases are inherently focused. Translating this tradi-tional intuition in theoretical terms, I propose that wh-phrases have an uninterpretable focus feature (see also Lasnik 1999 and Bošković 1998, 1999 who claim that the uninterpretable feature may reside on wh-elements in languages like Bulgarian e.g.). Furthermore, I assume that the wh-feature of wh-items in the examined languages is interpretable.

[109] Note that this view of the +EPP-feature is different from Chomsky's (1995:232) concept where the EPP reduces to the notion of feature strength. The +EPP-feature I propose corre-sponds rather to the notion of the EPP within the probe-goal system. The EPP according to this syntactic model is understood as a feature on a functional head that forces a phrasal element to move to its specifier. This amounts to saying that it is an 'attracting feature'. The strong focus feature of wh-elements is a feature that causes wh-elements to move towards a functional head with a corresponding interpretable feature. I assume that this difference exists for the following conceptual and empirical reason: I believe that the fact that wh-phrases cannot appear in-situ can neither be explained by the application of the notion of feature strength from the 1995-

flects the observation that wh-phrases in languages without multiple wh-questions obviously do not provide a slot in their structural representation capable of hosting another wh-phrase. Thus a wh-phrase does not allow another wh-element to establish a spec-head relationship with its D-head. Therefore a wh-phrase will not be able to attract other elements itself. (cf. parameter (c) of the Uniqueness Hypothesis in 235).

The last option to be excluded from the syntax of languages without multiple wh-questions is the iteration of a focus projection. I have proposed that this possibility has to be considered a matter of language specific parameterisation. Languages without multiple wh-questions do not exhibit a recursive FocP (cf. parameter (b) of the Uniqueness Hypothesis in 235).

To conclude, in this section I have shown that a minimalist syntactic theory may be a suitable theoretical model to account for the language variation with respects to the ability to form multiple wh-questions.

---

model nor by the notion of an +EPP-feature as in the probe-goal system (see Chomsky 1995 and subsequent publications).

why include under 'multiple whQs, 'unique' wh Q

CHAPTER 5
CONCLUSION

In this work I have shown that Somali, Berber, Italian and Irish are languages that obligatorily license wh-phrases in a structurally marked unique focus position. A wh-item occurs left-adjacent to a focus marker in Somali (cf. 230a), to a cleft marker in Berber (231a), to the complementizer *aL/aN* in Irish (cf. 233a) and to the finite verb in Italian (cf. 232a). According to the Head-Adjacency Generalisation (cf. 234) wh-phrases in Somali, Berber, Italian and Irish are licensed in the specifier position of a functional head endowed with a focus feature. Following the Uniqueness Hypothesis (cf. 235), focus in-situ, focus recursion and focus clustering (or, alternatively, licensing of wh-elements in multiple specifiers of a focus projection) are not possible. Since the information structure in wh-questions mirrors the information structure in declarative focus constructions, multiple wh-questions are excluded in Somali, Berber, Italian and Irish for the same reason as multiple foci are. These observations suggest that Somali, Berber, Italian and Irish constitute their own language type.

Thus, the language typology based on the criterion of multiple wh-question formation needs to be extended with an additional type. There are primarily two language types: languages that allow single wh-questions only and languages that allow multiple wh-questions:[110]

Table 5. The Typology of Multiple Wh-Questions

THE TYPOLOGY OF MULTIPLE WH-QUESTIONS			
LANGUAGES WITH MULTIPLE WH-QUESTIONS			LANGUAGES WITHOUT MULTIPLE WH-QUESTIONS
WH-IN-SITU LANGUAGES	WH-EX-SITU LANGUAGES	MIXED TYPE LANGUAGE	WH-EX-SITU LANGUAGES

The group of languages with multiple wh-questions shows a great variety of subtypes: a) ex-situ, b. in-situ and c) mixed type languages, as well as subtype

---

[110] Sabel (2004) also proposes that the languages that do not allow multiple wh-questions constitute a separate language type in the typology of wh-questions.

specific variations.[111] The group of languages that do not allow multiple wh-questions consists of members that license wh-phrases in a unique focus position located in the left periphery of the clause by a spec-head configuration. As far as I know, this language type consists only of overt wh-fronting languages. I have come across further languages, which do not allow multiple wh-questions. Branigan & MacKenzie (2000) report that Innu-aimûn (Algonquian) does not exhibit multiple wh-questions. They provide the following examples:

(259) a. **Auen** uîtshiepan Pûna enîshutshîshikânit?
who helped   Paul Tuesday
'Who helped Paul on Tuesday?'

b. *****Tshek^uishkueu auenua** uâtshiât?
which woman whom helped
'Which woman helped whom?'

c. *****Tshek^uishkueu** uâtshiât **auenua**?
which woman helped whom
'Which woman helped whom?'

d. **Mâ** tshi-tshissenim-âu tshetshî matuet-uk   Mânî?
Q   2-SG-know-2/3SG   if   called-1/3SG   Mary
'Do you know if I called Mary?'

e. ?*****Auen** uîtshiepan MUK^U PÛNA?
who helped   only Paul
'Who helped only Paul?'
(Branigan & MacKenzie 2000)

Example (259a) shows the proper position of wh-elements in Innu-aimûn. (259b) and (259c) show that multiple wh-questions are not possible in this language. Example (259d) presents evidence that a wh-phrase does not move to the left periphery for clausal typing reasons (or in order to check a strong wh-feature). The fact that wh-questions and the process of focusing are related phenomena in Innu-aimûn is suggested by (259e). This observation is also consistent with the generalisations about the investigated languages (Somali, Berber, Irish and Italian). Wh-elements are not compatible with focused phrases in a single clause. It is clear that Innu-aimûn fits in with my analysis of languages without multiple wh-questions and supports its basic claims. Happ & Vorköper (2006) observe that multiple wh-questions are not possible in German Sign Language (Deutsche Gebärdensprache (DGS)). In Stoyanova (2006) I have hypothesised that GSL is also a language with unique focus. Bruening (2004) points out that Passamaquoddy (Eastern Algonquian) also does not permit mul-

---

[111] I have not discussed the question exactly what kind of features, wh- or focus-features, drive the derivation of multiple wh-questions in every subtype of the languages that allow multiple wh-questions (for a feature-based typology of wh-questions see Sabel 2004).

tiple wh-questions and disallows wh-in-situ. This observation also seems to fit in with my investigation.

The two phenomena focusing and wh-question formation in languages without multiple wh-questions show a strict correlation, as they are both instances of the syntactic representation of unique focus. The analysis I have proposed makes the following typological prediction which turns out to be correct. There is no wh-in-situ language that does not allow multiple wh-questions (see also Cheng 1997:16f). The question whether the languages without multiple wh-questions show a variety of subtypes and, if so, which subtypes can be distinguished, remains subject to future research.

I will review the generalisations about the theory of multiple wh-questions made so far:

i)   Undoubtedly, wh-questions are connected crosslinguistically with a wh-feature. The Clausal Typing Hypothesis (Cheng 1997), which is closely related to the concept of a wh-feature, does not seem to make correct predictions about the formation of multiple wh-questions. First, obligatory wh-movement or insertion into a specifier position of a functional head and thus establishing a spec-head relation is not always for clausal typing purposes. Second, wh-in-situ (i.e. the occurrence of wh-elements in argument positions) is banned from the grammars of some languages that exhibit yes/no-particles (e.g., Somali, Berber and Irish). If one assumes that wh-raising can optionally be an instance of focus fronting in some languages, the Clausal Typing Hypothesis can be maintained only for languages in which wh-fronting is a syntactic process triggered by the presence of a strong wh-feature on a functional head, i.e. for languages which do not exhibit obligatory focus movement of wh-elements.

ii)   Besides the undisputable relationship between wh-questions and the theoretical notion of a wh-feature, wh-questions are also connected crosslinguistically with a focus feature. Focus based analyses do not make the proper predictions about the syntax of multiple wh-questions as well. Most important, there are languages exhibiting designated focus positions in their grammars, but nevertheless wh-questions in-situ do occur. Such theories cannot capture the optionality of wh-fronting in languages such as Malagasy.

Even if wh-question formation involves a process of clausal typing (no matter if this is achieved by a yes/no-particle, wh-movement to or insertion into a specifier of a functional head), there is good reason to believe that the focusing systems found across languages will be reflected in their interrogative systems. A fine-grained focus theory may explain the differences between languages with respect to the formation of multiple wh-questions. If we assume that wh-question formation is related to the available focusing strategy (or strategies) in a language then we expect to find a correlation between the licensing of focus and the licensing of wh-phrases. The languages of the world differ with respect to how focus is syntactically represented. There is evidence that some languages have focus in-situ only (Japanese).[112] Correspondingly, Japanese is a strict wh-in-situ language. Languages that show focus ex-situ only (Somali, Berber, Italian and Irish) are languages which have only wh-ex-situ. Languages like German and Malagasy show an optionality of focus in-situ and ex-situ. Differences occur in their interrogative systems. While Malagasy exhibits both wh-in-situ and wh-ex-situ, German allows wh-in-situ only in multiple wh-questions. As for Bulgarian, the language shows both focus in-situ and ex-situ. Nevertheless it is an obligatorily multiple wh-fronting language. How many potentially possible language types do we get with respect to the following four distinctive criteria: focus in-situ, focus ex-situ, wh-in-situ, and wh-ex-situ? Table (6.) represents the possible combinational options:[113]

Table 6. Focusing and Wh-Questions in Natural Languages

Criteria \ Languages	A	B	C	D	E	F	G	H	I
Wh-in-situ	+	+	-	+	+	+	-	+	-
Wh-ex-situ	+	-	+	+	-	+	+	-	+
Focus in-situ	+	+	-	+	+	-	+	-	+
Focus ex-situ	+	-	+	-	+	+	+	+	-

- Languages like Malagasy have all options, i.e. wh-in-situ, wh-ex-situ, focus-in-situ and focus ex-situ) and represent language type A.
- Languages like Japanese have wh-in-situ and focus in-situ (wh-ex-situ and focus ex-situ are excluded), hence they belong to language type B (see É. Kiss 1995).

---

[112] Note, however, that Japanese allows focus and wh-clefting, which means that wh-phrases may be in a designated structural position. I will not consider that fact, since I am not aware of a language that does not admit clefting.

[113] We do not expect to find languages without wh-questions and (or) languages without any available focusing strategy. Therefore at least one member in both the wh-row and in the focus row is valued positively.

- Languages like Somali, Berber, Italian and Irish have wh-ex-situ and focus ex-situ (wh-in-situ and focus in-situ are excluded), i.e. they are members of language type C.

The language types A, B and C present an exact correlation between the available focusing strategies and their interrogative systems. Several questions arise with respect to the classification in Table (6.):

1. Do languages like D, E, F, G, H and I exist?
2. How exact is the correlation between focusing and wh-question formation across languages?
3. How are the multiple wh-fronting, mixed type and optional wh-fronting languages spread across the language types as defined in Table (6.)?
4. How many different focusing strategies does a certain language have?
5. How many semantically different types of wh-questions can be attested crosslinguistically?

Note that there are different types of focus ex-situ languages. Languages like Hungarian exhibit focus ex-situ in the shape of a recursive FocP. Languages like Malagasy show a focus ex-situ option such as a focus cluster (or a single functional projection FocP with multiple specifiers). Languages like Somali, Berber, Italian and Irish exhibit a focus ex-situ strategy as a unique FocP. Therefore, it is plausible that the languages without multiple wh-questions fall into language type C.

I have concluded that the languages without multiple wh-questions considered so far have a unique focusing strategy in that they do not use different syntactic means in order to express information and contrastive focus. Many languages seem to make a syntactic distinction between these two interpretatively different focus types.[114] I have discussed real multiple wh-questions, which are generally connected with the expression of new information or the notion of pure

---

[114] Hungarian e.g., is argued to be a language which distinguishes between identificational (±contrastive) and information focus, in that the first is verb-related while the latter is not. Real wh-questions parallel the identificational focus strategy (see É. Kiss 1998b, Horvath 1998, Surányi 2004). Thus, multiple wh-questions corresponding to a recursive (identificational) FocP are assumed to allow both pair-list and single-pair readings (see Surányi 2004 for discussion). A pair-list reading is only obtained with multiple wh-questions of the Bulgarian-type, which are also possible in Hungarian. These are, however, wh-questions in which only the wh-phrase adjacent to the verb is interpreted as the focus of information that needs to be identified. The initial one may be replaced by the *all*-quantifier, which generally corresponds to already contextually activated or presupposed information (see É. Kiss 1998b and Surányi 2004 for discussion and examples).

non-contrastive identification. In this book I have contributed to the better understanding of the grammar of focus, wh-questions and the relation between these two phenomena. The remaining questions are subject to future research.

BIBLIOGRAPHY

Adams, M. 1984. Multiple interrogation in Italian. *Linguistic Review* 4: 1-27.

Andrzejewski, B. W. 1975. The role of indicator particles in Somali. *Afroasiatic Linguistics* 1(6): 123-191.

Baker, M. 1996. *The polysynthesis parameter*. New York & Oxford: Oxford University Press.

Barbosa, P. 2001. On inversion in wh-questions in Romance. In *Subject inversion in Romance and the theory of universal grammar*, A. C. J. Hulk & J.-Y. Pollock (eds), 20-59. Oxford University Grammar.

Barss, A., K. Hale, E. T. Perkins & M. Speas. 1991. Logical form and barriers in Navajo. In *Logical structure and linguistic structure. Crosslinguistic perspectives*, C.-T. J. Huang & R. May (eds), 25-47. Dordrecht, Boston, London: Kluwer.

Belletti, A. 1999. *'Inversion' as focalization and related questions*. Università di Siena, Ms.

Belletti, A. 2002. Aspects of the low IP area. In *The structure of CP and IP. The cartography of syntactic structures*. Vol. 2, L. Rizzi (ed.), 16-51. Oxford: Oxford University Press.

Belletti, A. 2003. *On the VP periphery*. Paper presented at the university of Frankfurt.

Benincà, P. & C. Poletto. 2002. Topic, focus and V2: Defining the CP sublayers. In *The structure of CP and IP. The cartography of syntactic structures*. Vol. 2, L. Rizzi (ed.), 52-75. Oxford: Oxford University Press.

Bhatt, R. & J. Yoon. 1991. On the composition of Comp and parameters of V2. *Proceedings of the tenth West Coast Conference on Formal Linguistics*: 41-52.

Boeckx, C. & K. K. Grohmann (eds). 2003. *Multiple wh-fronting*. [Linguistik Aktuell-Linguistics Today 64]. Amsterdam: John Benjamins.

Bošković, Ž. 1998. Multiple wh-fronting and economy of derivation. In *Proceedings of the sixteenth West Coast Conference on Formal Linguistics*, E. Curtis, J. Lyle & G. Webster (eds), 49-64. Leland Stanford University: CSLI Publications.

Bošković, Ž. 1999. On multiple feature checking: Multiple *wh*-fronting and multiple head movement. In *Working minimalism,* S. D. Epstein & N. Hornstein (eds), 159-187. Cambridge, Mass: MIT Press.

Bošković, Ž. 2000. Sometimes in [Spec, CP], sometimes in situ. In *Step by step. Essays on minimalist syntax in honour of Howard Lasnik*, R. Martin, D. Michaels & J. Uriagereka (eds), 53-87. Cambridge, Mass: MIT Press.

Bošković, Ž. 2002. On multiple wh-fronting. *Linguistic Inquiry* 33: 351-383.

Bošković, Ž. 2003. On wh-islands and obligatory wh-movement contexts in South Slavic. In *Multiple wh-fronting*, C. Boeckx & K. Grohmann (eds), 27-50. Amsterdam: John Benjamins.

Brandi, L. & P. Cordin. 1989. Two Italian dialects and the null subject parameter. In *The null subject parameter*, O. Jaeggli & K. Safir (eds), 111-142. Dordrecht: Kluwer.

Branigan, P. & M. MacKenzie. 2000. *How much syntax can you fit into a word? Late insertion and verbal agreement in Innu-aimûn*. Paper presented at WSCLA at the University of Toronto (24th March 2000), Ms.

Brody, M. 1990. Some remarks on the focus field in Hungarian. *UCL Working Papers in Linguistics* 2: 201-226.

Bruening, B. 2004. *Wh-indefinites, question particles, and wh-in-situ: There is no relation*. University of Delaware, Ms.

Brunetti, L. 2003. *A unification of focus*. To be published by Unipress, Padova. Ms.

Büring, D. 1997. *The meaning of topic and focus: the 59th street bridge accent*. [Routledge Studies in German Linguistics] London: Routledge.

Calabrese, A. 1984. Multiple questions and focus in Italian. In *Sentential complementation*, W. de Geest & T. Putseys (eds), 67-74. Dordrecht: Foris.

Calabrese, A. 1987. Focus structure in Berber: A comparative analysis with Italian. In *Studies in Berber syntax*, M. Guerssel & K. Hale (eds), 103-120. Cambridge: MIT.

Calabrese, A. 1992. Some remarks on focus and logical structures in Italian. In *Harvard working papers in linguistics* 1, S. Kuno & H. Thráinsson (eds), 91-127. Harvard University.

Campos, H. 1997. On subject extraction and the Anti agreement effect in Romance. *Linguistic Inquiry* 28(1): 92-119.

Carnie, A. 1995. *On the theory of movement and non-verbal predication*. Doctoral Dissertation, MIT.

Cecchetto, C. 2000. Doubling structures and reconstruction. *Probus* 12: 93-196.

Cheng, L. L.-S. 1997. *On the typology of wh-questions*. New York: Garland Publishing.

Cheng, L. L.-S. & J. Rooryck. 2000. Licensing wh-in-situ. *Syntax* 3(1): 1-19.

Choe, H.-S. 1987. An SVO analysis of VSO languages and parametrization: A study of Berber. In *Studies in Berber syntax*, M. Guerssel & K. Hale (eds), 121-158. Cambridge: MIT.

Choe, H.-S. 1995. Focus and topic movement in Korean and licensing. In *Discourse configurational languages*, K. É. Kiss (ed.), 269-334. Oxford: Oxford University Press.

Chomsky, N. 1981. *Lectures on government and binding.* Dordrecht: Foris.

Chomsky, N. 1986. *Barriers.* Cambridge Mass.: MIT Press.

Chomsky, N. 1995. *The minimalist program.* Cambridge Mass.: MIT Press.

Chomsky, N. 2000. Minimalist inquiries, the framework. In *Step by step. Essays on minimalist syntax in honour of Howard Lasnik*, R. Martin, D. Michaels & J. Uriagereka (eds), 89-156. Cambridge, Mass.: MIT Press.

Chomsky, N. 2001. Derivation by phase. In *Ken Hale: A life in language*, M. Kenstowicz (ed.), 1-52. Cambridge, Mass.: MIT Press.

Chomsky, N. & H. Lasnik. 1977. Filters and control. *Linguistic Inquiry* 8: 425-504.

Chung, S. & J. McCloskey. 1987. Government, barriers, and small clauses in Modern Irish. *Linguistic Inquiry* 18(2): 173-237.

Clark, R. 1990. *Thematic theory in syntax and interpretation.* London & New York: Routledge.

Cole, J. & C. Tenny. 1987. Coordination in Berber. In *Studies in Berber syntax*, M. Guerssel & K. Hale (eds), 49-78. Cambridge: MIT.

Conni, C. 2001. La cancellazione del complementatore che/that. *Italian journal of linguistics. Rivista di linguistica.* 13(1): 3-45.

Davies, W. D. & S. Dubinsky. 2004. *The grammar of raising and control. A course in syntactic argumentation.* Blackwell Publishing.

Doherty, C. 1997. Predicate initial constructions in Irish. In *Proceedings of the fifteenth annual meeting of the West Coast Conference on Formal Linguistics* [WCCFL XV], B. Agbayani & S. W. Tang (eds), 81–95. Stanford, Calif.: Stanford Linguistics Association.

Drubig, H. B. 2000. *Towards a typology of focus and focus constructions.* University of Tübingen, Ms.

Duffield, N. 1995. *Particles and projections in Irish syntax.* Dordrecht: Kluwer.

É. Kiss, K. 1995. Introduction. In *Discourse configurational languages*, K. É. Kiss (ed.), 3-27. Oxford: Oxford University Press.

É. Kiss, K. 1998a. Identificational focus versus information focus. *Language.* 74(2): 245-273.

É. Kiss, K. 1998b. Multiple topic, one focus? *Acta Linguistica Hungarica* 45(1-2): 3-29.

Ennaji, M. & F. Sadiqi. 1986. The syntax of cleft sentences in Berber. *Studies in Language* 10(1): 53-77.

Engdahl, E. 1986. *Constituent questions.* Dordrecht: Reidel.

Frascarelli, M. 1999. Subject, nominative case, agreement and focus. In *Boundaries of morphology and syntax*, L. Mereu (ed.), Amsterdam: John Benjamins: 175-194.

Frascarelli, M. 2000. *The syntax-phonology interface in focus and topic constructions in Italian.* [Studies in Natural Language & Linguistic Theory 50], Dordrecht: Kluwer.

Frascarelli, M. & R. Hinterhölzl. 2004. *Types of topics in German and Italian.* Paper presented at the Workshop: Information Structure and the Architecture of Grammar in Tübingen, 1st and 2nd February 2004.

Frascarelli, M. & A. Puglielli. 2004. The focus system in Cushitic languages. A comparative-typological analysis. In *Proceedings of the 10th Hamito-Semitic (Afrasiatic) Linguistics Meeting* (=Quaderni di Semitistica: Florence, 18-20 April 2001), P. Fronazaroli & P. Marrassini (eds), 1-28. Firenze.

Frascarelli, M. & A. Puglielli. to appear. Focus markers and universal grammar. In *Proceedings of the 4th International Conference of Cushitic and Omotic Languages*, M. Mous (ed.), Köln: R. Köppe Verlag.

Giorgi, A. & F. Pianesi. 1997. *Tense and aspect: from semantics to morphosyntax.* New York: Oxford University Press.

Grewendorf, G. 2001. Multiple wh-fronting. *Linguistic Inquiry* 32: 87-122.

Grewendorf, G. 2002. *Minimalistische Syntax.* Tübingen und Basel: UTB, A. Franke.

Guerssel, M. 1984. *Descriptive syntax of Berber.* MIT, Ms.

Happ, D. & M.-O. Vorköper. 2006. *Deutsche Gebärdensprache. Ein Lehr- und Arbeitsbuch.* Frankfurt am Main: Fachhochschulverlag.

Heine, B. & M. Reh. 1983. Diachronic observation on completive focus marking in some African languages. *Sprache und Geschichte in Afrika* 5: 7-44.

Hetzron, R. 1965. The particle *baa* in Northern Somali. *Journal of African Languages* 4(2): 118-130.

Hetzron, R. 1971. Presentative function and presentative movement. *Studies in African Linguistics*, Suppl. 2: 79-105.

Horvath, J. 1986. *FOCUS in the theory of grammar and the syntax of Hungarian.* Dordrecht: Foris.

Horvath, J. 1995. Structural focus, structural case, and the notion of feature assignment. In *Discourse configurational languages*, K. É. Kiss (ed.), 28-64. Oxford: Oxford University Press.

Horvath, J. 1998. Multiple wh-phrases and the wh-scope-marker. Strategy in Hungarian interrogatives. *Acta Linguistica Hungarica* 45: 31-60.

Jelinek, E. 1984. Empty categories, case and configurationality. *Natural Language and Linguistic Theory* 2: 39-76.

Kayne, R. 1994. *The antisymmetry of syntax.* Cambridge, Mass.: MIT Press.

Kayne, R. 1998. Overt vs. covert movements. *Syntax* 1(2): 128-191.

Kayne, R. 2002. Pronouns and their antecedents. In *Derivation and explanation in the minimalist program*, S. D. Epstein and D. Seely (eds), 133-166. Blackwell Publishing.

Kornfilt, J. 1997. *Turkish*. London and New York: Routledge.

Kuno, S. 1976. Subject, theme, and the speaker's empathy – A reexamination of relativization phenomena. In *Subject and topic*, Li, Ch. N. (ed.), 417-444. London: Academic Press.

Lamberti, M. 1983. Origin of focus particles in Somali. In *Sprache und Geschichte in Afrika*, R. Voßen & U. Claudi (eds), Vorträge, gehalten auf dem III. Afrikanistentag Köln, 14./15. Oktober 1982. Hamburg: Helmut Buske Verlag: 59-112.

Lasnik. H. 1999. *Minimalist analysis*. Blackwell Publishers.

Lasnik, H. & T. Stowell. 1991. Weakest cross-over. *Linguistic Inquiry* 22: 687-720.

Lecarme, J. 1999. Focus in Somali. In *The grammar of focus*. G. Rebuschi & L. Tuller (eds), 275-309. Amsterdam: John Benjamins.

Lee, F. 2000. VP remnant movement and VSO in Quiaviní Zapotec. In *The syntax of verb initial languages*, A. Carnie & E. Guilfoyle (eds), 143-162. Oxford: University Press.

Legate, J. 1997. *Irish predication: A minimalist analysis*. Masters thesis, University of Toronto.

Li, Ch. N. (ed.). 1976. *Subject and topic*. London: Academic Press.

Livnat, M. A. 1984. *Focus constructions in Somali*. Doctoral Dissertation, University of Illinois at Urbana-Champaign.

Manzini, M. R. & Savoia, L. M. 2002. Clitics: Lexicalization patterns of the so-called 3rd person dative. *Catalan Journal of Linguistics* 1: 117-155.

May, R. 1985. *Logical form. Its structure and derivation*. Cambridge Mass.: MIT Press.

Massam, D. 2000. VSO and VOS: Aspects of Niuean Word Order. In *The syntax of verb initial languages*, A. Carnie & E. Guilfoyle (eds), 97-116. Oxford, University Press.

McCloskey, J. 1979. *Transformational syntax and model-theoretic semantics: A case study in Modern Irish*. Dordrecht: Reidel.

McCloskey, J. 1990. Resumptive pronouns, A'-binding and levels of representation. In *The syntax of the Modern Celtic languages*, R. Hendrick (ed.), 199-248. San Diego: Academic Press.

McCloskey, J. 2001. The morphosyntax of wh-extraction in Irish. *Journal of Linguistics* 37: 57-84.

McCloskey, J. 2003. Resumption, successive cyclicity, and the locality of operations. In *Derivation and explanation in the minimalist program*, S. D. Epstein & D. Seely (eds), 184-226. Blackwell Publishing.

McCloskey, J. 2005. A note on predicates and heads in Irish clausal syntax. In *Verb first. On the syntax of verb-initial languages*, A. Carnie, H. Harley & Sh. A. Dooley (eds), 155-174. Amsterdam: John Benjamins.

McCloskey, J. & K. Hale. 1984. On the syntax of person-number and inflection agreement in Modern Irish. *Natural Language and Linguistic Theory* 1: 487-533.

Mereu, L. 1999. Agreement, pronominalization and word order in pragmatically-oriented languages. In *Boundaries of morphology and syntax*, L. Mereu (ed.), 231-252. Amsterdam: John Benjamins.

Meinunger, A. 1998. A monoclausal structure for (pseudo-)cleft sentences. In *Proceedings of NELS* 28, Tmanji, P.N. & K. Kusumoto (eds): 283-297.

Milsark, G. L. 1988. Singl-*ing*. *Linguistic Inquiry* 19(4): 611-634.

Molnár, V. 2001. Contrast from a contrastive perspective. In *Information structure, discourse structure and discourse semantics*, I. Kruijff-Korbayová & M. Steedman (eds), 99-114. Proceedings of the ESSLLI 2001.

Moro, A. 1997. *The raising of predicates*. Cambridge: Cambridge University Press.

Müller, G. & W. Sternefeld. 1996. Ā-chain formation and economy of derivation. *Linguistic Inquiry* 27: 480-511.

Munaro, N. 1998. Wh-in situ in the Northern Italian dialects. In *Studies on the syntax of Central Romance languages*. O. Fullana & F. Roca (eds), 189-212. Colleció 'Diversitas' 5: Universitat de Girona.

Munaro, N. 2003. On some differences between exclamative and interrogative wh-phrases in Bellunese: Further evidence for a split-CP hypothesis. In *The syntax of Italian dialects*, Ch. Tortora (ed.), 137-151. Oxford: Oxford University Press.

Noonan, M. B. 1997. Functional architecture and wh-movement: Irish as a case in point. *Canadian Journal of Linguistics/Revue canadienne de linguistique* 42(1-2): 111-139.

Oda, K. 2005. V1 and wh-questions: A typology. In *Verb first. On the syntax of verb-initial languages*, A. Carnie, H. Harley & Sh. A. Dooley (eds), 107-133. Amsterdam: John Benjamins.

Ouhalla, J. 1988. *The syntax of head movement. A study of Berber*. Thesis submitted in fulfilment of the requirements for the degree of Ph.D. in linguistics, University College London.

Ouhalla. J. 1991. *Functional categories and parametric variation*. London and New York: Routledge.

Ouhalla, J. 1993. Subject-extraction, negation and the anti-agreement effect. *Natural Language and Linguistic Theory* 11: 477-518.

Pesetsky, D. & E. Torrego. 2000. *T-to-C movement: Causes and consequences*. Ms.

Poletto, C. 2000. *The higher functional field. Evidence from North Italian*. Oxford: Oxford University Press.

Poletto, C. & J.-Y. Pollock. 2000. *On the left periphery of some Romance wh-questions*. Ms.

Puskás, G. 2000. *Word oredr in Hungarian. The syntax of A'-positions.* Amsterdam: John Benjamins.

Rackowsky, A. & L. Travis. 2000. V-initial languages: X or XP movement and adverbial placement. In *The syntax of verb initial languages*, A. Carnie & E. Guilfoyle (eds), Oxford: Oxford University Press: 117-141.

Reinhart, T. 1995. *Interface strategies.* [OTS Working Papers], Utrecht University.

Reinhart, T. 1998. WH-in situ in the framework of the minimalist program. *Natural Language Semantics* 6: 29-56.

Richards, N. 1997. *What moves where when in which Language?* Doctoral Dissertation, MIT.

Rizzi, L. 1982. *Issues in Italian syntax.* Dordrecht: Foris.

Rizzi, L. 1986. Null objects in Italian and the theory of *pro. Linguistic Inquiry* 17(3): 501-557.

Rizzi, L. 1990. *Relativesd minimality.* Cambridge, Mass.: MIT Press.

Rizzi, L. 1991. Residual verb second and the *wh*-criterion. In *Technical reports in formal and computational linguistics* 2, University of Geneva, 1-28. [Reprinted in *Parameters and functional heads*, A. Belletti & L. Rizzi (eds), 1996. 63-90. Oxford: Oxford University Press.]

Rizzi, L. 1997. The fine structure of the left periphery. In *Elements of grammar*, L. Haegeman (ed.), 281-377. Dordrecht: Kluwer.

Rizzi, L. 1999. On the position "Int(errogative)" in the left periphery of the clause. Università di Siena, Ms.

Rizzi, L. 2000. Reconstruction, weak island sensitivity and agreement. University Siena, Ms.

Rooth, M. 1992. A theory of focus interpretation. *Natural Language Semantics* 1: 75-116.

Roussou, A. 2000. On the left periphery. Modal particles and complementisers. *Journal of Greek Linguistics* 1: 65-94.

Rudin, C. 1988. On multiple questions and multiple wh-fronting. *Natural Language and Linguistic Theory* 6: 445-501.

Russell, P. 1995. *An introduction to the Celtic languages.* London: Longman.

Sabel, J. 1998. *Principles and parameters of wh-movement.* Habilitationsschrift, Frankfurt am Main.

Sabel, J. 2000. Partial wh-movement and the typology of wh-questions. In *Wh-scope marking*, U. Lutz, G. Müller & A. von Stechow (eds), 409-446. Amsterdam: John Benjamins.

Sabel, J. 2001. Deriving multiple head and phrasal movement: The cluster hypothesis. *Linguistic Inquiry* 32(3): 532-547.

Sabel, J. 2003. Malagasy as an optional multiple wh-fronting language. In *Multiple wh-fronting*, C. Boeckx & K. Grohmann (eds), 229-254. Amsterdam: John Benjamins.

Sabel, J. 2004. *Typologie des W-Fragesatzes.* Université catholique de Louvain, Ms.

Sabel, J. & J. Zeller. 2004. Wh-question formation in Nguni. Ms.

Saeed, J. I. 1984. *The syntax of focus and topic in Somali.* Hamburg: Helmut Buske Verlag.

Saeed, J. I. 1987. *Somali reference grammar.* Wheaton, MD: Dunwoody Press.

Saeed, J. I. 1999. *Somali.* Amsterdam: John Benjamins.

Saeed, J. I. 2000. The functions of focus in Somali. *Lingua Posnaniensis* 42: 133-143.

Schachter, P. 1973. Focus and relativization. *Language* 49(1): 19-46.

Shlonsky, U. 1987. Focus constructions in Berber. In *Studies in Berber syntax*, M. Guerssel & K. Hale (eds), 1-21. Cambridge: MIT.

Starke, M. 2001. *Move dissolves into merge: A theory of locality.* Doctoral Dissertation, University of Geneva.

Stenson, N. 1981. *Studies in Irish syntax.* Tübingen: Gunter Narr Verlag.

Stjepanović, S. 1999. *What do second position cliticization, scrambling, and multiple wh-fronting have in common?* Doctoral dissertation, University of Connecticut, Storrs.

Stoyanova, M. 2001. *Mehrfache W-Fragen.* Abschlußarbeit zur Erlangung des Grades Magistra Artium im Fachbereich Neuere Philologien der Universität Frankfurt am Main, Ms.

Stoyanova, M. 2004. The typology of multiple wh-questions and language variation. *Proceedings of Console XII*, S. Blaho, L. Vicente & M. de Vos (eds), 171-184.

Stoyanova, M. (2006) *Sprachen ohne multiple w-Fragen, Fokuspositionen und Strukturelle Verwandtschaften.*, Universität zu Frankfurt am Main, Ms.

Stoyanova, M. to appear. Topic and focus constructions in Somali and Berber. In *Frankfurter Afrikanistische Blätter* 18, S. Ermisch (ed.).

Surányi, B. 2004. *What does multiple foci reveal about multiple WH? Focus and answerhood conditions in Slavic- and English-type multiple interrogatives in Hungarian, and interpretative subjacency effects in Japanese.* Paper presented at the Workshop: Information Structure and the Architecture of Grammar in Tübingen, 1st and 2nd February 2004.

Svolacchia, M., L. Mereu & A. Puglielli. 1995. Aspects of discourse configurationality in Somali. In *Discourse configurational languages*, K. É. Kiss (ed.), 65-98. Oxford: Oxford University Press.

Svolacchia, M. & A. Puglielli. 1999. Somali as a polysynthetic language. In *Boundaries of morphology and syntax*, L. Mereu (ed.), 97-120. Amsterdam: John Benjamins.

Tsai, W.-T. D. 1994. On nominal islands and LF extraction in Chinese. *Natural Language and Linguistic Theory* 12: 121-175.

Vanden Wyngaerd, G. J. 1994. *PRO-legomena. Distribution and reference of infinitival subjects.* [Linguistic Models 19], Berlin, New York: Mouton de Gruyter.

Wratil, M. 2004. *Die Syntax des Imperativs.* Inauguraldissertation zur Erlangung des Grades eines Doktors der Philosophie im Fachbereich 10 der Johann Wolfgang Goethe-Universität zu Frankfurt am Main, Ms.

INDEX

Linguistik Aktuell/Linguistics Today

A complete list of titles in this series can be found on the publishers' website, *www.benjamins.com*

98   PIRES, Acrisio: The Minimalist Syntax of Defective Domains. Gerunds and infinitives. 2006. xiv, 188 pp.

97   HARTMANN, Jutta M. and László MOLNÁRFI (eds.): Comparative Studies in Germanic Syntax. From Afrikaans to Zurich German. 2006. vi, 332 pp.

96   LYNGFELT, Benjamin and Torgrim SOLSTAD (eds.): Demoting the Agent. Passive, middle and other voice phenomena. 2006. x, 333 pp.

95   VOGELEER, Svetlana and Liliane TASMOWSKI (eds.): Non-definiteness and Plurality. 2006. vi, 358 pp.

94   ARCHE, María J.: Individuals in Time. Tense, aspect and the individual/stage distinction. 2006. xiv, 281 pp.

93   PROGOVAC, Ljiljana, Kate PAESANI, Eugenia CASIELLES and Ellen BARTON (eds.): The Syntax of Nonsententials. Multidisciplinary perspectives. 2006. x, 372 pp.

92   BOECKX, Cedric (ed.): Agreement Systems. 2006. ix, 346 pp.

91   BOECKX, Cedric (ed.): Minimalist Essays. 2006. xvi, 399 pp.

90   DALMI, Gréte: The Role of Agreement in Non-Finite Predication. 2005. xvi, 222 pp.

89   VELDE, John R. te: Deriving Coordinate Symmetries. A phase-based approach integrating Select, Merge, Copy and Match. 2006. x, 385 pp.

88   MOHR, Sabine: Clausal Architecture and Subject Positions. Impersonal constructions in the Germanic languages. 2005. viii, 207 pp.

87   JULIEN, Marit: Nominal Phrases from a Scandinavian Perspective. 2005. xvi, 348 pp.

86   COSTA, João and Maria Cristina FIGUEIREDO SILVA (eds.): Studies on Agreement. 2006. vi, 285 pp.

85   MIKKELSEN, Line: Copular Clauses. Specification, predication and equation. 2005. viii, 210 pp.

84   PAFEL, Jürgen: Quantifier Scope in German. 2006. xvi, 312 pp.

83   SCHWEIKERT, Walter: The Order of Prepositional Phrases in the Structure of the Clause. 2005. xii, 338 pp.

82   QUINN, Heidi: The Distribution of Pronoun Case Forms in English. 2005. xii, 409 pp.

81   FUSS, Eric: The Rise of Agreement. A formal approach to the syntax and grammaticalization of verbal inflection. 2005. xii, 336 pp.

80   BURKHARDT, Petra: The Syntax–Discourse Interface. Representing and interpreting dependency. 2005. xii, 259 pp.

79   SCHMID, Tanja: Infinitival Syntax. Infinitivus Pro Participio as a repair strategy. 2005. xiv, 251 pp.

78   DIKKEN, Marcel den and Christina M. TORTORA (eds.): The Function of Function Words and Functional Categories. 2005. vii, 292 pp.

77   ÖZTÜRK, Balkız: Case, Referentiality and Phrase Structure. 2005. x, 268 pp.

76   STAVROU, Melita and Arhonto TERZI (eds.): Advances in Greek Generative Syntax. In honor of Dimitra Theophanopoulou-Kontou. 2005. viii, 366 pp.

75   DI SCIULLO, Anna Maria (ed.): UG and External Systems. Language, brain and computation. 2005. xviii, 398 pp.

74   HEGGIE, Lorie and Francisco ORDÓÑEZ (eds.): Clitic and Affix Combinations. Theoretical perspectives. 2005. viii, 390 pp.

73   CARNIE, Andrew, Heidi HARLEY and Sheila Ann DOOLEY (eds.): Verb First. On the syntax of verb-initial languages. 2005. xiv, 434 pp.

72   FUSS, Eric and Carola TRIPS (eds.): Diachronic Clues to Synchronic Grammar. 2004. viii, 228 pp.

71   GELDEREN, Elly van: Grammaticalization as Economy. 2004. xvi, 320 pp.

70   AUSTIN, Jennifer R., Stefan ENGELBERG and Gisa RAUH (eds.): Adverbials. The interplay between meaning, context, and syntactic structure. 2004. x, 346 pp.

69   KISS, Katalin É. and Henk van RIEMSDIJK (eds.): Verb Clusters. A study of Hungarian, German and Dutch. 2004. vi, 514 pp.

68   BREUL, Carsten: Focus Structure in Generative Grammar. An integrated syntactic, semantic and intonational approach. 2004. x, 432 pp.

67   MIŠESKA TOMIĆ, Olga (ed.): Balkan Syntax and Semantics. 2004. xvi, 499 pp.

66   GROHMANN, Kleanthes K.: Prolific Domains. On the Anti-Locality of movement dependencies. 2003. xvi, 372 pp.

65   MANNINEN, Satu Helena: Small Phrase Layers. A study of Finnish Manner Adverbials. 2003. xii, 275 pp.

64   BOECKX, Cedric and Kleanthes K. GROHMANN (eds.): Multiple Wh-Fronting. 2003. x, 292 pp.

63   BOECKX, Cedric: Islands and Chains. Resumption as stranding. 2003. xii, 224 pp.

62 CARNIE, Andrew, Heidi HARLEY and MaryAnn WILLIE (eds.): Formal Approaches to Function in Grammar. In honor of Eloise Jelinek. 2003. xii, 378 pp.

61 SCHWABE, Kerstin and Susanne WINKLER (eds.): The Interfaces. Deriving and interpreting omitted structures. 2003. vi, 403 pp.

60 TRIPS, Carola: From OV to VO in Early Middle English. 2002. xiv, 359 pp.

59 DEHÉ, Nicole: Particle Verbs in English. Syntax, information structure and intonation. 2002. xii, 305 pp.

58 DI SCIULLO, Anna Maria (ed.): Asymmetry in Grammar. Volume 2: Morphology, phonology, acquisition. 2003. vi, 309 pp.

57 DI SCIULLO, Anna Maria (ed.): Asymmetry in Grammar. Volume 1: Syntax and semantics. 2003. vi, 405 pp.

56 COENE, Martine and Yves D'HULST (eds.): From NP to DP. Volume 2: The expression of possession in noun phrases. 2003. x, 295 pp.

55 COENE, Martine and Yves D'HULST (eds.): From NP to DP. Volume 1: The syntax and semantics of noun phrases. 2003. vi, 362 pp.

54 BAPTISTA, Marlyse: The Syntax of Cape Verdean Creole. The Sotavento varieties. 2003. xxii, 294 pp. (incl. CD-rom).

53 ZWART, C. Jan-Wouter and Werner ABRAHAM (eds.): Studies in Comparative Germanic Syntax. Proceedings from the 15th Workshop on Comparative Germanic Syntax (Groningen, May 26–27, 2000). 2002. xiv, 407 pp.

52 SIMON, Horst J. and Heike WIESE (eds.): Pronouns – Grammar and Representation. 2002. xii, 294 pp.

51 GERLACH, Birgit: Clitics between Syntax and Lexicon. 2002. xii, 282 pp.

50 STEINBACH, Markus: Middle Voice. A comparative study in the syntax-semantics interface of German. 2002. xii, 340 pp.

49 ALEXIADOU, Artemis (ed.): Theoretical Approaches to Universals. 2002. viii, 319 pp.

48 ALEXIADOU, Artemis, Elena ANAGNOSTOPOULOU, Sjef BARBIERS and Hans-Martin GÄRTNER (eds.): Dimensions of Movement. From features to remnants. 2002. vi, 345 pp.

47 BARBIERS, Sjef, Frits BEUKEMA and Wim van der WURFF (eds.): Modality and its Interaction with the Verbal System. 2002. x, 290 pp.

46 PANAGIOTIDIS, Phoevos: Pronouns, Clitics and Empty Nouns. 'Pronominality' and licensing in syntax. 2002. x, 214 pp.

45 ABRAHAM, Werner and C. Jan-Wouter ZWART (eds.): Issues in Formal German(ic) Typology. 2002. xviii, 336 pp.

44 TAYLAN, Eser Erguvanlı (ed.): The Verb in Turkish. 2002. xviii, 267 pp.

43 FEATHERSTON, Sam: Empty Categories in Sentence Processing. 2001. xvi, 279 pp.

42 ALEXIADOU, Artemis: Functional Structure in Nominals. Nominalization and ergativity. 2001. x, 233 pp.

41 ZELLER, Jochen: Particle Verbs and Local Domains. 2001. xii, 325 pp.

40 HOEKSEMA, Jack, Hotze RULLMANN, Víctor SÁNCHEZ-VALENCIA and Ton van der WOUDEN (eds.): Perspectives on Negation and Polarity Items. 2001. xii, 368 pp.

39 GELDEREN, Elly van: A History of English Reflexive Pronouns. Person, Self, and Interpretability. 2000. xiv, 279 pp.

38 MEINUNGER, André: Syntactic Aspects of Topic and Comment. 2000. xii, 247 pp.

37 LUTZ, Uli, Gereon MÜLLER and Arnim von STECHOW (eds.): Wh-Scope Marking. 2000. vi, 483 pp.

36 GERLACH, Birgit and Janet GRIJZENHOUT (eds.): Clitics in Phonology, Morphology and Syntax. 2001. xii, 441 pp.

35 HRÓARSDÓTTIR, Thorbjörg: Word Order Change in Icelandic. From OV to VO. 2001. xiv, 385 pp.

34 REULAND, Eric (ed.): Arguments and Case. Explaining Burzio's Generalization. 2000. xii, 255 pp.

33 PUSKÁS, Genoveva: Word Order in Hungarian. The syntax of Ā-positions. 2000. xvi, 398 pp.

32 ALEXIADOU, Artemis, Paul LAW, André MEINUNGER and Chris WILDER (eds.): The Syntax of Relative Clauses. 2000. vi, 397 pp.

31 SVENONIUS, Peter (ed.): The Derivation of VO and OV. 2000. vi, 372 pp.

30 BEUKEMA, Frits and Marcel den DIKKEN (eds.): Clitic Phenomena in European Languages. 2000. x, 324 pp.

29 MIYAMOTO, Tadao: The Light Verb Construction in Japanese. The role of the verbal noun. 2000. xiv, 232 pp.

28 HERMANS, Ben and Marc van OOSTENDORP (eds.): The Derivational Residue in Phonological Optimality Theory. 2000. viii, 322 pp.

27 RŮŽIČKA, Rudolf: Control in Grammar and Pragmatics. A cross-linguistic study. 1999. x, 206 pp.

26 ACKEMA, Peter: Issues in Morphosyntax. 1999. viii, 310 pp.

25 FELSER, Claudia: Verbal Complement Clauses. A minimalist study of direct perception constructions. 1999. xiv, 278 pp.

24 REBUSCHI, Georges and Laurice TULLER (eds.): The Grammar of Focus. 1999. vi, 366 pp.

23 GIANNAKIDOU, Anastasia: Polarity Sensitivity as (Non)Veridical Dependency. 1998. xvi, 282 pp.

22 ALEXIADOU, Artemis and Chris WILDER (eds.): Possessors, Predicates and Movement in the Determiner Phrase. 1998. vi, 388 pp.

21 KLEIN, Henny: Adverbs of Degree in Dutch and Related Languages. 1998. x, 232 pp.

20 LAENZLINGER, Christopher: Comparative Studies in Word Order Variation. Adverbs, pronouns, and clause structure in Romance and Germanic. 1998. x, 371 pp.

19 JOSEFSSON, Gunlög: Minimal Words in a Minimal Syntax. Word formation in Swedish. 1998. ix, 199 pp.

18 ALEXIADOU, Artemis: Adverb Placement. A case study in antisymmetric syntax. 1997. x, 256 pp.

17 BEERMANN, Dorothee, David LEBLANC and Henk van RIEMSDIJK (eds.): Rightward Movement. 1997. vi, 410 pp.

16 LIU, Feng-hsi: Scope and Specificity. 1997. viii, 187 pp.

15 ROHRBACHER, Bernhard Wolfgang: Morphology-Driven Syntax. A theory of V to I raising and pro-drop. 1999. viii, 296 pp.

14 ANAGNOSTOPOULOU, Elena, Henk van RIEMSDIJK and Frans ZWARTS (eds.): Materials on Left Dislocation. 1997. viii, 349 pp.

13 ALEXIADOU, Artemis and T. Alan HALL (eds.): Studies on Universal Grammar and Typological Variation. 1997. viii, 252 pp.

12 ABRAHAM, Werner, Samuel David EPSTEIN, Höskuldur THRÁINSSON and C. Jan-Wouter ZWART (eds.): Minimal Ideas. Syntactic studies in the minimalist framework. 1996. xii, 364 pp.

11 LUTZ, Uli and Jürgen PAFEL (eds.): On Extraction and Extraposition in German. 1996. xii, 315 pp.

10 CINQUE, Guglielmo and Giuliana GIUSTI (eds.): Advances in Roumanian Linguistics. 1995. xi, 172 pp.

9 GELDEREN, Elly van: The Rise of Functional Categories. 1993. x, 224 pp.

8 FANSELOW, Gisbert (ed.): The Parametrization of Universal Grammar. 1993. xvii, 232 pp.

7 ÅFARLÍ, Tor A.: The Syntax of Norwegian Passive Constructions. 1992. xii, 177 pp.

6 BHATT, Christa, Elisabeth LÖBEL and Claudia Maria SCHMIDT (eds.): Syntactic Phrase Structure Phenomena in Noun Phrases and Sentences. 1989. ix, 187 pp.

5 GREWENDORF, Günther and Wolfgang STERNEFELD (eds.): Scrambling and Barriers. 1990. vi, 442 pp.

4 ABRAHAM, Werner and Sjaak De MEIJ (eds.): Topic, Focus and Configurationality. Papers from the 6th Groningen Grammar Talks, Groningen, 1984. 1986. v, 349 pp.

3 ABRAHAM, Werner (ed.): On the Formal Syntax of the Westgermania. Papers from the 3rd Groningen Grammar Talks (3e Groninger Grammatikgespräche), Groningen, January 1981. 1983. vi, 242 pp.

2 EHLICH, Konrad and Jürgen REHBEIN: Augenkommunikation. Methodenreflexion und Beispielanalyse. 1982. viii, 150 pp. With many photographic ills.

1 KLAPPENBACH, Ruth (1911–1977): Studien zur Modernen Deutschen Lexikographie. Auswahl aus den Lexikographischen Arbeiten von Ruth Klappenbach, erweitert um drei Beiträge von Helene Malige-Klappenbach. (Written in German). 1980. xxiii, 313 pp.